# Ways of Thinking
## about God

# Ways of Thinking about God

*Thomas Aquinas and the Modern Mind*

by EDWARD SILLEM

SHEED AND WARD · NEW YORK

Library of Congress Catalog Card Number 61-14655

*Nihil obstat: Adm. R. D. Canonicus Dionysius J. B.
Hawkins, S.T.D. Censor Deputatus. Imprimatur: H.
Gibney, Vicarius Generalis. Datum Southwarci die 28a
Novembris 1960.*

*Manufactured in the United States of America*

# CONTENTS

# FOREWORD

I feel that I ought to warn the reader that this is not just another book on the Five Ways of St Thomas; it does not even attempt any proof of the existence of God. It is rather a book on what St Thomas considered an argument for the existence of God ought to be. As St Thomas is generally held to be the author of the traditional proofs of God's existence, I have commenced my book with three chapters about theistic philosophy and the kind of interpretation widely put on the traditional ways of reasoning to God's existence both by their critics and their Thomist defenders.

Much of what I have written needs discussion, and I am presenting my work as an essay rather than as a fully documented book in the hope that it will be discussed, and that I shall learn a great deal from comments which expert Mediaevalists may be prompted to make. If their comments prove to be favourable, I may consider preparing a fully documented book later. So as to keep to the dimensions of an essay I have reduced the footnotes to a bare minimum, and in discussing modern opinions about the traditional arguments I have made no effort to be exhaustive in my references. I have only taken representative statements of commonly held opinions which a Thomist philosopher must consider in discussing the nature of a metaphysical argument for God's existence.

If the St Thomas Aquinas who appears in chapter VII strikes some readers as somewhat self-opinionated I trust he will blame this, and other faults he may find, on to me who am unequal to the task that cannot be avoided of having to address the modern world in Aquinas's name. I only hope that I will not be accused of being too flippant in constructing the kind of scene I have pictured in this chapter. I have tried this experiment because we surely need this sort of dialogue to help us re-think St Thomas today.

Finally, as this book goes to press Gilson's new book, *Introduction à la Philosophie Chrétienne* (Paris, J. Vrin), comes fresh from the printers, and the cursory reading which is all I have been able to give to it at the moment is enough to make me realize that it is closer to my theme than anything I have read elsewhere. May I suggest to those who finish this book, that they go immediately to Gilson's *Introduction*? Though he makes a number of statements that I could not accept, at least without qualification, we are certainly thinking about the work of St Thomas as a theologian in the same manner.

EDWARD A. SILLEM.

St John's Seminary
  Wonersh, October 1960.

## ACKNOWLEDGMENT

We are indebted to Messrs Longmans, Green & Co Ltd for permission to reproduce on pages 67 and 70 the three diagrams from *Existence and Analogy* by Dr E. L. Mascall.

# NOTE ON THE USE OF CAPITALS

Capitals are used when a statement is made directly about the full reality of God Himself, e.g. 'God's Being'.

When a statement refers to our ideas of God, capitals are not used, e.g. 'our idea of perfect being'.

A small e is used for God's essence, as essence is the complementary term to existence, and in God it only denotes the sum-total of His attributes.

Capitals are not used for 'necessary being' as the expression does not necessarily refer to God alone.

In composite statements, e.g. 'God's essence and being', a small b is used merely to fit in with the small e of essence.

# I

# ON NOT-SEEING AND SEEING THE PROBLEM

Today, as at all other times, philosophers discuss the arguments advanced by theists for the existence of God. Whatever their views about the validity of the arguments, or more radically, about the very possibility of our being able to establish by any kind of philosophical argument that God exists, most thinkers recognize that the existence of God is 'the philosophical question of most extreme importance, both theoretically and practically',[1] for the conclusion we reach in our reflections on this question has the most momentous consequences in the orientation of our thinking and of our daily living. Contemporary discussion of the question amongst English philosophers, however, scarcely does justice to its real importance. Since the war it has taken two different forms which are in marked contrast to each other. Many philosophers, influenced by one or other theory of analysis, take for granted that the existence of God is not a question for the philosopher to decide *qua* philosopher, for he is not called upon to reason to God's existence as to a conclusion we ought to be able to justify logically and so make intellectually respectable. All the philosopher is called upon to do is to ask those who believe in God to describe as accurately as they can how they think and speak of Him, so that he may try to find some method of determining the exact logical status of the kinds of statement about God believers make. Thus some inquirers into theism, and Christian theism in particular, like to test statements about God loving men, or God ruling the world, with the aid of the verification principle on the plea that statements about God, like statements about anything of which we may speak, must square with observations of fact by which we verify them as true; equally they must exclude, if they are true, the possibility of other facts which, were they to occur, would falsify our statements. A statement about

[1] A. C. Ewing: *The Fundamental Questions of Philosophy*, p. 221.

God which is consonant with one state of affairs, but does not exclude any other, so that we could adhere to its truth no matter what transpired, would not be a real assertion or statement at all. So, for example, the statement that 'God loves men' must square with the events and happenings of real life which God sanctions, and be consistent on the part of God with what we call love as we normally find it in the love of a parent for his or her children. Equally the statement must exclude the occurrence of misfortunes, the mere permission of which we normally judge to be incompatible with the real love of one person for another, especially of a parent for a child. If we find men suffering dire misfortunes we have before us happenings which falsify the statement that 'God loves men', for being omnipotent God could prevent them.

This kind of discussion, which goes on under the title of 'Theology and Falsification',[2] is as yet in its infancy (at least as a technique used by philosophers), and far from coherent. Quite clearly those who use the verification principle for the purpose of checking up on the meaning of theological statements have no accurate conception of how one can say that human fortunes and misfortunes verify or falsify a theological statement about God. To use the verification principle in this kind of way is to stretch its range of application beyond all reasonable limits. What happenings are we to take as verifying or falsifying the statements that God loves men, that God punishes sin and sinful men, that God is merciful to sinners, that God is just to all men? Human misfortunes might not disprove the statement that God loves men; they might verify instead some other theological statement as that sin is an incalculable evil for which man is responsible and for which he is justly punished by God. God's punishment of man for such an evil might not be incompatible with love on God's part. God's love, mercy, justice and patience are not so many qualities we can understand by seeing them in the light of what we regard as the fortunes and misfortunes of our earthly life. To judge the kind of love God may have and show us solely by what temporal or physical misfortunes He allows to

[2]cf. Papers on 'Theology and Falsification' in New Essays in Philosophical Theology, from now on referred to as NEPT, pp. 96–130. Also Alasdair MacIntyre's paper on 'Faith and the Verification Principle' in the volume entitled Metaphysical Beliefs, and I. M. Crombie's paper on 'The Possibility of Theological Statements' in the volume of essays entitled Faith and Logic.

befall us, to claim to recognize God's love for what it really is by seeing it in the light of standards of love known to men is utterly illogical, for if God is, as all Christians hold that He is, transcendent in His Being, He is also in His love and all His acts.[3] The kind of love which God may have and show us by His deeds may not be easily recognizable for what it really is by man's standards of love. When a philosopher chooses his own criteria of what love is (as he must do), and then fixes upon his own criteria of what God's love for men ought to be, he is not really verifying anything at all about God, nor falsifying anything about God, but only declaring on what terms he is prepared to accept the kind of being he arbitrarily thinks God to be. The most logical way of testing the Christian's statements about God's love for men would surely be to take the criteria by which God would have us judge of His love for men, and which He has actually revealed to us that we might be able to judge of His love for us in the events of the life and death of Jesus Christ.[4] A Christian knows how necessary it is to take every precaution against seeing the misfortunes of human experience, which might logically be used to test theological statements about man's sin, and obstinacy in sin, as though they were more relevant to the problem of God's love than that of the sinfulness of man. The very use of the verification principle with regard to statements about God only seems to be possible on anthropomorphic principles which are irreconcilable with the first principles of Christian theism.[5] So far are the fortunes and misfortunes of ordinary life from verifying or falsifying theological statements, that for the theist it is theological statements expressing belief about God that give meaning and purpose to the fortunes and misfortunes of life. So far from falsifying the statement that God loves

[3]The transcendence of God's ways in dealing with men, both sinners and saints, must be a major embarrassment to anyone trying to analyse theological statements empirically. Cf., for example, A. MacIntyre, *Metaphysical Beliefs*, p. 181, where he at first says that love in God must 'presumably mean something other than human love', and then he has to admit that it must mean 'just what we mean when we speak of love in human contexts'.

[4]cf. John iii. 16; Rom. v. 6–9; viii. 32; Eph. v. 1–2; 1 John iv. 8–10.

[5]No matter how popular its use may have been in recent years, the verification principle has never yet been satisfactorily stated, and as so far stated it itself eludes the laws it prescribes for meaningful statements.

cf. Professor W. H. F. Barnes's: *The Philosophical Predicament*, ch. VI, and E. L. Mascall's *Words and Images*, ch. I. Dr F. Waismann's paper on 'Verifiability', in the series *Logic and Language* I, is of particular interest.

him, suffering becomes acceptable and sometimes even desirable as a means to a higher, supernatural end when he sees it in the light of the truth that God loves him, and as a God-given chance to express his love for God. In brief, theological statements interpret facts: they should not be interpreted by facts.

Other philosophers follow the older path and look for some form of argument to establish that God exists. Only too often, however, the debate about the arguments for God's existence amongst these philosophers turns out to consist of little more than a number of philosophers pointing out what they consider to be the strong and weak points in the purely logical structure of select arguments which have been long regarded as traditional, and which have been universally recognized by philosophers as the crucial arguments in favour of theism. The arguments are invariably discussed in this way as though the existence of God was entirely a matter of logic rather than of metaphysics presented in conformity with the laws of logic, because most English philosophers prefer to avoid metaphysics as far as possible, or accept the not uncommon view that modern advances in philosophy have disposed of metaphysics once and for all. Logic and a method of analysis between them give us all that is required to sift the arguments thoroughly and show up in a clear light what we are entitled to claim for them. As a consequence of this expulsion of metaphysics the traditional arguments are discussed without any real effort being made to think them as the theologians and philosophers of the past thought them and would have us think them, or even without our making any effort to re-think them in accordance with the principles which make the arguments what they were originally supposed to be. English philosophers are not interested in studying what is old, nor in looking for anything new in the traditional arguments for the existence of God: they are still less inclined to seek for new philosophical arguments to replace the old. George Berkeley was one of the last of the world's great philosophers who made open claims to philosophize for himself about God and His existence, and prided himself on the originality of his ways of thinking about God.[6] Kant put an end to all such ventures in theistic philosophy by attacking the whole undertaking as a quest for the im-

[6]cf. E. A. Sillem: *George Berkeley and the Proofs for the Existence of God*, ch. I and VI.

possible: he argued in effect that one might as well try to square the circle as establish by reason that God exists. Since Kant's day philosophers have become disdainful of attempting anything new in their reflections about God. The dwindling numbers of theistic philosophers who have maintained their confidence in a reasoned theism have been so preoccupied with defending the traditional arguments against Kant, and with examining his reasons for rejecting them, that they have lost interest in making a reasoned theism a living venture. Many would regard anything new in theistic philosophy as a cheap novelty, or as a snare and delusion, presumably on the ground that, in the words of so eminent a thinker as Austin Farrer:

> It is indeed absurd to propose new grounds for belief in the existence of God. The belief has stood more than 2,000 years, if we are able to speak of the essentials of transcendental Theism. If belief has been reasonable, it has had a reason, and our only business must be to draw this out and re-state it. If we are the first to have found true reasons, we must condemn our predecessors in faith as simply superstitious.[7]

The question of the existence of God is thus often discussed as though, being old and set for all time by tradition, it cannot contain anything new. By force of circumstances many theists have come to think unrealistically about the existence of God, as though it were not, as it surely is, one of those questions which is at once ever ancient and ever new. It does not seem to occur to many writers on theistic philosophy that unless traditional ways of thinking about God germinate and give rise to thinking that is new and fresh within the framework of what is venerable and ancient, theistic philosophy must ossify completely.

\* \* \*

The use of the expression 'traditional arguments' gives rise to many difficulties when we think how it is used by many philosophers when referring to the arguments for the existence of God. When writing about the problems of theism many contemporary English philosophers are in the habit of basing their discussions on their own personal re-statements of what they take the traditional arguments to be, and one will look in vain for a serious study of the various forms which

[7] A. Farrer: *Finite and Infinite*, p. 3.

they have in fact taken during the course of their long history. It is clear that for most of the philosophers I have in mind a study of their history would be superfluous. They treat the arguments as if they had persisted permanently the same throughout time,—as if, in other words, never having undergone any development, they have no history worthy of the name. They are all too prone to take for granted that the somewhat conventional and lifeless forms in which they are wont to summarize the arguments give us exactly the very arguments which Kant refuted in his 'Critique of Pure Reason', and that the arguments Kant had before him were the same as those which were known to Suarez, and before him to the mediaeval schoolmen. This is not a little surprising, because, more scientific reasons apart, the arguments which are looked upon as 'traditional' in the *philosophia perennis* are presented in quite a surprising variety of ways, despite the conventional outline of the way in which they are summarized, and receive a notable variety of interpretations. One would have thought that, being aware of this anomaly, modern writers would have made some allowance for deeply rooted varieties in the very texture and fabric of the arguments belonging to past centuries, especially in the work of thinkers who were pioneers in philosophy and strangely different from each other in the character of their thinking (as the thinkers of the Middle Ages certainly were), and that as a consequence contemporary discussion would have been shaped to some extent by its carefully considered estimates of one or other form which an argument had taken in the course of its history. But strangely enough, we rarely find anything of the sort coming from the pen of an English philosopher. Clement Webb published his *Studies in the History of Natural Theology* in 1915, and we have not had anything comparable to it since that time.[8] It seems to be taken for granted that no theist will appeal from a modern summary of an argument to some source from which the argument is supposed to be derived. And yet from the point of view of a convinced theist of the Thomist persuasion much of the contemporary discussion about the validity of the arguments is unsatisfactory

[8]I am not considering here works about our knowledge of God written by theologians since 1915 of which there are a large number.

I must make a last minute qualification of this statement in the text, for as this book goes to the printers Professor James Collins has published his *God in Modern Philosophy*.

because contemporary versions of the so-called 'traditional' arguments differ appreciably from the older versions which we find in the writings of the mediaeval scholastics, even as the mediaeval arguments differ appreciably from those of the ancient Greek philosophers from whom they are ultimately derived. Thus one has the impression time and again that a contemporary philosopher is writing up and then criticizing one of the 'traditional' arguments for the existence of God which no body of philosophers from the past, least of all from the high Middle Ages, would recognize as an argument they had ever committed to paper or parchment.

What, then, are the 'traditional' arguments for the existence of God? In what context are we to place them? And in accordance with what principles are we to discuss them?

\* \* \*

Anyone who is going to write about theistic argument nowadays must take some account not only of this confusion as to what the 'traditional' arguments really are, but also of at least some of the numerous criticisms which are brought against any kind of argument for the existence of God. In bygone ages the metaphysical or cosmological arguments for the existence of God had more friends than foes, but in our time they have certainly more foes than friends in the ranks of the professional philosophers.[9] In English philosophical circles they have barely any friends left, apart from a handful of thinkers who believe in the truth of a metaphysics of being as conceived by the mediaeval schoolmen. A discussion of the arguments may be counted upon to provoke a veritable barrage of objections and difficulties which of course vary a good deal from time to time in the points they attack, but which tend to revive from a fresh standpoint the reputedly crippling refutations of all theistic argument made by Hume and Kant. Thus the theist who is prepared to defend the validity of the arguments in any form will be allowed little peace from the ceaseless barrage of objections to which he will inevitably be subjected, and which might well dissuade him from defending them in writing at all.[10]

[9]cf. W. R. Sorley: *Moral Values and the Idea of God,* ch. XII.
[10]Those who are not familiar with contemporary discussions about theistic philosophy in England, and who would like to have some idea of the kind of

The trouble created for the theist by this unceasing fire of destructive criticism is, however, the least of the many that a theistic philosopher in my position has to face. To be perfectly frank, I find the views of some of my fellow Thomists more difficult than most of the objections raised against theism by philosophers! There can, after all, be few easier occupations for a philosopher than finding difficulties in our human ways of thinking about God, and critics of a reasoned theism would do well to remember that thought about the infinite God Who created heaven and earth, Who is inscrutable in His judgements and undiscoverable in His ways (cf. Rom. xi. 33), Who is eternal life and unlimited Being, is and always has been full of difficulty and mystery to countless millions of thoughtful Christians. The mystery of God's Being has been racking the minds of Christians since the time of St Paul; it has been discussed by theologians for centuries under the title given to it by the pseudo-Dionysius of 'the Divine Names'.[11] But whereas a difficulty makes many modern philosophers cry out against the effort to think of God, and sometimes set the reality of God aside as imaginary or meaningless, Christians profess a theism which would scorn a God who presented no great difficulty, no depth of mystery to the mind. Cardinal Newman expressed the mind of all theists when he wrote: 'Of all points of faith, the being of a God is, to my own apprehension, encompassed with most difficulty, and yet borne in upon our minds with most power.'[12] If the work of the philosopher is to consider those realities which excite our wonder because they present us with the kind of difficulty which we know to be ultimately intelligible

---

objections philosophers bring against the 'traditional' arguments, have only to study such works (to mention but a handful) as Professor Laird's *Theism and Cosmology,* Professor Paton's *The Modern Predicament,* Professor Ayer's *Language, Truth and Logic,* the volume of *New Essays in Philosophical Theology* edited by Professor Flew and Alasdair MacIntyre, Professor Wisdom's paper on 'Gods' reprinted in *Logic and Language,* first series, and in *Philosophy and Psycho-Analysis,* and Dr Ronald Hepburn's challenging book *Christianity and Paradox.* One of the most lively attacks on all forms of reasoned argument for the existence of God, however, is still Edouard Le Roy's famous 'cahier' entitled *Le Problème de Dieu* which was published in 1930. Though scarcely known in England now, it merits reading as it represents an attitude of mind not uncommon amongst English theists who believe in God, but not in reason giving us any knowledge of Him.

[11]cf. Ch. de Moré-Pontgiband, S.J., *Du Fini à l'Infini,* ch. 1.

[12]J. H. Newman: *Apologia pro Vita Sua,* part VII, 'General Answer to Mr Kingsley'.

and which for this reason we call a 'mystery' (such as we find when we reflect on the nature of knowledge, of life and the soul, of free will, and the ultimate nature of matter), then mere difficulties, so far from bringing discredit, should rather incline the minds of philosophers to look with favour on a reasoned theism. The fact of the matter is, however, that the line of cleavage between the supporters and the critics of the arguments for the existence of God does not lie so much in difficulties inherent in reasoning about God, as in the fundamental divergence of view by which they are sharply separated even before they start thinking about God, on questions concerning the nature of the human mind and its powers of knowing. Those who reject the arguments usually hold in some way or the other, but at least quite uncompromisingly, that reason is the measure of reality, or of what we can know about reality, and thus they revolt against anything that reason finds difficult to conceive. Those, on the other hand, who defend the arguments hold that reality is the measure of reason, so that they have no difficulty at all in accepting as a reality perfectly intelligible in itself something which is full of difficulty to reason because beyond the limited reach of our powers of understanding. For those who defend the arguments, Aristotle's attitude towards the mysteries of the Being of God is more logical than that of the modern critic, for he *does* look for mysteries in God, and he certainly relishes those he finds. He writes, for example:

If, then, God is always in that good state (of thinking) in which we sometimes are, this compels our wonder; and if in a better this compels it yet more. And God *is* in a better state. And life also belongs to God; for the actuality of thought is life, and God is that actuality; and God's self-dependent actuality is life most good and eternal.[13]

And again in connexion with the life of God:

The nature of the divine thought involves certain problems; for while thought is held to be the most divine of things observed by us, the question how it must be situated in order to have that character involves difficulties.[14]

[13]Aristotle: *Metaphysics,* Book Λ, ch. 7, 1072b, 23–28 (translation by W. D. Ross, Oxford University Press).
[14]Aristotle: *Metaphysics,* Book Λ, ch. 9, 1074b, 15–18 (translation by W. D. Ross, Oxford University Press).

The theist rejoices in this kind of way in the reality of the mystery of God Who is supremely intelligible in Himself and clearly understood to be so, though He is utterly beyond our powers of comprehension. He will find thought about God fraught with difficulties, but not vitiated by contradictions. The modern philosopher, by contrast, is all too ready to proclaim as a contradiction the slightest difficulty he experiences in thinking about God without even taking the trouble to probe beneath the surface for a possible way out of his difficulties.

Let us take some examples of the kind of 'difficulty' against a reasoned theism that certain philosophers sensationally throw at us as an evident 'contradiction' or 'absurdity'. Professor A. N. Prior, who is a very able logician, finds that the Christian way of speaking of God as good, and also as being His own goodness, is absurd: he regards this a sheer nonsense and as sufficient of itself to expose the futility of the idea of God. Logic, he says, permits us to say one thing or the other, either that God is good, or that God is His own goodness, but it forbids us to say both at once. 'We cannot have it both ways, and use a word as an abstract noun and a common noun at once, as you try to do in your sentence "God is his own goodness"—that's just bad grammar, a combining of words which fails to make them *mean*—like "Cat no six".'. He urges against our position that 'you have established a complete difference between "God" and all the other words we use for naming things; but the difference is that this word, as you use it, does not and cannot name anything whatever—you refuse to put it through the proper motions of "naming"'.[15] Professor Prior just takes for granted that this is the end of the matter, that for all these hundreds of years theologians have had nothing else to say about this little difficulty in logic, and that there cannot be anything beneath the surface that he has overlooked.[16] But there is nothing more serious in this 'contradiction' than in the little child's question about God: 'and what must God do on Sunday?' Professor Findlay, in a paper entitled *Can God's Existence be Disproved?*, begins by describing satisfactorily what kind of being a Christian takes God to be, and what it is which requires that we should not just venerate and respect Him as we do the saints, but worship and

[15]A. N. Prior: 'Can Religion be Discussed?' from NEPT, pp. 5–6.
[16]St Thomas explained how it is we speak in this way of God in the *Summa Theologia*, I, qu. 3, art. 3, ad 1.

adore Him with the supreme adoration of λατρέια. He then quietly asserts that these very requirements of what we take God to be entail that His existence is impossible, the reason being that 'the modern mind feels not the faintest axiomatic force in principles which trace contingent things back to some necessarily existent source, nor does it find it hard to conceive that things should display various excellent qualities without deriving them from a source which manifests them supremely.' This, as it stands, is, of course, mere rhetoric, for the point at issue is whether or not there is something wrong with the modern mind and what it finds easy: the point to be decided is not what is hard or easy, but what is correct and incorrect, what is true and false. The only reason Professor Findlay advances against the theistic position is that Kant considered that there are no necessary facts of existence, and that we could only speak of the divine existence as necessary:

> If we made up our minds to speak theistically *whatever the empirical circumstances might turn out to be.* This, doubtless would suffice for some, who speak theistically, much as Spinoza spoke monistically, . . . but it wouldn't suffice for the full-blooded worshipper, who can't help finding our actual world anything but edifying, and its half-formed tendencies towards righteousness and beauty very far from adorable.[17]

And once again we are back with the illogicalities of the use of the verification principle, with the consequent surrender before difficulties which it is the very purpose of the arguments to take into consideration. The difficulties are not examined by Professor Findlay, but just used to decide the issue by saying that God does not exist. In so far as what Professor Findlay says of the modern mind is true, we can understand how it is that philosophers nowadays find reasoning about God's existence too far removed from all that they take to be meaningful and thinkable for theistic argument to be intelligible to them.

We can take for granted, then, that nothing will be easier for contemporary philosophers than finding difficulty upon difficulty in any kind of reasoned theism likely to satisfy a Christian simply because it is impossible to think about God in the kind of way so many philosophers hold we ought to think, namely, about phenomena as distinct

---

[17]J. N. Findlay: 'Can God's Existence be Disproved', in NEPT, pp. 53–54.

from being. This, however, need not make a theist in my position imagine that contemporary objections against the arguments for God's existence constitute the most formidable problem that he has to face. A theist who philosophizes nowadays about his theism lives no doubt under fire, but there is no need to exaggerate the severity of the shelling to which he is being subjected just because he must take notice of it. He might as well be heartened with the assurance that some of the noise around him is due to the firing of guns which, though levelled threateningly on his position, are only using 'blanks', and a certain amount to the firing of guns which have not the supply of armour-piercing shells they need to bring about the destruction which they seem bent on effecting. In fact often enough the fire is directed not at the positions we actually occupy, but at positions which for some reason or another we are represented as occupying. As this is the case, rather than expend all our energies on counter attack, we can afford to conserve them for more necessary work; and so, after inspecting in the next chapter the most serious threats to our real position, which, of course, we must take every precaution to ward off, we will proceed to our main task of inspecting our own position and internal affairs. Having expended time and energy on effecting various internal reconstructions and improvements, we ought as a result to be the better equipped to meet those of our adversaries who really are using lethal weapons, and who really are attacking with serious difficulties the position we hold.

Let me give an example, in addition to that provided above by Professor Prior, of an eminent philosopher using blank for live ammunition, presumably to frighten those who are nervy about the use of reason in discussing the problems of theism. In the book from which I quote Bertrand Russell is presenting briefly the argument, or what he takes to be the argument, for the existence of God as the First Cause, and after summarizing it very ambiguously he comments as follows:

> I may say that when I was a young man and was debating these questions very seriously in my mind, I for a long time accepted the argument of the First Cause, until one day, at the age of 18, I read John Stuart Mill's Autobiography, and I there found this sentence: 'My father taught me that the question, "who made me?" cannot be answered, since it immediately suggests the further question,

"who made God?" ' That very simple sentence showed me, as I still think, the fallacy in the argument of the First Cause. If everything must have a cause, then God must have a cause. If there can be anything without a cause, it may just as well be the world as God, so that there cannot be any validity in the argument. It is of exactly the same nature as the Hindu's view, that the world rested upon an elephant and the elephant upon a tortoise; and when they said, 'how about the tortoise?' the Indian said, 'suppose we change the subject.' The argument is really no better than that.[18]

Dr Hepburn repeats the same kind of thing in a few brief sentences which, one would have thought, a serious philosopher could only write with his tongue in his cheek. He puts to himself an objection: 'Suppose, however, we allowed that the universe might in fact demand a cause. Suppose we agree that it cannot "owe its existence to itself", but must owe it to some other being. Would this concession be enough to rid the argument of its difficulties?' To this he replies as follows:

> Only if, for one thing, we could be sure that the being who caused the universe to exist did not himself require a cause of a still higher order. If everything without exception demands a cause, then God must have *his* cause too. God, replies the Thomist, is the author of his own existence. But then, his critic can point out, here *is* an exception to the rule: not everything demands a cause, after all. And if this is so, how do I know that the world demands a cause, or everything in the world? Admit exceptions, and the cosmological argument at once loses its purchase.[19]

Quite plainly Bertrand Russell's knowledge of the argument he is summarizing is not derived, any more than Mill's, from any study of the argument at first hand in a source of acknowledged importance, nor does his statement of the argument betray any effort to think very deeply on the problems from which it arises, anyway after he was 18.[20] Similarly Dr Hepburn's account of the way the term 'cause' is supposed to be bandied around by the traditional arguments bears no relation whatever to the way theists conceive of the world as caused,

---

[18]Bertrand Russell: *Why I am not a Christian*, pp. 3–4.

[19]Ronald W. Hepburn: *Christianity and Paradox*, pp. 165–6.

[20]The presentation of the Five Ways in the *History of Western Philosophy*, p. 477, and in the *Wisdom of the West*, pp. 158–9, confirms the fairness of this statement.

or of God as its cause, and if there is one statement which is entirely incompatible with the basic idea that St Thomas advanced about God, and which no Thomist could say as a Thomist, it is that God might under any condition whatever be the author or cause of His own existence. What these two examples provide us with is not philosophy, but a little display of dialectical fireworks which are supposed to produce the impression of a bombardment by heavy artillery.

The problems about the validity of the argument for the existence of God which, I suggest, are the most serious do not come from the critics who indulge in his kind of polemic.

*     *     *

The problem which I wish to suggest is the most perplexing and absorbing in interest for the theist in my position concerned with vindicating the reasonableness of the Christian belief in God, is neither the diversity of interpretations put upon the 'traditional' arguments by philosophers who have never studied them in the reality of their historical development, nor the objections brought against them by so many contemporary philosophers, but the diversity of interpretations put upon the most celebrated version of the arguments, the famous Five Ways of St Thomas Aquinas, by those whose studies have been expended for many years on the actual text, both of the arguments themselves and generally of the writings of the holy doctor. Let anyone study the text of St Thomas's Five Ways with the aid of such important works as (to mention but a handful) Reginald Garrigou-Lagrange's *Dieu, Son Existence et Sa Nature*, A. D. Sertillanges's *La Philosophie de St Thomas d'Aquin*, Dr R. L. Patterson's *The Conception of God in the Philosophy of St Thomas Aquinas*, E. L. Mascall's *He Who Is* and especially his later *Existence and Analogy*, Pedro Descoq's *Praelectiones Theologiae Naturalis*, or Dom Emmanuel Gisquière's *Deus Dominus*, or with the aid of shorter but no less penetrating studies of St Thomas's Five Ways as we find in A. Grégoire's *Immanence et Transcendence*, in chapter III, article 3 of F. Van Steenberghen's *Ontologie*, in the third chapter of Gilson's *Le Thomisme* (translated into English as *The Christian Philosophy of St Thomas Aquinas*), or the chapter entitled 'Der Aufstieg zu Gott' from G. M. Manser's *Das Wesen des Thomismus* (not to mention any of the numerous articles which have been in earnest debate in periodicals during the past thirty years),[21] and I am sure he will be left wondering, as I was, (a) what after all St Thomas really thought about the arguments for the existence of God which were known in his day, and (b) how he thought of the arguments which he put into the first part of his *Summa Theologica,* in Quacstio 2, art. 3, as Five Ways to establish God's existence. These problems, which we will study closely in chapter 5, are probably almost unknown to most of the contemporary critics of theistic argument in England of whom I was speaking in the previous sections, for most of the scholars engaged in discussing them live in an intellectual world unknown to contemporary English academic philosophers. Nevertheless I trust that this circumstance will not induce anyone who has read thus far to put my book down at this point suspecting that I am shirking the issue by discussing the problem on my own ground. I trust I can assure those who are interested in contemporary discussions about our knowledge of God, and many of my Thomist confrères for that matter, that their reading will not be without interest or surprise.

The problem with which I am primarily engaged in this book is, then, whether or not something of capital importance has been overlooked by the Thomist scholars themselves which needs to be set right in the foreground of the interpretation to be put on St Thomas's arguments for the existence of God, and which must be kept in mind when we are trying to meet the difficulties and objections which modern philosophers find in the very nature of theistic reasoning. The solution of this problem probably contains the key to the difficulties experienced universally, but most acutely by Thomist philosophers themselves, as to what the 'traditional' arguments for the existence of God really are, and in accordance with what principles we are to assess them.

[21]We ought to add as of special interest the volume *Sulle 'Cinque Vie' di S. Tommaso* by five different writers, one writing on each of the Five Ways, published at Rome by the Officium Libri Catholici, as Volume VII of the series 'Doctor Communis'.

# 2

## SOME CRUCIAL ISSUES TO BE FACED

Before we settle down to our main task and embark on our study of St Thomas, we had better take a look at some of the crucial issues involved in a serious discussion about the proofs for the existence of God, as when all is said and done, we will have to place St Thomas in the midst of the philosophers who reject the proofs.

Whatever their differences of view about the interpretation and the validity of the traditional arguments, there is fortunately a measure of agreement amongst philosophers today on certain fundamental points which St Thomas shares fully with them, and which is more extensive than it looks when presented summarily in three headings as I present it here.

First, it seems to be widely agreed that the *a priori* or ontological argument, both in its original Anselmian and in its later Cartesian forms, is invalid, for, as both Aquinas and Kant agreed, 'existence is not a predicate'.[1] This point has been so thoroughly discussed by both sides that there is no need to say anything about it here. The fallacy involved in the ontological argument was splendidly analyzed by the late Professor Moore in his well-known paper, 'Is Existence a Predicate?', which is invaluable at least in showing what existence is not.[2]

Second, it seems to be agreed that, of the numerous kinds of argument that have been put forward (metaphysical, physical, moral, anthropological, etc., as well as arguments based on religious and mystical experience), the metaphysical arguments (or the arguments which Kant called 'cosmological' and which are sometimes referred to

---

[1] cf. D. J. B. Hawkins: *The Essentials of Theism,* pp. 64–73; J. J. C. Smart: in NEPT, pp. 33–34; H. J. Paton: *The Modern Predicament,* ch. XII; E. L. Mascall: *Existence and Analogy,* ch. II.

[2] Reprinted in *Logic and Language* (second series).

as the 'causal' arguments) are from the strictly philosophical point of view the most important, for not only do they claim to demonstrate that God exists, but also to enable us to understand how we must think about His nature and attributes. Other kinds of arguments may show that there is a supreme being of some kind, and apologetically they may be of considerable service because they are less exacting in the demands they make on a man's abilities for sheer hard thinking. But these arguments cannot establish that the supreme being to which they argue is in fact the infinitely perfect God, nor can they help very much in showing how, by dealing with the problem of the divine attributes, we ought to conceive the supreme being, and hence from the strictly theological and philosophical points of view they fail to go all the way that an argument for the existence of God has to go. Philosophers differ in their estimates not of the importance, but of the validity of the metaphysical arguments, and the fundamental cleavage between them in matters of theism arises from the totally different ways in which they visualize the structure of the arguments.

Third, it seems to be agreed that the most important source to which we have to look for a statement of the traditional metaphysical or cosmological arguments is the *Summa Theologica* of St Thomas Aquinas. Dr Paton is speaking for everyone when he writes: 'The classical exposition of the cosmological argument may be found in the *Summa Theologica* of St Thomas—in the famous "Five Ways" of proving the existence of God.'[3] Were he alive today St Thomas could not deny that the Five Ways are in his *Summa Theologica,* nor that philosophers and theologians attach a singular value to them as proofs, but we shall have to see what he would have thought about them being regarded as *his* arguments for the existence of God.

*     *     *

As many critics appear to derive their knowledge of the structure of the traditional arguments from the analysis Kant made of them in his 'Critique of Pure Reason',[4] or at least appear to have been in-

---

[3]H. J. Paton: *The Modern Predicament,* p. 192, cf. also E. L. Mascall: *Existence and Analogy,* p. 66.

[4]Kant: *Critique of Pure Reason,* in the section on the 'Transcendental Dialectic', Book 2, ch. iii, sec. 5 (pp. 507–14 of Kemp Smith's translation).

fluenced to no small extent by his analysis, it may be as well, before attempting anything else, to give the bare outline of Kant's demonstration of the impossibility of any cosmological (or metaphysical) argument for the existence of God. A large number of philosophers seem to be firmly of the opinion that Hume and Kant between them disposed of the arguments once and for all, so that later re-statements of the old arguments given by Christian apologists in their efforts to save them are, in Dr Hepburn's words, 'no more significant of life than the twitchings of a body already dead'.[5] Kant's critique of the traditional arguments remains to this day the most radical of all, for it bears not merely on particular points of particular arguments, but on the whole plan or structure of the metaphysical arguments, and on the idea of our attempting to think of God at all. Kant, and those many critics who have been influenced by his ideas, are certainly not using anything but live ammunition in discussion against the supporters of reasoned theism.

Kant held that two processes of reasoning are necessarily involved in any complete argument for God's existence; in the first of these we argue from the contingent beings known to us in experience to necessary being, and in the second we advance to the decisive step of arguing from necessary to infinite or perfect Being. He held, however, that the first process alone, arguing as it does from the contingent beings of the world to a necessary being as their cause, deserves to be considered as cosmological and as causal; the second and decisive stage in the total argument, so far from being cosmological, i.e. grounded on an analysis of experience, or causal in nature, is merely a variant of the ontological argument, and it is added on to the first process in an effort to prove that an absolute or necessary being is, as we Christians believe God is, infinite and perfect Being. Hence the traditional arguments which claim to be grounded solely on experience are in fact the product of a subtle and unwarranted commingling of a causal analysis of the data of experience (coming from the first part of the argument) with lines of reasoning which have no support from experience whatever, and are in fact logically invalid (coming from the second).

Dr Paton has restated the criticism of Kant very clearly in his book *The Modern Predicament*. The traditional arguments, he contends, are

[5]R. W. Hepburn: *Christianity and Paradox*, p. 156.

based on the various kinds of imperfection we find in the data of experience, and they try to argue from these imperfections in all things known to us to the infinite perfection of God Who is the cause of all things.[6] But we cannot get further by arguing in this way from the imperfections in things than establishing a mere fragment of the desired conclusion that God exists; the most that we can legitimately conclude from the data is that some kind of being exists which is the cause of the phenomena with which we are familiar in experience, and which is not contingent as are the objects of experience. To prove that this cause is the one, infinitely perfect God, nay the God Who is the creator of all things in heaven and earth, assistance is required from some more fruitful source than mere experience. The advocates of the traditional arguments have as a consequence had to seek help from an outside source which, of course, they had to make for themselves as unfortunately there is no such source within experience. This they eventually and mercifully stumbled upon in the form of the ontological argument invented in the eleventh century by St Anselm. The schoolmen contrived to knit, or engraft a slightly modified form of St Anselm's argument on to their cosmological reasonings and thus free themselves from the difficulty which threatened the success of their efforts to establish God's existence by argument. Kant claimed he had detected and distinguished between the two separate processes of reasoning which the mediaeval theists had arbitrarily run into one, and had thus exposed the traditional arguments as invalid. Since the difficulty which the proponents of the arguments at first encountered is insurmountable, Kant concluded that we cannot establish the existence of God by philosophical argument. The traditional arguments are metaphysical by nature, and not merely cosmological; and as Kant held that pure metaphysics is uncritical (or falsely assumed) knowledge because it is divorced from experience, and that reason can only think about, or have genuine knowledge of the sensible data of experience, it follows that reason cannot provide the second process required to complete the total argument, and thus that we cannot establish by philosophical

[6]Like Kant Dr Paton distinguishes the cosmological arguments from the argument from design which argues from perfections found in the created universe. He examines the argument from design on its own after the cosmological arguments.

reasoning that God exists. Dr Paton sums up the situation as the Kantians see it as follows:

> The cosmological argument cannot prove the existence of God without the aid of the ontological argument, and this may be the underlying reason why the ontological argument had to be invented. If the ontological argument is valid, the cosmological argument is superfluous. If the ontological argument is invalid, the cosmological argument must be invalid too. The religious man has to walk by faith and not by sight; and in view of the difficulty of this discussion he may be tempted to thank God that it has pleased Him not to save His people by means of dialectic.[7]

Dr Paton illustrates this, the traditional Kantian criticism of the cosmological arguments, with the aid of an ingenuous example: he asks us to imagine a people damned in hell discussing the possibility of establishing the existence of God by reasoned argument (an imaginative venture which, on strictly Kantian principles, should be outlawed for we have no experience of hell to assure us that its unfortunate inmates would need to demonstrate God's existence in this cold-blooded way imposed on earthly seekers after the truth):

> If the cosmological argument holds at all, it must hold for any world in which objects are the effects of causes other than themselves. Hence it would be valid even if the only world we experienced were Hell—provided we were able to trace a relation of cause and effect between one torment and the next. As we should hardly be justified in conceiving as God a first cause whose sole known product was an inferno, it seems that the cosmological argument, even if it can prove the existence of something, cannot prove without the aid of further premises that this 'something' is God.[8]

Further, Kant disagreed with Hume's denial that there is anything necessary in the cause-effect relationship and considered that there is an element of necessity so long as we restrict the use of the relationship to the phenomenal world. But Kant considered that though we can infer the existence of a phenomenal cause for effects we find within the

[7]H. J. Paton: *The Modern Predicament*, p. 200.
[8]H. J. Paton: *op. cit.*, p. 191.

universe we cannot possibly use the principle of causality meta-physically or meta-empirically to show that there is a cause of the entire universe which is not itself within or of the universe. Human reason can only be used within the world of experience, for the cate-gories of the mind are of their nature applicable solely to sensible phenomena; hence they cannot be used to infer the existence of a being which is not a possible object of experience: 'so employed, the principle of causality, which is only valid within the field of experience, and outside this field has no application, nay, is indeed meaningless, would be altogether diverted from its proper use.'[9] Hence the principle of causality is of no avail in theistic argument. The first process of reasoning from contingent to necessary being cannot even establish that the necessary being is of a trans-empirical order of reality.

These criticisms made by Kant of the claims of a reasoned natural theology had the devastating effect of shattering the widespread agreement which used to exist amongst philosophers and theologians that we are able to establish the existence of God by reason. During the past 150 years Kant's opinion that the traditional arguments are invalid has firmly held the support it rapidly gained amongst philo-sophers. Even those who reject the main principles of his philosophy admit that he was right in his view about the impossibility of our being able to think of God's Being without becoming involved in some kind of antinomy or contradiction. In England at the present time the only philosophers who are prepared to defend the traditional arguments from the things of the world we know in experience are a handful of scholastic thinkers who stand by the integrity of the mediaeval science of metaphysics as the science of being, and of all that pertains to things inasmuch as they are beings (which is quite a different conception from anything Kant took metaphysics to be). Their voice is, however, scarcely audible in contemporary philosophical debates, and the work of scholastic philosophers from the continent on matters of meta-physics and natural theology is just brushed aside as better left alone. It is rare that we find an ally in an English philosopher owing no allegiance to scholasticism expounding the traditional arguments or defending them against Kant. Some years ago Mr A. E. Taylor made an outstanding defence of the cosmological arguments against Kant in

[9]Kant: *Critique of Pure Reason*, loc. cit., (p. 528 of Kemp Smith's translation).

his article on 'theism' in *Hastings' Encyclopaedia of Religion and Ethics*,[10] and recently Mr J. J. C. Smart defended the argument against Kant's criticisms in his article on 'The Existence of God' which was reprinted in the *New Essays in Philosophical Theology*, but only to reject it for another, and (shall we say) more up-to-date reason.[11] Outside scholastic circles, however, such defences of the traditional arguments against Kant are rare indeed, and, as we have remarked, we are faced with the amazing spectacle of the widespread acclamation by all manner and kind of philosophers of his reasons for rejecting the arguments as valid. All that the critics will grant is that the traditional arguments are of interest as rationalizations of man's persistent belief that an eternal Being on whom we somehow depend exists. The unfailing fascination which the arguments have for each generation of thinkers just witnesses to the vitality of this most cherished belief, it does not, alas, show that the belief itself is rationally justifiable.

\*     \*     \*

An objection against the traditional arguments which is gaining support nowadays, possibly as a result of recent trends in logic, is concerned with the notion of necessary being. Dr Paton raises the objection in a comparatively gentle manner, arguing that our concept of a necessary being is purely negative in content: all it means is that:

> God does not exist in time and space; and He has no cause, no condition, no ground, other than Himself. Even when we are told that He is a necessary being, we are not using the word 'necessary' in the sense in which it is applicable to contingent beings. As applied to God it does not mean 'necessary subject to a condition': it means 'necessary subject to no condition'. When we drop the condition which is ordinarily supposed to make necessity intelligible, do we get an absolute necessity which can be regarded as supremely intelligible? Or are we merely playing with words?[12]

To meet this difficulty of being left with merely negative concepts with which to think of God, Dr Paton argues that the proponents of the cosmological argument have had to 'make the negative concept of a

[10]cf. vol. 12, pp. 274–81.
[11]J. J. C. Smart: NEPT, pp. 36–37.
[12]H. J. Paton: *op. cit.*, p. 199.

non-contingent or necessary being into a positive one', and they do this by arguing first that a necessary being is its own ground, condition or cause, and explaining that as a consequence 'a necessary being is one whose non-existence is inconceivable—that is, it is one whose essence is the ground of its existence', and thus they have to fall back on the ontological argument for the 'non-existence of a being can be inconceivable only if we possess a concept which guarantees the existence of its object—the concept of an essence which is also a ground of existence'.[13] The concept of 'necessary being' seems therefore to be incoherent.

Mr J. J. C. Smart follows the more topical and ruthless line that necessity pertains solely to judgements and propositions, and not to existent things. It is therefore meaningless to talk of a necessary being. One might talk of the necessity of our thinking that God exists, and even of concluding a line of reasoning with the proposition 'God exists', but it is absurd to say that God necessarily exists. Talk about 'necessary being' just reveals complete ignorance of the difference between logical and real categories.[14] Mr Smart thus rejects the traditional arguments because he maintains that the first process mentioned by Kant of arguing from contingent to necessary being is invalid. On this score he must also reject the second process of the argument but, as we have just mentioned, he does not reject it for the reason given by Kant. Mr Smart seems to think that when we talk of God as the necessary being we mean that God is *logically* necessary, or that the traditional arguments argue to God as a logically necessary first cause, but he objects that 'logically necessary being' is a contradiction just like a 'round square'. Dr Hepburn examines the use of the concepts of contingency and necessity in a similar way, pointing out that the terms normally apply to propositions and not to things. Taking the word 'necessary' in its logical sense, the term 'necessary being' can mean that the proposition 'God exists' is necessary, and that God's non-existence is inconceivable. On this understanding of the expression he holds that the arguments demand 'a regress from beings whose non-existence is conceivable to a being whose non-existence is *in*conceivable', and this

[13]H. J. Paton: *op. cit.*, p. 199. cf. T. Penelhum: 'Divine Necessity', an article in *Mind*, April 1960, p. 181.
[14]J. J. C. Smart: *op. cit.*, pp. 37–39.

is impossible (for it is the ontological argument). There can be no such regress arguing from contingent being to a necessary being as in the popular version of the argument from contingency 'for its terminus would be not only infinitely remote but also logically impossible'. The other way of taking the necessity we ascribe to God is 'as saying something about God's mode of existence itself', as saying that God is (in the words he quotes of A. C. A. Rainer) 'complete actuality, indestructibility . . . independence of limiting conditions'.[15] But Dr Hepburn finds this sense equally open to objection, for characteristics such as these have to be understood in terms of causality. 'To call God completely actual and independent of conditions are ways of stating that he is the being who causes all things, but owes his existence to nothing, and cannot forfeit his existence through the action of any other being.' Dr Hepburn argues like Kant, that the application of the idea of causality in any form to God is full of difficulties for cause-words have their natural application when used to connect one limited thing with another limited thing, and they ought not to be compelled to connect infinite being with anything, nor to connect the totality of things to anything. Thus we should not speak of God as the cause of all things, nor of God as owing His existence to, nor forfeiting His existence through some other being. Such expressions have no meaning, and thus the theist's habit of speaking of God as necessary, as completely actual, as indestructible, and independent of limiting conditions really does not make any sense.[16] 'Necessity' is therefore a term which cannot be used of God, and all the arguments which employ the idea in connexion with God are invalid.[17]

\*       \*       \*

[15] A. C. A. Rainer: NEPT, p. 68.

[16] R. W. Hepburn: *op. cit.*, pp. 160–5; 171–4. cf. J. Laird: *Theism and Cosmology*, pp. 98–102.

[17] cf. A. J. Ayer: *Language, Truth and Logic* in which the logical positivist theory, that all statements are either necessary and tautologous because they express definitions or the formal consequences of definitions, or empirical and thence only more or less probable statements of fact, is admirably set forth. The theory is then used to show that the Christian idea of God, or any other idea of God as a transcendent being is meaningless on p. 44ff. E. L. Mascall deals with Ayer's theories in ch. 1 of *Words and Images*. As Professor Ayer has himself abandoned, or at least modified many of his earlier views, I do not regard them as constituting a real threat to a reasoned theism.

A final type of objection which is also given considerable prominence by contemporary writers bears on the indiscriminate use theists make of causality in their arguments for God's existence. Some philosophers argue that the idea of cause can only be applied to particular things, and 'that the concept of cause is not applicable to the total',[18] that is to say the whole universe. The statements that God is the cause of the universe as a whole, or that the universe as such is an effect produced by the creative activity of God have no meaning. This is a basic contention of Bertrand Russell who argues that it is as fallacious to argue that because particular things have a cause therefore the totality of things have a cause as well, as it is to argue that because every man has a mother, therefore the human race must have a mother as well. This objection has been made with considerable acumen by Dr Hepburn. He writes:

> When we are seriously speaking of absolutely everything there is, are we speaking of something that requires a cause, in the way that events *in* the universe may require causes? What indeed can be safely said at all about the totality of things? For a great many remarks that one can make with perfect propriety about limited things quite obviously can*not* be made about the cosmos itself. It cannot, for instance, be said meaningfully to be 'above' or 'below' anything, although things-in-the-universe can be so related to one another. . . . Our problem is this. Suppose we could draw up a list of questions that can be asked about objects in the universe, but cannot be asked about the *whole* universe: would the question, 'Has it a cause?' be on that list? One thing is clear. Whether or not this question is on the prescribed list, we are not entitled to argue as the cosmological argument does that *because* things in the world have causes, therefore the sum of things must also have *its* cause.[19]

In other words the logical principles governing the use of the word 'whole' are quite different from those governing the use of the word 'part', and in like manner the logic of the word 'thing' is quite different from that of the word 'universe'. We cannot, therefore, argue that because things may be effects of other things which are their causes,

[18]Russell: *Why I am not a Christian*, p. 152; cf. also A. C. Ewing: *op. cit.*, pp. 223–4.
[19]R. W. Hepburn: *op. cit.*, pp. 167–8.

therefore the universe may be an effect of which God is the cause. The notion of cause and effect only applies to particular things, and therefore we cannot just switch it as it stands 'to a cosmic setting'. It seems that 'while the world is indeed the *theatre* of causes and effects, we are not entitled to claim that it is itself an effect of some super-cause'.[20]

Dr Hepburn emphasizes the basic importance of the scientific idea of the cause-effect relationship as referring to the ordering and group-ing of events into uniform patterns observed experimentally. Those who accept this Kantian idea of causality must inevitably think that the 'natural habitat of "cause" words' must be the things we know from experience and observation. But if this is the proper meaning of causality, then the cosmological argument is of no avail,

> For if we argue from the existence of a world to a First Cause, we are not in this case recording some observed concomitance of events, or stating a causal law according to which certain sets of events vary reciprocally. We are instead *uprooting* the vocabulary of cause and effect from its habitat in the language, in order to relate the known *to the unknown and unknowable*. It is not the case that every time we have observed a universe, we have noticed a First Cause causing it, and that therefore we feel justified in saying, 'No universes without First Causes'.[21]

*          *          *

These are difficulties aimed at destroying the whole conception of theistic argument in any form and clearly they must be taken into con-sideration before we finish our study of St Thomas's proofs for the existence of God. The objections of Kant are directed against the entire structure of an argument for the existence of God based on experience; it is the opinion of many that they expose the artificiality of the appar-ently solid edifice of one compact argument, the logical futility of the final process of the reasoning, and the theological ineptitude of the first in that whatever necessary being might mean, it cannot help towards establishing the existence of God. For our critics difficulties raised by methods of analysis, especially linguistic analysis, serve to justify

[20]R. W. Hepburn: *op. cit.*, pp. 168–9.
[21]R. W. Hepburn: *op. cit.*, p. 160.

in new ways the criticisms Kant made. One objection maintains that the concept of necessity is inapplicable in any way to God, so that we cannot look either for logical or for real necessity in our arguments. This objection completed Kant's demolition of the idea of necessity as used in the arguments. Another objection rejects the idea of there being any cause-effect relationship between God and the world as a whole. Between them these objections demolish the entire fabric of any metaphysical argument. There are, of course, numerous other objections, but none threaten the position of the rational theist so totally. We can raise difficulties which attack particular points in the arguments here and there, and discuss them later on as occasion arises.

# 3

## THOMIST ATTITUDES TO THE FIVE WAYS

The attitude prevailing amongst most Thomist philosophers regarding the Five Ways is straightforward enough. It is that St Thomas asked the question 'utrum Deus sit' in the famous article 3 of Quaestio 2 in the first part of the *Summa Theologica*, and that following his usual method of asking and answering one question in each article, he answered the question in the same article, giving five arguments showing that God exists. Thus when we examine the exposition of the proofs for the existence of God in the work of a modern Thomist we find long and detailed studies given to each particular step of each of the five arguments as they are given in the text of article 3.[1] I have no wish to quarrel with what the scholars who adopt this attitude have to say when they are actually commenting on the text of this article, nor to enter into the controversies on which they are engaged concerning details of interpretation. I am not primarily concerned here, as they are, with the particular stages and details of the reasoning traced out by St Thomas in each of the Five Ways. I am concerned with a matter in which these Thomist writers show very little, if any, interest, namely, the overall conception of theistic reasoning within the plan of the *Summa Theologica*. I am concerned with the idea St Thomas had of the structure of theistic argument as such, and not with the particular lines followed by each argument he gave. The only real quarrel I have with these Thomists is with the conclusion they draw from the arguments, rather than with their interpretations of the arguments.

During the past fifty or so years Thomist writers have, on the whole, been almost exclusively preoccupied with (*a*) interpreting accurately each of the Five Ways, and determining the probative force of the reasoning of each Way as an argument for God's existence, and

[1] We have a good example of this attitude in the papers *Sulle 'Cinque Vie' di S. Tommaso* referred to in the footnote on p. 15.

(b) using these Ways for the purpose of dealing with modern difficulties and objections, with most of which, of course, St Thomas was not concerned when he wrote the *Summa*. They have in fact and quite understandably, been bending all their efforts to explaining the Five Ways to present-day readers with a view to defending them from the objections raised by Kant and other philosophers. Recently some Thomists on the continent have begun to take into consideration the atheist philosophy of Marxist Communism, and have used the Five Ways to show that with them we can defend the basis of Christianity from a purely materialist philosophy. Father Charles Boyer, for example, in the preface to the papers referred to in the above footnote, writes in this spirit: 'Se qualche cosa è urgente per l'onore di Dio e la salvezza degli uomini, è certamente il combattere l'ateismo, illustrando le prove classiche dell'esistenza di Dio.'[2]

No doubt this effort of modern Thomists is necessary, and no doubt St Thomas has much to say in contemporary debates about the existence of God. But a too exclusive emphasis on apologetics, and an all too ready assumption that the Five Ways, on their own and apart from the context in which they exist, are all that is needed in any emergency in any age, must engender an attitude of mind which will fail more or less completely to think of them as St Thomas himself thought of them when he wrote the first part of the *Summa*, and as the readers for whom he wrote would actually have thought of them. Most readers of the *Summa*, as of any other work belonging to a bygone age, would consider that in our reading we must keep an eye open for all kinds of peculiarities of style, treatment, vocabulary, etc., due solely to historical circumstances, and that we should always try to distinguish between what a writer is saying and the particular way in which he may have expressed what he is saying. Dr Mascall is only stating a truism when he writes that 'St Thomas's own exposition of the argument (for the existence of God) was, of course, adapted to the circumstances of his time and was deeply influenced by the sources from which he derived it',[3] and Van Steenberghen is surely wholly justified in protesting against the way in which modern Thomist philosophers take the Five Ways out of their context in the *Summa* and serve them

[2]C. Boyer: *op. cit.*, p. 1–2.
[3]E. L. Mascall: *Existence and Analogy*, p. 66.

up as they stand with complete assurance that they are all that we need for a reasoned theism in our own day.[4] But, strange as it might seem, the rigid Thomist will have none of this: he persists in regarding the Five Ways as perfect for all time, just as we find them in article 3. Umberto Degl'Innocenti, and others, have expressed their annoyance with Van Steenberghen for drawing attention to historical reasons accounting for weaknesses in the arguments as given in article 3, but there can be no doubt that in the opinion of most people Van Steenberghen's attitude is correct in principle, and equally that of the rigid Thomists who think like Umberto Degl'Innocenti is unsound in principle.[5] It may well be that some of the conflicting interpretations given to the Five Ways by modern Thomists owe their origin in some measure to difficulties they have encountered in re-thinking the old arguments as they stand in a climate and atmosphere vastly different from that in which they were originally conceived, instead of studying them first in the native surroundings in which they originated and then adapting them where necessary with a view to dealing with modern problems. For example, the modern Thomists cannot agree as to whether we have five separate and complete arguments in article 3, or five versions of, or variations on one and the same argument, or whether only the first three Ways are really one argument; they are widely opposed on the interpretation to be put on the fourth Way, for which we have at least three different interpretations, and there is little agreement as to whether we can regard the fourth Way as standing on its own feet, or as based upon the first three Ways as on its necessary foundation. They fail to determine how the fifth Way stands to the others, and precisely what it demonstrates. Above all Thomists seem to avoid facing both the question about the relationship between article 3 and the following Quaestio 3, and the difficulty which has been simmering in the background for centuries that, if the Five Ways are separate arguments, and each one is accepted as valid on its own, how we are to establish that the five beings we attain in the arguments are one and the same God. No one that I know of has faced this problem as

[4]F. Van Steenberghen: 'Le Problème Philosophique de l'Existence de Dieu', in the *Revue Philosophique de Louvain* (1947), pp. 5–20; 141–68; 301–16.
[5]U. Degl'Innocenti, O.P., 'La validità della "III via",' p. 42–43 of the *Doctor Communis* volume.

it deserves and as clear-sightedly as Dr Mascall in chapter 4 of his
*Existence and Analogy*. It is very difficult to hold that St Thomas left
these problems unsolved and that if we read the *Summa* as he intended
it to be read we shall fail to find these problems solved.

*        *        *

To study the way St Thomas conceived the problem of the nature
of theistic argument as such we must adopt a different attitude to
article 3. There is, first of all, no reason whatever to imagine that St
Thomas wrote the Five Ways with any other readers in mind than
those who lived in the thirteenth century, and we can be quite certain
that while writing he never envisaged any of the problems which we
have mentioned in the last chapter as bequeathed to us by Kant and
post-Kantian philosophers. Second, in order to appreciate what he
intended to say in writing the Five Ways we must study not only the
contents of article 3, but also the context of contemporary mediaeval
debates into which the contents of the article fit. I suggest, therefore,
that we would be well advised to study the Five Ways neither ab-
stractly on their own as though they did not belong to some natural
surroundings, nor in the context of the Kantian and post-Kantian
philosophers which is alien to them, but first and foremost in their
natural surroundings where, after all, they have their proper roots.
To know a man we must have studied him first in his family circle and
in the surroundings of his home country, and not presume to judge him
solely from how he fits or fails to fit into far removed and even completely alien surroundings. Similarly before we begin to fit them into
the context of the controversies of later centuries, we must study the
Five Ways in the context of the controversies of the time when they
were written, and we shall then be the better able to see them as
Aquinas himself saw them, and as he intended his readers to see them.

I feel quite certain that many readers will be saying to themselves,
as they realize that I am suggesting the need for starting on a new
inquiry, that St Thomas's Five Ways are thoroughly well known
already to all philosophers worthy of the name, and that being the
case, this attempt at something like re-introducing a classic in a new light
is (to say the least) highly pretentious. Is not the chance of making a new
discovery in, or casting fresh light upon, something that is famous and

familiar even to the youngest novice, most improbable? and is not the suggestion, that something with which we are closely acquainted, and have been closely acquainted for years, but seldom studied as it ought to be, rash and intemperate? Nothing more need be said in reply to suggestions like these than ask those who are interested to take up the text of St Thomas on this, or almost any other vexed problem, and, forgetting their own problems as well as those of modern times, put themselves as they read as far as they can into the Angelic Doctor's frame of mind by thinking themselves back into the thirteenth century, working for months at a stretch with him as he writes in his cell: anyone who seriously tries to do this in even quite a small way will soon realize how difficult the *Summa Theologica* is to read, especially in certain sections, and even how unfamiliar a great deal of it really is.[6] There is, after all, as everyone knows a world of difference between being acquainted and familiar with things or persons and really knowing or understanding them. We do well not to shirk further investigation when people say that some Quaestio or article of the *Summa* is well known lest we overlook much that is of importance, or that St Thomas would himself have regarded as important, though it may not feature prominently in the mind of modern Thomist philosophers because it is irrelevant to the problems of later times. Scholars who are even moderately familiar with mediaeval studies, and more especially expert mediaevalists who know of the intricacies of historical investigation into the sources of the ideas and arguments of the schoolmen, or who try to trace the development of ideas on any topic during the life of a theologian or in the course of some era, will appreciate the wisdom of Victor White's remarks at the beginning of his paper, 'Prelude to the Five Ways'. He writes:

> It has become extraordinarily difficult to read the text of St Thomas Aquinas as he wrote it, or as it would have been read by his contemporaries. Few even attempt to read it until they have been thoroughly initiated into the later developments of Thomism with the aid of introductions and manuals, and it becomes hard to read the original except through their spectacles and without their preoccupations in mind. Those sections of the text which have a parti-

[6]David Knowles: *The Historical Context of the Philosophical Works of St Thomas Aquinas,* Aquinas Society Paper, No. 30.

cular interest and importance of their own may all too easily be read torn out of their context in the closely-knit unity which is the *Summa Theologica*, and disregard for what precedes or follows them in the original text can all too easily distort their meaning and purport. There is also the risk that we seek in the *Summa* for contributions to controversies which had not yet arisen when it was written, or answers to questions which the original text had already excluded.[7]

Father White's next sentence provides me with the foundation on which many of my reflections on St Thomas's handling of the question of God's existence are based, and on the soundness of which I stand in presuming to suggest that there is something fresh for which we can look in the text if we adopt a different and a more scientific attitude towards it: 'our reading of the *Quinque Viae*—the so-called "Five Ways" of proving the existence of God—in the *Summa* (1, ii, 3) is perhaps rather especially liable to be blurred in these ways.' Our reading of article 3 is indeed especially liable to be blurred if, being absorbed with modern controversies, we become almost forcibly prevented from reading the text save as we think St Thomas might be reading it with us at the moment if he had returned to give us a hand with the task of dealing with modern and contemporary problems. Article 3 is one of those passages to which Father White refers as 'having particular interest and importance of their own', so that they are 'all too easily read torn out of their context in the closely-knit unity which is the *Summa Theologica*'. We tend to forget that St Thomas wrote the whole of Quaestio 2 of the *Summa* with the controversies of his own day in mind, and with no other readers than the students of the theology schools in a thirteenth-century university, and the educated laity seeking instruction from a trained theologian, being so much as envisaged; St Thomas must have envisaged whatever he may have had in mind as fitting into the situation that existed in the theological world at the time he wrote the *Summa,* for there is no reason why he should have thought in terms of any other situation. We have no justification for presuming that he would have written article 3 just as it stands had he been engaged in dealing with our philosophical problems and difficulties about proving the existence of God, and therefore before we

[7]Victor White, O.P., *God the Unknown*, p. 35.

use it as best we can (as is perfectly permissible provided we make due allowance for the change of context and situation which prevailed then and which prevails now), we ought to take the greatest care to place the article 'in the closely-knit unity of the *Summa*', and study it in the light of what precedes and follows. By so doing we shall at least be trying to read the *Summa* as it would have been read by theologians in the thirteenth century, and seeing in it what St Thomas wished us to find in it.

For the time being, then, we will put Kant's criticism of theistic argument and all the other pressing difficulties of modern philosophy out of our thoughts, no matter how forcefully they may clamour for first place in our estimation of their importance. Similarly we will put modern interpretations of the Five Ways out of our minds as far as we are able. Without wishing to quarrel with those who have studied the different steps in the argument of each of the Five Ways, we propose to adopt an altogether different, but perfectly realistic and scientific line. We will ask how St Thomas conceived the arguments he gave in article 3 as fitting within his overall plan of the *Summa*, and especially of the first part in which he treats of God. We will ask how in particular he conceived article 3 of Quaestio 2 as following on the two preceding articles of that Quaestio, and as leading on to Quaestio 3 and those which follow. If we try to think in this way as objectively as possible we shall perhaps find that there are points of unusual interest about the Five Ways which are overlooked in the debates about the 'traditional arguments', but which ought to be taken into consideration by anyone who refers to St Thomas as connected with them.

# 4

## WHAT PRECEDES THE FIVE WAYS

In the first Quaestio of the *Summa* St Thomas treats of *Sacra Doctrina*, of Sacred Teaching. He considers what Sacred Teaching is (qualis sit), and to what it extends (ad quae se extendit). The wary reader will realize at once that with this term he is confronted, at the very beginning of the *Summa Theologica*, with a formidable difficulty with which he may have to wrestle for a long time till he finds an answer which is wholly satisfactory. He has to decide what St Thomas meant by this term, *Sacra Doctrina*. Fortunately we are able to by-pass the problem by giving a solution which is adequate enough for our purposes, and (I trust) accurate as far as it goes, though it is far from complete. I must refer the reader who is interested in studying the problem further for its own sake to the excellent works of Father Van Ackeren, S.J.,[1] Father Congar, O.P.,[2] and Father Victor White, O.P.,[3] to all of whom I am profoundly indebted in the writing of this, as of the sixth chapter.

For St Thomas *Sacra Doctrina* did not mean what we nowadays refer to as 'religious doctrine', that is to say truths about the Catholic religion in which instruction is to be given. The expression meant roughly the same as Catholic teaching, in the twofold sense of (a) the activity of instructing men undertaken by authorized teachers, and (b) instructing them in the truths availing to salvation. As Father Van Ackeren points out, *Doctrina* meant for St Thomas 'the action of a person who causes knowledge in another', and *Disciplina* meant 'the reception of knowledge from another'.[4] Father White points out that we have a clue to the meaning of the term *Sacra Doctrina*, as St Thomas

[1] Gerald Van Ackeren, S.J., *Sacra Doctrina* (Officium Libri Catholici, Rome).
[2] M. J. Congar, O.P., *Bulletin Thomiste*, V, pp. 490–500, and the article on 'Théologie' in the D.T.C., colums 341–502.
[3] Victor White, O.P., *Holy Teaching* (Aquinas Society Paper).
[4] G. Van Ackeren, *op. cit.*, p. 54.

used it in Quaestio 1, in the opening words of the Prologue in which he sketches the work of the *Catholicæ Veritatis Doctor,* which, he says, includes not only the instructing or developing of those advancing in knowledge (doctor non solum provectos debet instruere), but the forming of beginners (incipientes erudire). The word *Doctor* is used here to denote, not an academically qualified lecturer who has received the degree of 'doctor', but a teacher commissioned by the Church to instruct men in the Catholic faith, who in the Middle Ages may have been a bishop, a parish priest, a licensed preacher or a university lecturer holding a chair in a theological faculty. The students St Thomas had in mind when writing the *Summa Theologica* were not exclusively students within a university, but all those who wished to learn about the Catholic truth as genuine students. It seems that he also wrote for the benefit of those lecturing in theology and actually engaged in instructing the rising generation of theological students within the universities. These students would have completed their course in the arts faculty and so be well versed in the liberal arts, and have acquired a sound knowledge of the works of Aristotle which had been finding their way into the arts faculties of the mediaeval universities during the first half of the thirteenth century. Their instruction in *Sacra Doctrina* presented the *Doctor Catholicae Veritatis* with all kinds of new problems which doubtless St Thomas hoped his *Summa* would help to solve. In brief, then, there is no doubt he had especially in mind students who had passed as clerics from the arts faculties into the theology schools, but there is nothing in the text of the *Summa* to suggest that he had them alone in mind.

Father White points out that in the Prologue, and in the whole of Quaestio 1, St Thomas bases his idea of what Sacred Teaching is on his ideal of the teacher-learner relationship, and in particular on the elementary pedagogical principle that the teacher should have the interests of his pupils uppermost in his mind. As he is writing for students St Thomas says that he intends to treat the truths of the Catholic faith 'secundum ordinem disciplinae', or in an order that will facilitate learning; and since he is writing especially for beginners he intends to avoid the somewhat haphazard and unpedagogical ways in which in those days *Sacra Doctrina* was often studied in the lecture room as a result of adhering rigidly to a text on which the lecturer gave his commentaries, and to supply something to improve upon the hopeless task (from the student's point of view) of having to learn by following a series of public disputations on select questions. He proposes instead to treat his subject briefly and clearly, as briefly and as clearly as the subject will allow, and make the instruction of the students in their subject ever his prime concern. Implicitly Aquinas is saying that the students of those days would be better off without the Commentaries on set texts and highly specialized disputations, or at least that they needed something else as a foundation for study. His intention, therefore, is to deal with those truths which belong to the Christian religion in a way that suits the beginner, and facilitates his formation: 'Propositum nostrae intentionis in hoc opere est, ea quae ad christianam religionem pertinent, eo modo tradere, secundum quod congruit ad eruditionem incipientium.'[5]

\* \* \*

The first article of Quaestio 1 is not without an interest of its own. St Thomas does not follow the line that Sacred Teaching is plainly necessary in its own right and standing in no need of justification, and then try to justify what was in his day the innovation of the philosophical disciplines (as a number of the more conservative theologians of the time, following the Augustinian-Anselmian principle of *Credo ut intelligam* used to consider more suited to the theologian). In a way that would have scandalized a St Bernard, St Thomas accepts the necessity of the purely human and the philosophical disciplines which are the work of unaided reason (even 'illa theologia quae pars philosophiae ponitur', as distinct from that theology 'quae ad sacram doctrinam pertinet'),[6] and he argues that besides these disciplines a teaching coming from God by divine revelation is necessary for all men. This teaching, however, is necessary not because man has any natural desire or necessity for the knowledge it imparts, but because God has called and destined all men for an end which is beyond their nature, indeed beyond all natural being, because especially given by God as a supernatural or divine gift. If men are to be able to live in this world with a

[5]['Our intention in this book is to treat of all that belongs to the Christian religion in a way that is suited to the formation of beginners.']
[6]Art. 1, ad 2; cf. also art. 5. cf. I *Sent.*, Prologus, qu. 1, art. 1.

view to attaining this end and so saving their souls from the consequences of sin, they must have a knowledge of this end. Sacred Teaching is thus not necessary to man as the natural sciences are, because man
is what he is, but because God plans to make him something he can
never make himself, something supernatural. Sacred Teaching is
therefore necessary to men, not absolutely because men naturally seek
to know what God has to teach them, but hypothetically or granted
that God's plans for man's eternal life happen to require it, and that
man is freely going to accept the gift of God. Likewise men seek this
divine knowledge not absolutely because their nature require it, but
only if they are seeking God as their end and their salvation in God.
Sacred Teaching, therefore, is a God-given gift as is salvation itself of
which it is an integral part. It is essential to man's final well-being as
supernaturally ordained by God in the sense that, like all the supernatural gifts of God, it positively contributes towards a man's perfection: it is no mere condition of salvation contributing nothing positive
of its own, but a factor which itself advances us towards our final well-
being and salvation.[7]

Here, as in the fourth chapter of the first book of the *Contra
Gentes,* St Thomas grants that in principle human reason is no doubt
able to attain some knowledge of God by itself, but in practice this
will only be attained by a few people, and after much time has been
expended in seeking for it, and 'cum admixtione multorum errorum'.[8]
Lack of ability in reasoning, lack of time, inclination or opportunity
will inevitably mean that most men will fail to reach even that smatter-
ing of certain knowledge which it is theoretically within their power to
attain. If, then, God wills that man's salvation is to be found exclusively
in Him and in the enjoyment of His Being, evidently men need to be
instructed from on high by God Himself in the truth about God, and
the knowledge of God given to men is evidently a part of His gift of
salvation to man. Thus St Thomas introduces the theme that *Sacra
Doctrina* instructs all men in the truth about God, so that they may
know Him, not as the philosopher knows Him in his quest for speculative knowledge to satisfy a natural thirst of his intellect, but as God

[7] cf. also I *Sent.,* Prologus, qu. 1, art. 3. *Summa Theologica,* II–II, qu. 1, art. 6,
ad. 1.
[8] cf. also *Summa Theologica,* II–II, qu. 2, art. 4.

has made Himself known to us and wishes to be known by us, i.e. as being Himself man's eternal life. Sacred Teaching is a supernatural theology totally different from the natural theology of the philosophers. As Father White says so clearly, the investigations of the philosopher into the Being of God cannot 'lead to the healing and saving truth which depend on God's free grace and calling', and he concludes 'whatever claims may therefore be made for such 'natural theology', it cannot meet the concrete needs of all men, nor indeed bring the good news of God's mighty and loving *salus* to any. Yet on some acknowledgement of this "dependent tota hominis salus quae in Deo est".'[9]

*        *        *

In articles 2–8 St Thomas explains his ideas about the nature of Sacred Teaching, and we must remember that, though these ideas have been accepted, or at least known almost universally for several centuries by theologians, many of them were real innovations and were regarded as such in the thirteenth century. For his contemporaries the most striking thing about the teaching of the holy doctor was its novelty, 'new arrangements of the subject-matter, new methods of proof, new arguments adduced for the conclusions; in short, no one who heard him could doubt that his mind was full of a new light from God'.[10] He seemed to some to be 'another Moses, for God first spoke to him in the spirit, and then sent him out to be the leader of his brethren, not without signs and great wonders'.[11]

Sacred Teaching is, he maintains in article 2, knowledge or *scientia*. Once again I agree fully with Father White that we cannot translate *scientia,* as used here in this article, in the way that some do, to mean what we now call 'science'. St Thomas is showing in this article not that Sacred Teaching is a 'science', but that it gives us genuine knowledge and certainty, and not just some kind of opinion or a number of conjectures on which we might be urged to look favourably. He is dealing with the difficulty that because we can only believe the truths which God reveals, because our intellectual response to God teaching can only

[9] V. White, *op. cit.,* p. 11.
[10] cf. Kenelm Foster, O.P., *The Life of Saint Thomas Aquinas: Biographical Documents,* p. 33.
[11] cf. Kenelm Foster, O.P., *The Life of Saint Thomas Aquinas: Biographical Documents,* p. 35.

be one of belief, seeing that we cannot possibly know the truths of faith in such a way as to be able to understand and prove them by reason, faith cannot give us knowledge. To this St Thomas replies that, because we can only believe and never know in the sense of understand what revelation teaches, we cannot conclude that what we believe is not knowledge (*scientia*) but a mere probability, for what we are taught comes to us from the understanding or perfect knowledge which God, our Teacher, has. We believe what God understands, so that we share in the knowledge God has of Himself and which the saints possess; but we do not share God's knowledge so perfectly as to have an understanding of what we are given to know for on earth we only know in a glass darkly: 'Et hoc modo sacra doctrina est scientia, quia procedit ex principiis notis lumine superioris scientiae, quae scilicet est Dei et beatorum.'[12] Sacred Teaching is thus, for St Thomas, a knowledge subalternate (to use the technical term) to that of God and the saints in heaven, even as, to repeat his own example, the knowledge that a musician has of the arithmetic he uses is accepted on faith from a mathematician, and so subalternate to the mathematician's knowledge of mathematics. The mathematician knows, in the sense of understands, arithmetic; the musician accepts by belief what knowledge he has of arithmetic without (necessarily) understanding what he believes, and this is sufficient for the purposes for which he needs it in his music. Because his knowledge of arithmetic is based not on his own thinking, but on the superior knowledge of the mathematicians, it is genuine knowledge, and not just the musician's own private opinion about mathematical truths he does not understand.[13] What the one knows and understands, the other knows not by understanding, but by belief; but in both cases there is knowledge (*scientia*). Thus Father White writes:

> So far from proving that theology is a science on our side, the article establishes by implication that *sacra doctrina* precisely is not: no more than is the arithmetic of the musician. But being accepted in faith it is, as the next article finely puts it, a certain imprint in us of God's own knowledge.[14]

[12]'[And it is in this way that Holy Teaching is a science. It is based on principles which belong to a more perfect kind of knowledge, namely that of God Himself and the saints].' Art. 2.

[13]cf. M. D. Chenu: *La Théologie comme Science au XIIIe Siècle*, pp. 71–85.

[14]V. White, O.P., *op. cit.*, p. 13.

In articles 3 and 4 St Thomas introduces a basic theme which runs right through the rest of the Quaestio, and indeed the whole of the *Summa:* it is that *Sacra Doctrina* is one *scientia* (again taking 'scientia' to mean knowledge), because although it may treat about many different kinds of persons, things and events, it none the less treats of them all only in so far as we have been taught about them by God, and in so far as they are fitted by God within the plan He has, and which He has revealed to us, of our salvation. He points out that the unity of *Sacra Doctrina* is assured by the unity of its formal object, that is to say by the uniformity of the way in which everything which we are given to know is made known to us. We know all that we do know because God has revealed it and just as God has revealed it. In article 7 he adds the further reason that *Sacra Doctrina* has only one proper subject, and it is God Himself: everything else that is revealed to us is only revealed in so far as it is connected in some way with God: 'Omnia autem tractantur in sacra doctrina sub ratione Dei vel quia sunt ipse Deus, vel quia habent ordinem ad Deum, ut ad principium et finem.'[15] This idea, that *Sacra Doctrina* treats solely of God as its proper subject, or that God Himself is the formal object of theology, was new in St Thomas's day. He did not accept the older idea that Sacred Teaching treats of the biblical narrative of the fall and redemption, which is a narrative of the long series of prophecies and of historical events stretching throughout time recorded in the Old and New Testaments, for *Sacra Doctrina* is not biblical exegesis; nor did he even accept the idea that it treats of the person and work of Jesus Christ, nor of the total Christ, 'idest caput et membra',[16] as its distinctive subject. As we shall explain at greater length later, any such ideas of the proper subject matter of *Sacra Doctrina* were ruled out for Aquinas because he was convinced that Sacred Teaching is not only knowledge but scientific knowledge; as he adhered to the Aristotelian principle that science is only of the universal and necessary, and never of the particular or contingent, he could not find the subject-matter of *Sacra Doctrina* in the historical narratives of the Bible nor in the events of Christ's human life. God, however, is

[15] '[But in Holy Teaching all things are considered from the point of view of God, either because the things considered are God Himself, or because they refer to God as to their origin or end].' Art. 7; cf. also art. 3, ad. 1 cf. I *Sent.*, Prologus, qu. 1, art. 4.

[16] Art. 4.

necessary being: He alone is *per se* necessary in Himself, and thus the science of *Sacra Doctrina* must have God alone as its proper subject, and consider all other things, including the person and work of Jesus himself, 'secundum ordinem ad Deum',[16] as related to God. Thus *Sacra Doctrina* is one knowledge, one science, for all things are considered in relation to the one God, as He has made them known to us in His Revelation, and it is more speculative than practical (even though given with a view to our attaining salvation) because it considers human actions not for what they are in themselves, but as the work of God in us leading us to Himself.[17] As God knows Himself and all things in the knowledge He has of Himself, so Sacred Teaching resembles God's knowledge in that it gives us knowledge of God and all other things in this knowledge we are given of God (and not apart from it).

I cannot do better in closing this section than refer the reader to the incomparable pages in which Cardinal Newman has expressed his mind on the science of theology, for on this topic he and Aquinas agree exactly:

> Say that no other religious idea whatever were given but it (i.e. that of God), and you have enough to fill the mind; you have at once a whole dogmatic system. The word 'God' is a theology in itself, indivisibly one, inexhaustibly various, from the vastness and the simplicity of its meaning. Admit a God, and you introduce among the subjects of your knowledge, a fact encompassing, closing in upon, absorbing every fact conceivable.[18]

\*     \*     \*

As God is the sole subject of *Sacra Doctrina,* St Thomas so planned his *Summa Theologica* that all its parts should converge on the central theme of God Himself: 'omnia tractantur sub ratione Dei'.[19] Let us see now how St Thomas works this plan out, so far as his planning affects his treatment of the arguments for the existence of God. At the beginning of Quaestio 2 he inserts a short Introduction, the importance of which cannot be over-estimated, giving the basic lines of the plan

---

[16]Art. 7, cf. also II–II, qu. 1, art. 1; qu. 4, art. 6, ad. 1.
[17]Art. 4.
[18]J. H. Newman: *Idea of a University*, Discourse 2, sec. 3 (p. 26).
[19]cf. Per Erik Persson: 'Le Plan de la Somme Théologique et le rapport "Ratio-Revelatio" ', in the *Revue Philosophique de Louvain*, Nov. 1958, pp. 545–72.

he proposes to follow in constructing the vast edifice of the *Summa*. This Introduction serves as an admirable link connecting Quaestio 1 on *Sacra Doctrina* with the following Quaestio 2, *De Deo: an Deus Sit*. In its widest sweep the *Summa*, he says, will treat of God in the first part, of the movement of rational creatures to God in the second part, and of Christ, 'qui, secundum quod homo, via est nobis tendendi in Deum', in the third part. St Thomas then shows how he proposes to treat about God in the first part. He proposes to fit everything under three main treatises, first he will consider what pertains to the divine essence (and this he does in Quaestiones 2–26), then of the Trinity of the divine persons (which he does in Quaestiones 27–43), and finally of God as the source and creator of all things, of the kinds of thing which He creates, and of God's government of all that He creates (as he does in Quaestiones 44–119). He then proceeds to specify in greater detail how he will deal with the study of the divine essence. Again he introduces three headings: 'primo considerandum est an Deus sit; secundo, quomodo sit, vel potius quomodo non sit; tertio considerandum erit de his quae ad operationem ipsius pertinent, scilicet de scientia et voluntate et potentia'.[20] Thus, for St Thomas the question of establishing the existence of God is a part of the vaster question about the essence of God, and it is planned to be treated not for its own sake, but for the sake of showing what the divine essence is. There are, in other words, three major theological questions for St Thomas about God, and they concern the divine essence, the Trinity of Persons in God and God the creator. There is no separate *theological* question about God's existence: the question about God's existence is only raised at all in connexion with the study of what God is.

The modern scholastic philosopher usually divides his natural theology into three distinct parts and treats first of the existence of God, second of God's essence or nature, and finally of God's activity outside Himself. These divisions which the modern philosopher needs to make in natural theology, starting with one reserved for the existence of God, are sound enough from the point of view of modern philosophy, with all the philosophical problems that have to be considered in proving

[20]'[First we must consider whether God is; second, how He is, or rather how He is not; and third, all that pertains to the divine activity, that is to say, God's knowledge, will and power].'

God's existence. Fundamentally the philosopher is concerned to show that God exists as the cause of the universe, and he is only concerned with God inasmuch as He is the cause of all being. He can only seek such knowledge of what God is as he can gather from proving that He is the cause of all things. The philosopher, then, is only concerned with God in so far as He explains the being of the universe, and in so far as the universe points beyond itself to Him. But St Thomas is clearly not planning his *Summa Theologica* in the way that a philosopher nowadays needs to plan his natural theology. When they treat Quaestio 2 of the *Summa* as corresponding with their discussion of the proofs for God's existence and Quaestio 3 onwards as corresponding with this treatment of the divine essence, the modern Thomists are twisting St Thomas's clearly stated plan to suit their own. St Thomas is clearly not planning his *Summa Theologica* in the way that a philosopher plans his natural theology, for one reason because, writing as a theologian, he provides no separate question *an Deus sit* to be treated on its own before he comes to the second question of the divine essence. St Thomas is concerned with God as He has revealed Himself to us, with what God has told us about Himself, or in technical terms with the divine essence itself, and not simply with God as the cause of created things. He has no need as the philosopher has to prove that God exists before he treats of the divine essence. St Thomas has more than assured us of his certainty of God's existence, and that he knows full well that all his readers share his certainty, from the very beginning of the *Summa* in saying what he means by *Sacra Doctrina* and in defining what he means by that branch of theology which differs from philosophical theology because it gives us knowledge from the living God. He is only compelled to consider the ways in which we can establish the existence of God by reason in so far as this is required to make what God has revealed about Himself (His essence) intelligible to reason. In other words, the question of the existence of God, and equally that of how God does not exist (which is necessary to show how different God is from all created things) is regarded by him, not as a separate question to be treated on its own philosophically, as though it had nothing to do with the revelation of God, before treating the divine essence, but as involved in the theological study of God's essence. The sequence of his thought, then, is quite clear. He passes directly from his study of Sacred Teaching to his study of the divine essence: there is no justification for thinking that he introduced the query 'utrum Deus sit' for its own sake, as a kind of philosophical interlude, especially when he himself states explicitly that he introduces it because it is involved in the consideration of a problem which, from the theological point of view, is more ultimate, and as helping towards the solution of that problem. As Father White says:

> The *Summa Theologica* is not, as is sometimes supposed, a *potpourri* of theology and philosophy; it is wholly a *Summa* of Theology concerned with the *Sacra Doctrina,* the Holy Teaching of salvation given by God's revelation. But because it is that, it can *use* philosophical argument for its own end—which is *hominis salus*—the health or salvation of man. It in no way substitutes a 'natural theology' for revelation, nor does it appeal to reason for what only revelation can impart.[21]

The whole of Quaestio 2, *De Deo: an Deus sit,* is therefore put into the *Summa* for the sake of unravelling in the following Quaestiones the theological problem of God's essence, or of expounding by reason what God has revealed of Himself.

During the Middle Ages the 'problem of God' (if we may be pardoned the use of the expression) was a theological problem, and it was concerned with determining, not whether God is, or whether we can establish that He is by reason, but with what He is, and by what thinking processes we can attain a knowledge of what He has revealed about Himself. St Thomas treats of the divine essence in Quaestiones 2–11, of how we can know his essence in Quaestio 12, and of the divine names in Quaestio 13. The planning of the treatise on God in the *Summa* is thus in perfect keeping with the theological outlook of the thirteenth century. But if he agrees with his contemporaries in concentrating his attention on the study of the divine essence, St Thomas differs from

[21]V. White, O.P., 'Prelude to the five ways', from *God the Unknown,* p. 44.
The view of many writers I am rejecting here as false is well summarized by Professor John Baillie: 'St Thomas thought he could harmonize the two traditions by simply placing them side by side—a process which may be described as synthesis by juxtaposition. The Greek tradition, as we saw, gave him his *natural* knowledge, and the Biblical tradition his *revealed* knowledge. The former provided the first chapters in theology, and the latter the more advanced.' cf. *Our Knowledge of God,* p. 127.

them in that he regards the line of reasoning to be followed in determining what God is, so far as reason can do this under the guidance of
faith, as really one with that by which we come to a reasoned knowledge of God's existence, or at least with that by which we commence
reasoning to His existence from the things of this world; in other words
we determine what God is by continuing the arguments commenced
to establish that He is, and show that He exists in a way which is unlike
that in which anything we know from experience exists. In this way
the question 'utrum Deus sit' comes, for St Thomas, within the question 'quid Deus sit', of what God has revealed Himself to be.

It is interesting to note that St Thomas laid down exactly the same
line of procedure for the theological study of God in the first book of
the *Contra Gentes,* in chapter 9 of which he lays down the order and
method he is going to follow in his work. Again he says that he will
treat first of the divine essence, 'primo occurit consideratio de his
quae de Deo secundum seipsum conveniunt'; then he proposes to treat
of God as the cause of creatures, 'de processu creaturarum ab ipso'; and
thirdly of the order of creatures to God as to their last end. (He leaves
the Trinity to the fourth book because the *Contra Gentes,* being written
in defence of the reasonableness of the faith, presents the truths of revelation which reason can understand more fully before the greatest
mysteries of the faith.) Finally he concludes by stating explicitly why
and how he is going to give the arguments of reason for the existence
of God: 'inter ea vero quae de Deo secundum seipsum consideranda
sunt, praemittendum est, quasi totius operis necessarium fundamentum,
consideratio qua demonstratur Deum esse. Quo non habito, omnis
consideratio de rebus divinis necessario tollitur.'[22] This is categorical:
the proofs for God's existence are required as the indispensable foundation on which the whole of a speculative theology of the divine essence,

[22]'[Before all the questions to be considered about God as He is in His own
Being, we must place first of all, as the necessary foundation of the whole inquiry,
the arguments showing that God exists. If these are wanting, there cannot
possibly be any considerations about God Himself.]' I regard the *Contra Gentes* as a
*Summa Theologica* as it is clearly stated to be in Book I, ch. 2. In ch. 9 the passage
just quoted is preceded by a section in which St Thomas says that his intention is
to manifest the truth about God which 'faith proposes and reason investigates',
and therefore I regard all Book I as written under the direction of faith and not as
pure philosophy. cf. Chenu: *Introduction à l'Etude de St Thomas d'Aquin,* pp.
251–3.

or of what we know of God *secundum seipsum* from revelation, can be built.

* * *

We return now to Quaestio 1 to continue our study of St Thomas's conception of *Sacra Doctrina*. After showing that God is the proper subject about Whom we are taught in Revelation, St Thomas takes up one of the great questions of his day, as to whether Holy Teaching is a 'science' in the technical sense of the term. He explicitly raises this question, not in article 2, but in article 8 with the query 'Utrum haec doctrina sit argumentativa', though in fact he had been forced to touch upon the matter earlier in answering the second objection of article 5. Sacred Teaching, as such, is the knowledge of God we have received from Him. Science, as such, represents a human way of knowing with certainty: it investigates the processes by which we can demonstrate, or cast some light upon events that we know happen and statements that we know to be true, but do not fully understand because we cannot explain why the events happen or why the statements are true. For Aristotle science is a knowledge of events through their causes enabling us to see why and how events come to pass as they do. Sacred Teaching will become a science, then, as it investigates how and up to what point we can rationally demonstrate what God has made known to us, or up to what point we can think reasonably and consistently the great mysteries of faith which God has revealed. But though St Thomas was always in favour of treating Sacred Teaching as a science, paradoxically enough he would be the first to insist that the least important thing about it is that it should be regarded as a science. Unlike any purely human form of knowledge, the holy knowledge we have from revelation acquires nothing new, at least in the way of knowledge, nor does it give us any increase in certainty as a result of being treated as a science. There is no sense in which men can add to the content of God's revelation, nor in which they can improve on the certainty of divine faith, for the certainty of faith, based as it is on the authority of God, is far more secure than any certainty of natural reason.[23] Further, no one could ever acquire faith for himself by being taught *Sacra Doctrina* as a science: on the contrary, as we can

[23] Art. 5.

only acquire the knowledge we have about God and divine things by faith, only the believer can make a science of Sacred Teaching. For St Thomas the first principles of the science of Sacred Teaching, the principles from which all our efforts to think and reason commence, and which stand to this divine science as the first principles which are *per se nota* stand to a human science, are accepted from God as true by faith. Only the believer who accepts the articles of faith taught by Christ and His Church as certainly true, as the scientist accepts the truth of his first principles, can possibly make a science of the knowledge God has given us.

*Sacra Doctrina* is presented by St Thomas in the form of a dialogue between 'revelatio' and 'ratio', or more precisely, as a dialogue between the teacher of Catholic truth and his pupil. The teacher presents the truths of revelation to his pupil in as reasonable a manner as possible in order to make them the more intelligible and so acceptable to him. The pupil is presumed to know his philosophy and his logic, though the teacher must be prepared for his pupil's reasoning to be faulty and to lead him into serious difficulties, especially when he is confronted with such high mysteries as those revealed by God. *Sacra Doctrina* is a science, then, for one reason because it calls for such a dialogue between a teacher and a pupil. But the truths of revelation themselves do not need, nor do they in any way call for the support of our reasoning; it is *we* who need to approach, and may benefit by approaching the mysteries of faith in a scientific spirit, in that by reasoning about these mysteries much will become manifest to our minds we might easily fail to see. The science of Sacred Teaching 'accipere potest aliquid a philosophicis disciplinis, non quasi ex necessario eis indigeat, sed ad majorem manifestationem eorum quae in hac scientia traduntur'. Sacred Teaching can use human sciences, as we may find the need of them in the way that a superior may employ an inferior, but it uses them, 'non propter defectum vel insufficientiam ejus, sed propter defectum intellectus nostri', so that thereby our minds may be the more easily led to the truths which are above their powers of understanding.[24] After all a man who approaches his own life and everything

[24]The science of Sacred Teaching '[can borrow from philosophical sciences, but not because this teaching itself stands in any need of them; it borrows merely in order to bring into clearer relief the knowledge it gives to us].' Sacred teaching uses the philosophical sciences ['not because of some defect or insufficiency of its own, but out of regard for the defects of our minds.'] Art. 5, ad. 2; also art. 8, ad. 2.

in life in a thinking way is not liable to accept, nor could he reasonably accept, the truths of faith, even though they are revealed by God, if they seem to him to be unreasonable; God commands the homage of our intellects by demanding that we believe truths that are *above* reason, but He could not possibly demand that anyone believe what is, or strikes him as being unreasonable or against reason. Thus *Sacra Doctrina* is a 'science' (or 'argumentativa' as St Thomas vividly expresses the matter),[25] not intrinsically and in its own nature, but 'quoad nos et propter necessitatem humanae rationis': in its own nature *Sacra Doctrina* is knowledge (scientia) and wisdom (sapientia), in fact 'sacra doctrina maxime dicitur sapientia'.[26] It is arguable that for St Thomas, as he writes in the *Summa*, Sacred Teaching only becomes a science in the technical sense, or 'argumentative', for the purposes of instructing students, and thus for the pastoral purpose of teaching; such, at least, is the opinion of Father White who adds that 'if St Thomas had any idea of the intrinsic value of the construction of a systematic, scientific discipline called theology as an end in itself, and independently of the requirements of the preaching and teaching of the faith and of the cure of souls, he is strangely silent about it in his introduction to his own *Summa*'.[27]

It seems, however, that Father White is here exaggerating; he is pressing too far an idea which is perfectly sound in itself, that in the *Summa* St Thomas insisted on *Sacra Doctrina* being regarded as a science for purposes of teaching. But surely this does not justify our concluding that this is the only reason why it should be treated as a science. St Thomas surely held that *Sacra Doctrina* should be a science for purposes of teaching because it must become a science when we try to think systematically about divine truth. Whether we are students or not, we need to think discursively as this is the only way we can think, and if we believe God's revelation we must think the truths He has revealed discursively as we think anything else, and therefore we cannot avoid treating them scientifically. Thus in the commentary on Boethius's *De Trinitate*, which most experts date as belonging to the middle of his early teaching career in Paris, but later than the *Commentary on*

---

[25]In I *Sent.*, Prologus, qu. 1, art 5, he uses the term 'artificialis'.
[26]Art. 6.
[27]V. White, O.P., *Holy Teaching*, p. 17.

*the Sentences,* St Thomas says that we have a science of divine truths simply because in thinking we reason discursively from what we understand clearly or treat as a principle to some conclusion which, before we see formally as a conclusion, we do not understand. Thus in the measure that we reason about the truths of faith, and find the explanation of one in another, e.g. as we find the ultimate reason for our bodily resurrection in the bodily resurrection of Christ, we are arguing from principles to conclusions in accordance with fixed laws, and are thus thinking of the truths of faith scientifically. Thus St Thomas writes: 'quod cum scientiae ratio consistat in hoc quod ex aliquibus notis alia ignotiora cognoscantur, hoc autem in divinis contingat; constat quod de divinis potest esse scientia',[28] in other words it is just our thinking about the truths of faith which demands that we should treat them scientifically. In the *Summa* St Thomas must have taken this for granted, and just limited himself to giving a pedagogical reason requiring that *Sacra Doctrina* should be a science because he was especially interested with the work of instructing pupils in Catholic doctrine.

\*       \*       \*       \*

In the Commentary on Boethius's *De Trinitate* St Thomas also deals with the question of the use of philosophical arguments within the framework of the science of *Sacra Doctrina,*[29] and he mentions three kinds of work that reason may be called upon to perform in the service of divine truth. First, it may be called upon to prove the *praeambula fidei,* and amongst these he explicitly mentions the truth that God exists, that He is one and 'the suchlike' which, he says are proved in philosophy and which faith presupposes. Second, it may be called upon to provide analogies from natural things to illustrate a truth of faith, as St Augustine did in writing about the Trinity. And third, it may be called upon both to reason with the man who denies an article of the faith, and to meet the difficulties of the man who does not believe in any article of faith, in some cases, not even in the existence of God.

[28]'[Since scientific thinking consists in making certain unknown things known by connecting them with something which is known, and we are able to come to a knowledge of many things treated in sacred teaching which are not of themselves intelligible to us, it is clear that sacred teaching is capable of becoming a science.]' In Boetii: *De Trinitate,* Prooem, qu. 2, art. 2.

[29]In Boetii: *De Trinitate,* Prooem, qu. 2, art. 2.

It is quite certain that St Thomas held that we can prove the existence of God by reason, and that philosophers had actually proved it. In the *Contra Gentes,* for example, he distinguishes between two kinds of truth about God, the one being supernatural and revealed, the other being naturally accessible to our minds. There are, he says, certain truths about God, as that He exists, is one 'and the suchlike' which reason can attain: 'quae etiam philosophi demonstrative de Deo probaverunt, ducti naturalis lumine rationis'.[30] The theologian needs to become a philosopher if he has to discuss God with an atheist or an agnostic, and if he cannot convince him of the rational necessity of accepting God's existence, he must content himself with meeting and dissipating his objections. St Thomas attached considerable importance to this work of the theologian in defending the foundations of the faith and watching over the integrity of the essential prerequisites of faith, the *praeambula fidei.* Nothing, however, suggests that when he was writing article 3 of Quaestio 2 of the *Summa Theologica,* and chapter 13 of the first book of the *Contra Gentes,* St Thomas was trying to prove the existence of God purely as a philosopher for the purposes of defending the *praeambula fidei.* So far from considering these *praeambula* to faith, he was considering our faith in the divine essence. Hence we cannot conclude from the fact that he discussed the existence of God in the way he did in these two *Summae,* that he regarded the arguments he used just as they stand as suited to the use of the philosopher at all times, in all emergencies and to meet all difficulties. Indeed, one of the most striking features of article 3 and chapter 13 is that they present the arguments for the existence of God without raising any serious philosophical difficulties against them (the two objections of article 3 count for very little in comparison with the kind of thing we have studied in chapter 2), and this ought to be a pointer to the fact that both article 3 and chapter 13 were written by a theologian theologizing, and not by a philosopher philosophizing. On this point I find myself forced to disagree with Father White who considers that the Quinque Viae were put into the *Summae* by St Thomas because he was philosophizing to meet the position of the atheist:[31] in neither *Summa* does he suggest that this is the purpose for which he includes the arguments. As we have

---

[30]*Contra Gentes,* ch. 3. cf. also *Summa Theologica* I, qu. 2, art. 2, ad. 1.
[31]V. White, O.P., 'Prelude to the Five Ways', in *God the Unknown,* p. 50ff.

seen St Thomas states in both *Summae* that he needs the arguments for God's existence for what they contribute to the believer's study of the divine essence.

*        *        *

Now let us take up Quaestio 2 and survey summarily the contents of articles 1 and 2. First of all, in article 1, St Thomas asks whether God's existence is 'per se notum', which we can translate as evident, or known of itself so that it does not need to be demonstrated or made known. St Thomas decides that God's existence is not evident of itself to our minds, that we do not just spontaneously know of God's existence, and he concludes that, though of itself it is so knowable because supremely intelligible, none the less as far as we are concerned 'indiget demonstrari per ea quae sunt magis nota quoad nos, et minus nota secundum naturam, scilicet per effectus'.[32] This idea is, of course, all a part of St Thomas's conviction that human reason is not the measure of reality, but that reality measures it, and equally that as the human mind is a very limited power it must find the supreme realities too intelligible for its understanding just because they are above (but not against) its ways of reasoning. St Thomas approves of Aristotle's famous metaphor: 'For as the eyes of bats are to the blaze of day, so is the reason in our souls to the things which are by nature most evident of all.'[33]

In article 2 he points out that God's existence can, in principle, be made known to us from the things which are known to us of themselves, namely the things of the universe which we know naturally from experience, for in fact these things are the work of God's causal or creative activity. If, therefore, we can first establish that they are effects, we can argue from them to their cause, for 'posito effectu necesse est causam praeexistere'. St Thomas will formally establish, for the purposes of the argument, that the things we know are effects in the Five Ways, which are, as Dr Mascall so pointedly argues, ways for establishing the existence of God by showing that the universe and

[32]God's existence '[needs to be demonstrated from those things which are better known to us (than God), but less knowable in themselves, that is to say, through effects]'.

[33]Aristotle: *Metaphysics,* Book α, ch. 1, 993b, 9–11. St Thomas: *Summa Theologica,* 1, qu. 1, art. 5, ad. 1.

all it contains are an effect of another's activity: 'As I see it, the ultimate function of the Five Ways is to make it plain, by calling attention to five outstanding features of finite being, what the fundamental characteristic of finite being is.'[34]

If *Sacra Doctrina,* considered as a science, is a dialogue between faith and reason, and equally between teacher and pupil, then quite logically St Thomas commences the *Summa Theologica* with a Quaestio about our natural knowledge of God, but it is important to remember that he is not writing even this Quaestio as a philosopher, or perhaps we might say more accurately that he is not writing as a philosopher to answer a philosophical problem for its own sake. He is writing in the interests of sound theology about and against a theological opinion current during the thirteenth century. He is rejecting the view that we have some kind of intuitive knowledge of God's existence, and trying to show that naturally human reason has no intuitive certainty of the truth that God exists. We have to establish this truth by reasoning. Thus in Quaestio 2 he is concerned with showing how reason on its own, without faith, can in principle, and has in fact attained a knowledge of God's existence.

Father Victor White explains how an objection sometimes raised againt St Thomas's arguments for the existence of God is easily answered once the objector has seen the theological plan of the *Summa* as sketched in the opening articles of the second Quaestio. The objection is raised against Quaestio 2, article 2

> To the effect that, before having even attempted to demonstrate that there is a God, he lays down that this can be demonstrated— and indeed that the very name *Deus* can be derived—only from effects. . . . Thus, it is urged, St Thomas begs the whole question in advance: he assumes that given phenomena are effects, and therefore have a cause, and indeed a divine cause; the very point to be proved and a palpable *petitio principii.*[35]

Father White grants, of course, that if St Thomas had been writing as a philosopher he would be committing a *petitio principii* by arguing in this way. But seeing that he is writing Quaestio 2 as a theologian, the same theologian who had shortly before written the whole of Quaestio 1

---

[34]E. L. Mascall: *Existence and Analogy,* p. 71 and p. 169; *He Who Is,* pp. 69–70.
[35]V. White, O.P., 'Prelude to the Five Ways', in *God the Unknown,* p. 36.

fully convinced that God exists and has made a revelation to all men, he is not writing as a philosopher presupposing what he wants to prove, viz. that God exists. He is expounding in a methodical manner the truths of faith he believes and which he has been commissioned to teach, giving reasons to justify them to the mind, and showing how reason stands in their regard. In article 2 writing as a theologian, he is pointing out that since the things we know in experience are the effects of God's creative activity, we must be able in principle to argue from them to the existence of God. In the actual arguments (as given in article 3), however, St Thomas reasons, not from his knowledge that things are the effects of God, but from the way things reveal themselves to us in experience; he argues that, being imperfect in various ways as they are, they must be the effects of some cause. He avoids *petitio principii* because he gives us, not his own arguments, but those of pagan philosophers who knew nothing of the Christian doctrine of creation. Thus St Thomas does not prejudice the actual arguments for the existence of God he gives in article 3 by bringing into it as a premise the truth he is trying to prove.

In article 3 St Thomas takes up the question: 'utrum Deus sit', which might quite fairly be expanded, or rather re-worded in the context within which it is put as 'how do we know or prove by reason that God, in Whom we believe and Who has made a revelation to us, exists?' for throughout Quaestio 2 St Thomas is really dealing with our knowledge of God's existence. He gives his view that God's existence can be established in five Ways, 'Respondeo dicendum quod Deum esse quinque viis probari potest.' In the body of the article he gives one by one of each of these Five Ways, and concludes each Way with a statement about God existing.[36]

[36]cf. R. A. Markus: 'A Note on the Meaning of "Via",' an article in *Dominican Studies,* 1954, especially p. 241.

# 5

## THE ENIGMA OF THE FIVE WAYS

We come now to article 3 and the 'traditional' arguments for the existence of God, which, of course, I am presuming the reader has before him. I am also presuming that he has with him the arguments which we have already had occasion to mention in chapter 13 of the first book of the *Contra Gentes*, for, as Father Motte pointed out some years ago,[1] in studying the Five Ways we do well to keep in mind the earlier arguments of the *Contra Gentes*. As we have already remarked on the close agreement on the basic strategic principles followed by St Thomas in these two *Summae* in constructing a theological treatise on God's Being, our proposal to follow Father Motte's suggestion in this chapter should not cause any surprise. In particular St Thomas's method of handling the question of God's existence in the two works is exactly the same and stands out clearly in relief amidst the numerous minor points of difference there are, especially in the actual arguments given to show that God exists. St Thomas commenced his work on the *Contra Gentes* towards the end of his first period of teaching at Paris, probably a little before 1259, and he finished the fourth and last book in Italy during the pontificate of Pope Urban IV sometime before 1265. He probably wrote the first part of the *Summa Theologica* in Italy between 1266–8, so that a period of about eight years elapsed between the time he wrote the proofs for the existence of God in the *Contra Gentes* and those of article 3 in the *Summa Theologica*. Now that we are coming to grips with the more detailed study of our special problem we can profitably take these two versions of the arguments together, for between them they give us the maturest thought of the master on the whole problem of establishing the existence of God. Of the two versions of the arguments there can

[1]A. R. Motte, O.P., 'A Propos des "Cinq Voies"', from the *Revue des Sciences Philosophiques et Théologiques*, Oct. 1939, pp. 577–82.

be no doubt that that from the *Summa Theologica* is in every way superior, so that we will centre our study on article 3, and consult chapter 13 as a guide in interpreting article 3.

A number of curious points should strike the reader, especially if he is a philosopher rather than a theologian, as he progresses in his study of the Five Ways. If the reader is familiar with St Thomas's style and method of writing, and with the scholastic technique of investigating problems in the *Quaestio* and *Article,* article 3 will stand out as not a little different from, and set in marked contrast to the articles around it. These points, which we shall take one by one, with a section given to each, make up what I call the 'enigma of the Five Ways'.

\*        \*        \*

One of the first of these curious points which ought to strike the reader, especially after his study of the earlier articles, is an uncharacteristic lack of originality in most of the contents of this article. This is, indeed so pronounced that the reader can scarcely avoid entertaining the suspicion that with conscious and deliberate intent St Thomas is refraining as far as possible from expressing his own ideas while grappling with the question he has put, 'Utrum Deus sit'—so far, at least as he has grappled with it in article 3. This apparent absence of his personal contribution to the arguments not unnaturally gives rise to considerable disappointment with those philosophers who look to him for light in their perplexities, for it is just on vital issues such as this of the existence of God that many seek for his personal contribution, and are not, save possibly on rare occasions, disappointed at failing to find it. In this instance, however, it seems that St Thomas has not risen to the occasion, that he has deliberately, for some reason or the other, thrust others as it were into his chair to speak in his place, and that there is very little of Thomas Aquinas in what is perhaps one of the most famous passages he ever wrote. Up to this point he has shown himself only too ready to advance and defend views of his own, and as an inevitable result the reader expects him to display the same excellent qualities of originality and profundity of thought when he actually comes to grips with the main problem of proving that God exists. But in the third article, whatever good qualities it may display, the reader does not find what he might expect and even hope to find, and as a consequence the Five Ways have for many the appearance of an ill-timed anti-climax. The Five Ways, we are told time and again, do not engender that sense of conviction which we feel the personal thought and attention of the angelic doctor might well have engendered. Such is the appearance of things to the inquiring outsider who does not profess to be one of the Thomist brotherhood, nor even to profess the Christian's faith in God.

Let us take yet another glance back at the first two articles of Quaestio 2 just to see on what lines St Thomas commenced his treatment of the problem of our knowledge of God's existence. But before we read them we had better once more put ourselves on our guard against reading into his thought, as he has expressed it in writing, what we, faced with our own problems, might well wish him to have said, or imagine he might be trying as best he can to say, and secondly we had better recall the point we made in the last chapter, that the first Quaestiones of the *Summa Theologica* were written neither for nor against philosophers, but for, and, to a certain extent, against theologians.[2]

St Thomas wrote articles 1 and 2 to refute the widely accepted view of theologians of his day that we need not prove the being of God, the ESSE DEI, but only the divine attributes, and thence to show how we can think of each of them. Hugh of St Victor epitomized the general view current at the time in a formula that was often quoted by St Bonaventure: 'Deus enim sic ab initio notitiam sui ab homine temperavit, ut sicut numquam quid esset totum posset comprehendi, ita numquam quia esset prorsus posset ignorari.'[3] Men cannot be ignorant of God's existence: so far from needing to be proved, the *Esse Dei* was considered by many theologians to be a first principle of thought (similar to the principle of contradiction) in the light of which every other truth we can know actually becomes known. If a man did not know of the *Esse Dei* he could not know anything whatever, for the self-evidence of the first principles accounts for our ability

[2] cf. E. Gilson: *Le Thomisme* (5th edit.), pp. 72–73; *The Christian Philosophy of St Thomas Aquinas*, pp. 47–48.

[3] '[From the beginning God so disposed the knowledge of Himself by man, that even as he should never be able to comprehend totally what He is, so he should be incapable of ever not knowing that He is].' Hugh of St Victor: *De Sacramentis*, liber 1, pars. 3 (P. L. CLXXXVI, col. 217). cf. St Bonaventure: I *Sent.*, dist. VIII, art. 1, qu. ii.

to perceive the evidence we find in the things we know. The first point which St Thomas raises, as he approaches the consideration of the existence of God, concerns this supposed self-evidence which many theologians of the day considered to be a characteristic of the knowledge we have of His existence. He asks in the first place 'utrum Deum esse sit per se notum', even as he had asked the question about twelve years before at the beginning of the *Commentary on the Sentences*.[4] St Thomas is repeatedly considering the same question during the course of his lifetime. We find him discussing it in the first book of the *Contra Gentes*: 'De opinione dicentium quod Deum esse demonstrari non potest cum sit per se notum'; again in the most explicit manner possible in the *De Veritate*: 'Utrum Deum esse sit per se notum menti humanae, sicut prima principia demonstrationis, quae non possunt cogitari non esse',[5] and in the *Commentary on Boethius's De Trinitate*: 'Utrum Deus sit primum quod a mente cognoscitur'.[6] Whereas the view of many Augustinian theologians of the day was that the existence of God, the first truth, is the first principle of all thinking, and the most intelligible and meaningful of all truths, St Thomas contends that it is certainly not a first principle of human thinking, that it is not evident to us, whatever it may be for other intelligent beings (such as the angels), so that it is possible for a man to think and not find anything intelligible in the idea of God existing. He maintains that there is a genuine need for us to establish the truth of God's existence by means of other principles of thought (as the principle of causality), and other beings which are known to the human mind of themselves, and initially more evident and certain to us than the truth of God's being. We need to prove the truth of God's existence by means of metaphysical principles knowable to reason, and not their truth by means of the knowledge we are assumed to have of God's existence. We know naturally of God's Being from created things, and not created things from God's Being. For St Thomas God is undoubtedly more intelligible in Himself than created things: if he were not *Sacra Doctrina* would not be the highest form of knowledge. But we, unaided by faith, do not know either 'de Deo, quid est', nor even 'de Deo, an sit' intuitively or im-

[4]*I Sent.*, dist. III, qu. i, art. ii.
[5]*Contra Gentes*, I, ch. 10. *De Veritate*, qu. 10, art. 12.
[6]*In Boetii de Trinitate*, Prooem., qu. I, art. 3.

mediately. God's existence needs to be proved as a consequence 'per ea quae sunt magis nota quoad nos, et minus nota secundum naturam, scilicet per effectus'.[7]

Here, then, in article 1 we find St Thomas philosophizing, but not for the sake of philosophers, against whom he has to defend a thesis so as to establish some philosophical position for philosophical purposes. He is philosophizing against theologians and in a theological context in order to show them some philosophical truths of theological consequence about the nature of the human mind and the real sources of the knowledge it may attain of God, and, as we have seen, he continues to philosophize for theological purposes in the same way in article 2. Thus St Thomas is really theologizing in articles 1 and 2. Each article is like an original composition, giving the master's own personal ideas on the matters under discussion. Having, then, displayed so excellently his qualities as an original and independent thinker in these first two articles of Quaestio 2, and thus continued in the strikingly independent style he had maintained throughout Quaestio 1, the reader naturally expects him to manifest the same qualities when he actually comes to grips with what we now regard as the central issue of demonstrating the existence of God, for, after all, St Thomas himself has been insisting on the necessity of proving His existence. But in the third article he does not appear to acquit himself in at all the same excellent style, and as a consequence the Five Ways give by comparison the impression of being different from, or at least out of keeping with, the two earlier articles. Perhaps this makes the modern practice prevalent amongst philosophers of extracting article 3 from its context so very easy to do, and so very easy to get away with.!

\*     \*     \*

A second curious point which must strike the reader as distinctive of article 3, again especially if he is a philosopher, is the extreme brevity of the whole treatment it affords to this, the crucial and most involved problem of philosophy. Mr. J. J. C. Smart, in his paper on 'The Existence of God', drew attention to this characteristic which he seems to think is distinctive of all the traditional arguments for the existence of God:

[7]Art. 1.

> One very noteworthy feature which must strike anyone who
> first looks at the usual arguments for the existence of God is the
> extreme brevity of these arguments. They range from a few lines
> to a few pages. St Thomas Aquinas presents five arguments in
> three pages! Would it not be rather extraordinary if such a great
> conclusion should be got so easily?[8]

Mr Smart is evidently anxious not to minimize St Thomas's efforts:
five arguments 'in three pages' is as generous as it is arbitrary a piece
of reckoning. It sounds more like a modern printer's estimate for
making a pocket edition of the *Summa* than a mediaeval copyist's report
on his parchments! Be that as it may, the situation is rather worse than
Mr Smart states: we need do no more than say that to fill three pages
with the Five Ways one would have to use very small pages, or very
large type. If, then, we accept the view that the Five Ways give St
Thomas's arguments for the existence of God in full, then we will
have to say that he gave far less attention to this great philosophical
problem than Aristotle gave in proving the existence of the first
Unmoved Mover in book $\Lambda$ of the Metaphysics, or than St Augustine
did in the second book of the *De Libero Arbitrio*, or than Descartes in
the *Discours de la Méthode* and in the *Meditations,* or than Berkeley
either in the *Principles of Human Knowledge,* or in the *Dialogues between
Hylas and Philonous.* As, furthermore, he refrains from discussing the
philosophical problems involved in arguing for the existence of God, it
seems rather difficult to hold, then, either that St Thomas is writing
article 3 as a philosopher, or that he intended to give in this article
alone what he would have presented as complete philosophical arguments for God's existence had he been writing a *Summa Philosophiae.*

*        *        *

A third curious point, which certainly ought to strike the reader
very quickly, arises from the fact that, instead of giving arguments of
his own based on his own philosophy, St Thomas seems to have
brought together arguments which he has found elsewhere, and which
give the impression at first of having been selected from a wide and
diversified range of sources. The reader is thus understandably left with
the impression that St Thomas is reproducing a number of arguments

[8]J. J. C. Smart: 'The Existence of God', in NEPT, p. 29.

which were regarded as 'traditional' in his day. But closer examination shows that he has not made use of versions of arguments that were current in the Middle Ages at all. He has evidently worked from arguments that were becoming known to theologians in the thirteenth century, but instead of taking any of these new arguments as it stands from a mediaeval writer, he has gone directly to what he regarded as the ultimate sources of these arguments, and notably to Aristotle. It would be impossible, and it is certainly unnecessary, for us to attempt to go into the long and complicated debates concerning the exact passages of Aristotle's works from which St Thomas derived what he did from the philosopher. On this delicate matter we will say as much as we need for our present purposes later in this section. In chapter 13 of the *Contra Gentes* St Thomas himself tells us in a general way as much as we really need to know. He commences this long chapter by saying first that, as it is not idle (vanum) to demonstrate that God exists, he will give 'rationes quibus tam philosophi quam doctores Catholici Deum esse probaverunt', the reasons by which philosophers and Catholic teachers have shown that God exists.[9] If we imagine these words being put at the beginning of the Five Ways we can see quite clearly why there seems to be so little of Thomas Aquinas in article 3. Chapter 13 contains four of the five Ways of article 3: it gives St Thomas's first idea of the first, second, fourth and fifth Ways, so there does not seem to be any reason why we should not read these opening words of chapter 13 at the beginning of article 3. If the four arguments of chapter 13 are arguments of philosophers and Catholic teachers, then four of the five Ways are as well. Returning now to chapter 13 St Thomas continues: 'Primo autem ponemus rationes quibus Aristoteles procedit ad probandum Deum esse.' As we have just said, there is no doubt that St Thomas had in mind arguments he knew in the works of, for example, the Persian philosopher, Avicenna, the Jewish theologian, Moses Maimonides, and especially of his own fellow Dominican and Master, St Albert. But as the arguments of these mediaeval writers were based, sometimes as variants, on Aristotle, and as his own special interest lay in introducing Aristotle to his brother theologians, St Thomas evidently decided to go directly to the main source and take Aristotle as the spokesman of the philosophers who

[9]cf. also *Contra Gentes* I, ch. 9, sec. 3.

have given proofs to show that God exists. In chapter 13 he gives first in great detail Aristotle's argument from motion for the first Unmoved Mover. He follows this with a second argument which comes directly from Aristotle, but which was not used by him to prove the existence of God, or even of a god. Aristotle's line of reasoning was first used as an argument for the existence of God as the first efficient cause by Avicenna, Alan of Lille and St Albert the Great,[10] and St Thomas is clearly following their lead in using it for the same purpose. Finally he gives a third argument from Aristotle based on the existence of degrees of being, and once again though Aristotle never used the reasoning to demonstrate the existence of God, St Thomas takes Aristotle's text as others had done before him and constructs a proof for God's existence from it. Thus in chapter 13 of the *Contra Gentes* St Thomas gives us the first, second and fourth Ways of article 3 taken directly out of Aristotle, without giving any adaptations from contemporary Aristotelians. The fourth and last argument of chapter 13 represents the efforts of the Catholic teachers to prove the existence of God. St John Damascene is, however, the only Catholic teacher to whom St Thomas refers. In his *De Fide Orthodoxa*[11] St John does give a teleological way of arguing to the existence of God, but clearly neither of St Thomas's two presentations of this argument is borrowed from the text of the *De Fide Orthodoxa*. St Thomas's arguments bear very little resemblance to that contained in the source to which he refers. He adds the remark, however, 'quam etiam innuit Commentator in 2 Physicorum', thus coupling the name of Averroes with that of the Catholic teacher as one of his sources even for this argument which at first the reader might have thought he had taken as typical of the Christian teachers. If we compare this fourth argument in chapter 13 with the fifth Way of article 3, however, we will find that there are considerable differences between the two versions; in the *Summa Theologica* he does not refer to any authority, nor declare any source from which he may have borrowed his argument, but we cannot attach much significance to this because in the whole of the article he only once refers to a source,

---

[10]cf. E. Gilson: *Le Thomisme*, p. 99; *The Christian Philosophy of St Thomas Aquinas*, p. 66.

[11]St John Damascene: *De Fide Orthodoxa*, liber I, ch. 3, (P.G. XCIV, col. 793-7).

and then only incidently in the course of the fourth Way where he refers to Aristotle. None the less, though there are numerous instances of an argument from design in the works of philosophers and Christian writers which he might have quoted verbatim, it seems that in the *Summa Theologica* St Thomas has given us his own version of the argument, and that in the fifth Way we have after all a section of the famous article 3 in which St Thomas is giving us something of his own. It is only because we have become so accustomed to his way of presenting the argument that we spontaneously conclude that, as he is discussing one of the oldest arguments for God's existence, he is reproducing an old form of the argument. It is particularly interesting to note that he enlarged on the argument from design in chapter 42 of the first book of the *Contra Gentes,* while proving that God is one, but in a manner decidedly reminiscent of Aristotle.[12] It is arguable that the fifth Way of article 3 is really an original summary or contraction of the kind of argument from design St Thomas thought out on Aristotelian principles, so that all the five Ways of the *Summa Theologica,* unlike the four of the *Contra Gentes,* come from Aristotle.

It may very well be considered rash to state bluntly and categorically the details of chapter and line for the sources of the arguments used by St Thomas, seeing that the whole matter is still warmly controverted. It is, however, advisable to say something about the sources if only to provide myself with as much evidence as I can find for the points I wish to make at the end of this section. However, these points are, I trust, still substantially sound even if it should turn out that I am deceived in some of these references to sources. As a working hypothesis I am satisfied that the first Way of chapter 13 was derived from Aristotle's *Physics,* Book VII and VIII, and that of article 3 from his *Metaphysics,* Book $\Lambda$, chapter 6, 1071b, 3ff. Maurice Bouyges may well be correct in suggesting that in writing the text of the Five Ways St Thomas may have been using the text of the Latin translation from the Arabic of Averroes's *Great Commentary* on the *Metaphysics* in Book a, chapter 2, 994a, 11–19, in the Bekker edition, in which lines Aristotle is showing the impossibility of an infinite regress in a series of causes.[13]

---

[12] cf. also St Thomas's *Commentary on the Metaphysics,* liber XII, lectio 12.
[13] M. Bouyges: 'Pour l'Interprétation des "Quinque Viae" de St Thomas d'Aquin', in the *Recherches de Science Religieuse,* Oct. 1949, pp. 594–5.

The second Way is attributed by St Thomas in chapter 13 to Aristotle's *Metaphysics,* evidently Book α, chapter 2, 994a, 1ff. The source of the third Way of article 3, which does not occur at all in chapter 13 of the *Contra Gentes* (though an argument which is often unjustifiably taken to be the same occurs in chapter 15 as an argument for the eternity of God), has been discussed by scholars for a long time, but I am taking for granted that Dr Dermot O'Donoghue has settled the main problems by showing that this Way comes directly neither from Avicenna, nor from Moses Maimonides (as at one time seemed likely to many scholars), but directly from Aristotle, and most probably from the *De Caelo,* Book 1, chapter 12. St Thomas's argument as stated in article 3 is very different from the popular argument from contingency. The proof is not *ex contingenti ad necessarium,* but *ex possibili et necessario* to *ens per se necessarium,* and if the reader studies Aristotle's *De Generatione et Corruptione,* 335a, 32—b, 10, and his *Metaphysics* at 1032a, 15–20, 1039b, 25–30, 1050b, 10–25, with Aquinas's Commentaries on these texts, he will see how the argument is based on the phrase 'possibile esse et non esse'. Dr O'Donoghue rejects the earlier theories of Dom Chambat and Henri Holstein that the third Way came from chapter 6 of Book Λ of the *Metaphysics.*[14] Finally, the fourth Way comes most probably from Aristotle's *Metaphysics,* again Book α, chapter 1, 993b, 19–31, and Book Γ, chapter 4, 1008b, 32–1009a, 5.

Presuming that in giving these details about the sources of the Five Ways I am not seriously in error, it is easy to see, and for some it may be a first redeeming feature of article 3, that St Thomas has shown considerable skill, first in selecting the proofs which he sought not from the writing of St Augustine, St Anselm, or a well-known Christian theologian, but directly from the works of the pagan philosopher, Aristotle, who never had a theologian's interest in establishing God's existence, and whose writings were still little known by theologians at the time that St Thomas wrote. The selection of the arguments seems to have been made by St Thomas purely empirically: he happens to have given five arguments, because presumably, he found five with

[14]D. O'Donoghue: 'An Analysis of the "Tertia Via" of St Thomas', in the *Irish Theological Quarterly,* 1953, pp. 129–51. Also A. Finili, O.P., 'Recent Work on the "Tertia Via" ', in *Dominican Studies,* 1954, pp. 22–47.

which he was satisfied, but he might have selected four, or six or ten had he found the number of satisfactory arguments. There does not seem to be any ground for thinking, as some writers have thought in the past, that systematic or philosophical considerations of any kind determined that there had to be five, no more nor less, arguments. As Père Motte said: 'L'origine empirique de l'énumération n'en demeure pas moins l'un des éléments indispensables de l'interprétation.'[15] St Thomas wanted to demonstrate that God exists, not that there are five ways of demonstrating His existence.

St Thomas has shown considerable ingenuity, secondly, in casting the arguments, and especially the first Way, into the brief, incisive form in which we find them in article 3, and in which they have been widely known ever since the thirteenth century. This has no doubt had much to do with their becoming universally accepted as 'traditional' arguments. No one can question the fidelity of the first four Ways to the Aristotelian originals from whence they were derived. If they go beyond and enrich Aristotle's own ideas, they do not betray them. The first Way of article 3 is certainly an enrichment of Aristotle's argument based on the old cosmology as we find it in chapter 13; but the third Way of article 3 seems to be far more cosmological in structure than any modern Thomist likes to think.

Thirdly, St Thomas carefully arranged the Five Ways in a certain order, so that they do in fact knit together as a group to form into a certain unity. The first and fifth Ways are based on change, the first on an analysis of the actual process of change, and the fifth on its origin, orientation and fulfilment. The second and fourth Ways are based on an analysis of the ontological structure of things as sources of activity and as fitted within a hierarchically conceived system of reality or of being. The third Way is based on the metaphysical character of the being of the things we know, for ultimately it is based on an analysis of their manner of existence.[16] Again, in the first four Ways St Thomas seems to be working his way deeper and deeper in metaphysics, beginning with data which are easier to analyse, e.g. change and causality, and then working his way by stages from a study of the

---

[15]A. R. Motte, O.P., *op. cit.*, p. 580.

[16]D. Dubarle, O.P., 'L'Existence de Dieu', a paper in the volume entitled *De la Connaissance de Dieu*, pp. 46–47.

activity to a study of the being of things, dealing first with the manner in which they exist (third Way), and then with the problem of their limitation (fourth Way). In the fifth Way he studies things in the universe as the effects of a mind. Thus the Five Ways take five aspects of the objects we know in the world to show that they are all the effects of a cause. Thus, as Mgr. De Raeymaeker says, the Five Ways develop in concentric circles, each one serving to strengthen the reasoning of those that have preceded, with the fourth Way (not the third Way as most modern Thomists hold) coming to the heart of the whole issue by showing that there must be a being which is the entire perfection (maxime ens) of all things as the formal and perhaps efficient cause of things.[17] Such, at least, seems to be the way that St Thomas conceived the ordering of the Five Ways.

*     *     *

A fourth curious point about article 3 comes clearly to view now. It is that St Thomas seems to know nothing about arguments for the existence of God which were considered 'traditional' in the Middle Ages in the way that we speak of his arguments for God's existence as 'traditional'. If he does know of such arguments he is remarkably silent about them. The reader of today may well be struck by the apparent lack of originality in the arguments St Thomas gives in chapter 13 and article 3, but he cannot conclude from this that Thomas's own contemporaries would have reacted in this way to his proofs and said that he was just giving his own versions of 'traditional' arguments. During the thirteenth century St Thomas's attempt to produce arguments culled almost exclusively from the writings of Aristotle would have appeared as strikingly new and not a little daring. If anything his contemporaries might well have formed the impression that he intended to sweep aside quite ruthlessly the arguments which were known to the Fathers, and which they might have regarded as traditional amongst the Doctores Catholici, and thence substitute new arguments in their place.[18] St Thomas evidently did not think highly of St Augustine's argument for God's existence in the second book of

[17]L. de Raeymaeker: La Philosophie de l'Etre, pp. 316–7.
[18]There does not, however, seem to be any evidence to show that this was in fact the way they reacted to article 3.

the *De Libero Arbitrio,* and he refrained from mentioning any of the numerous passages in which St Augustine speaks of man coming to know of God from the spectacle of the universe. He says nothing at all about the arguments of St Anselm in the *Monologion,* nor of those of St Gregory of Nyssa, for example, in his *Theological Discourses.* He just ignores the whole tradition of Platonic thinking, which many of the Fathers used to expound the teaching of the faith about God, no doubt because he found it unsatisfactory from the point of view of its philosophical foundations, for it does not make sufficiently clear that it is from the world of things, as known effects, from the material universe, that reason gathers such knowledge as it can attain of God.[19] In other words, the Platonic tradition did not try to establish that God exists as the cause of the universe, or on the foundation theme that all things are effects of God's activity, as in article 2 he had insisted must be done. It is the line of argument followed in articles 1 and 2 which, in St Thomas's mind, calls uncompromisingly for the Aristotelian approach. Thus we ought to remember that, even though the Five Ways are all borrowed from other thinkers, so that they do not strike us nowadays as highly original, the very idea of looking to a pagan philosopher for a number of arguments of a purely philosophical character, and using them substantially unchanged as they exist in their original form, was highly original in the thirteenth century. Hence Thomas Aquinas is, after all, to be found in article 3, not perhaps as we might expect or wish to find him nowadays strikingly in evidence in each particular argument, but more subtly, in the master idea of the whole article. In the thirteenth century it was still possible to find new and original arguments for the existence of God, or new ways of presenting old arguments, despite the fact that the Christian faith had been known for well over a thousand years.

In the *Contra Centes* the first Way is given in its native Aristotelian, physical form, i.e. it is based on the ancient astronomy with its distinction of the sub-lunary and supra-lunary worlds, and with the ancient conception of the heavenly spheres together with their movers. No doubt St Thomas decided to reproduce the argument in this form as it stands in Aristotle's *Physics* because he wrote the *Contra Gentes* to

[19] cf. *Contra Gentes* II, cf. 4 where St Thomas contrasts the theologian's and the philosopher's knowledge of God.

expound and defend Christian theology to philosophers who, like Siger of Brabant a little later, were pressing to extreme lengths a rigid Aristotelianism both in what we would call philosophy and in science.[20] It may be that St Thomas himself was satisfied with the old physics as far as it went, for in the Middle Ages everyone else was satisfied with its principles. But in the *Summa Theologica* he has, on his own responsibility, presented Aristotle's argument freed of all associations with the ancient physics, cosmology and astronomy, as a metaphysical argument based on our experience of change, and thus his presentation of Aristotle's argument, transposed and elevated on to a new plane, is highly original. Neither the second, third nor fourth Ways can in any sense of the term be considered as arguments that were regarded by Christian theologians or philosophers in the thirteenth century as traditional. In fact, of the Five Ways only the first and fifth had been used as proofs which could be regarded as ancient in any sense of the term, and of these only the fifth could be regarded as in some sense traditional. St Thomas's second, third and fourth Ways are original adaptations of Aristotle's text. René Arnou points out that several theologians during this period of the early thirteenth century were giving arguments for the existence of God, and he refers to a number in the writings of such men as William of Paris, Richard of St Victor, William of Conches and Alan of Lille as anticipations of the Five Ways, but there is in fact very little likeness between the arguments we find given by these writers and the Five Ways of article 3.[21]

After all, then, Thomas Aquinas is very much present in article 3, and only apparently eclipsed by Aristotle.

\*    \*    \*

A fifth curious point about the Five Ways has been ably brought to our attention by Dr Mascall in chapter 4 of his *Existence and Analogy*. He points out that the first Way, which argues back to a first Unmoved Mover by having recourse to the principle of Aristotle

[20]cf. Chenu: *op. cit.*, p. 250 where he argues that the *Contra Gentes* was written against *Gentiles* in Paris, and not in Spain to whom, according to the legend, missionaries were being sent by St Raymond of Penafort equipped with the *Contra Gentes*.

[21]R. Arnou, S.J., *De Quinque Viis Sancti Thomae ad Demonstrandum Dei Existentiam: Textus selectos*, p. 98.

that an infinite series is impossible, 'does not necessitate any immediate influence exerted by God upon the being first considered'.[22] A is moved by B, B is moved by C, C by D and so on, until one has to postulate a mover Z which is not itself moved. This argument cannot do more than establish that Z moved Y, not that Z moved and continues to move all the other movements back to and including that of A. It may be that *ultimately* A is moved by Z, but A's movement is not *immediately* due to Z. A's movement is derived from Z's influence mediately via a whole series of intermediate moved movers. This, however, is not the way in which St Thomas visualized the causal influence of God on His creatures: he holds that though there are many secondary causes acting in the universe to produce effects which God wills, God is none the less the primary cause Who is Himself immediately active in the production of each effect. What, then, is the point of basing the argument on the principle 'non est procedere in infinitum'? Dr Mascall answers that the principle is used to show, 'not that we *cannot* proceed to infinity, but that it does not get us any nearer the solution of our problem if we do. . . . Non est procedere in infinitum, not in the sense that the infinite regress is impossible but that it leads us no nearer to the solution of our problem.'[23] In other words to solve the problem of the movement of A it is necessary to look elsewhere than amongst mobile things, and turn our attention to an immobile being. The argument establishes this, but no more than this. It cannot establish that the first Unmoved Mover not only initiates the series of moved movers, but that it itself stands outside and above the series because it sustains the whole series in being. St Thomas does not in the text of article 3 make plain 'that the first mover, just because it is itself unmoved, must be of a radically different nature from all the other terms in the series; that it is, in fact, not merely at the beginning of the series, but outside it'.[24] To borrow Dr Mascall's little diagrams, the argument only establishes

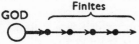

[22]E. L. Mascall: *Existence and Analogy*, p. 72.
[23]E. L. Mascall: *Existence and Analogy*, pp. 73–74.
[24]E. L. Mascall: *Existence and Analogy*, p. 74.

it fails to make clear

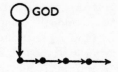

and in fact, to establish the existence of God, it ought to establish

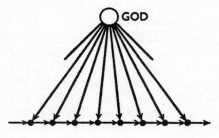

The same criticisms can be made of the second and third Ways, both of which employ the principle 'non est procedere in infinitum' in a regressive series, for after all 'any argument based upon the notion of a regress can never prove more than that God acts at the beginning of the sequence, whether that sequence be a temporal sequence or not'.[25]

The fourth Way differs from the first three in that it does not make any use of the principle *non est procedere in infinitum*. St Thomas uses this argument, which he also found in Aristotle, to insist on the fact that where some things are more perfect than others, all within the realm where comparisons can be made are imperfect and finite. Thus if a being possesses a perfection, it possesses it in a limited degree; if it does not merely possess the perfection, either it has not the perfection at all or it is that perfection supremely, so that the beings which are finite and limited possess what perfections they have in immediate dependence on some being which is not limited or finite at all. In other words, St Thomas is arguing that all the beings we know in experience depend for what they are on some being which is not limited nor finite. And here he drops the argument, for Aristotle went

[25]E. L. Mascall: *Existence and Analogy*, pp. 75–76.

no farther. Again Aquinas's main objective in the fourth Way, as in the other three, is to prove in yet another way that all the things we know are effects, but in the fourth Way he determines more precisely the immediacy of the dependence of each effect as limited in being on the Cause on which it ultimately depends, and the transcendence of this Cause with regard to the entire finite order of things.

* * *

A sixth curious point which should strike the reader about article 3 concerns the third Way, which does not occur in chatper 13 of the *Contra Gentes*. In chapter 15 St Thomas gives an argument for the eternity of God which is regarded by many Thomists as an alternative form of the third Way of article 3. However, this argument in chapter 15 does not seem to have been derived from Aristotle like the third Way of article 3. As the argument of article 3 comes almost verbatim from Aristotle, and that of chapter 15 seems to be based on Aquinas's own metaphysics, including his theory of the real distinction of being and essence, it is very difficult to see how the one argument is only a variant of the other, as many modern Thomists think. Degl'Innocenti's effort to show that the argument of chapter 15 is really equivalent to the third Way of article 3 looks very feeble to anyone who has realized that the third Way comes from Aristotle's *De Caelo* and is based on the ancient Cosmology.[26] It may be that the argument of chapter 15 is a valid argument for the existence of God, but we cannot conclude from this that it is basically the same argument as the third Way. Professor Van Steenberghen is surely justified in holding, as anyone who is familiar with the extensive literature devoted to the study of this Way must know quite well, that the third Way, as we have it in the *Summa Theologica*, is bristling with philosophical difficulties.[27] But surely the best way to meet the difficulties is to try to see the Tertia Via as St Thomas himself saw it, and then at least we can set about remedying them more easily than we can by trying to read the argument in a

[26]U. Degl'Innocenti: *La Validità della Tertia Via* in the series 'Sulle Cinque Vie', pp. 41ff.

[27]F. Van Steenberghen: *Ontologie*, pp. 160–1; *Acta III Congressus Thomistici Internationalis*, pp. 239–40; cf. 'Le Problème Philosophique de l'Existence de Dieu' in the *Revue Philosophique de Louvain*, 1947, pp. 141–68 for many pointed observations about the Five Ways.

way that plainly does violence to the text. Most Thomists in recent years seem to abandon the attempt to defend the third Way as it stands, and just put the argument from chapter 15 of the *Contra Gentes* in its place. This is quite feasible in practice, provided they do not convey the impression that in article 3 St Thomas really meant us to read the argument of chapter 15 rather than the third Way. There is no getting round the fact that in the third Way of article 3 St Thomas meant us to read the argument of Aristotle.

Without discussing whether or not the third Way is valid, despite all its difficulties we can at least say that St Thomas could only have put this argument forward unpruned, as it stands in Aristotle's text, in an age which was so thoroughly Aristotelian in mind and heart that he could afford to yield, as many of his contempories did in the thirteenth century, to his at times excessive fidelity to Aristotle's written word.[28] It is important to understand, however, that the kind of interpretation of the third Way given by most modern writers, both Thomist and non-Thomist as well as anti-Thomist, namely that it argues from contingent to necessary being as a purely metaphysical argument, and that it is the most important of the five arguments given by St Thomas, has no foundation either in article 3 of the *Summa Theologica,* or in chapter 13 of the *Contra Gentes.* This argument from contingency, known to Leibniz and Kant, does not exist in either article 3 or chapter 13.

*     *     *

This leads me to the seventh of the curious points to be observed about Five Ways. This point has not attracted the general attention of commentators which, it seems, it ought to have done. As we have said, at the beginning of article 3 St Thomas puts the query 'utrum Deus sit', and it is the invariable practice of the angelic doctor to answer the query he puts at the beginning of each article, and not to finish the article till he has answered the query raised. But article 3 seems to be an exception: St Thomas does not answer the query 'does God exist?' at the end of the article, and furthermore it does not appear that he intended to do so. He gives five arguments purporting to prove that God exists, but they do not go so far as to reach the required conclusion. All five of them break off in a most abrupt manner with some such

[28]F. Van Steenberghen: *Acta III Congressus,* p. 240.

statement as 'et hoc omnes intelligunt Deum', 'quam omnes Deum nominant', 'et hoc Dicimus Deum'. The third Way for example eventually reaches the conclusion, 'Ergo necesse est ponere aliquid quod est per se necessarium, non habens causam necessitatis aliunde, sed quod est causa necessitatis aliis', and without more ado St Thomas adds 'quod omnes dicunt Deum'. Now surely the whole problem that is being discussed by St Thomas in the context of the *Summa Theologica* is, DO all men, and do we Christians and Christian theologians in particular, call any of the five beings (the unmoved mover, the un-caused cause, the being which is per se necessary, the sovereign Being, and the 'aliquid intelligens' of the fifth Way) God, and if anyone does so, *ought* he to do so? The real answer to the query put at the beginning of the article should be something like this: 'therefore, this Being we have proved to exist must be and can be no other than God'—not that all men call some being whose existence they claim to prove 'God'. In any case we might well ask 'all' who? Should 'omnes' be translated as 'all men'? There is ground for considering that St Thomas has not yet finished his proof for the existence of God at the end of article 3. He has established that the beings we know from experience in the universe are effects, and that therefore there must be some cause not itself an effect to explain the different ways in which they are the effects of some causal activity; this marks a stage, an important stage, in the total argument, in that it gives us a foot-hold, or establishes a bridge-head within territory beyond ordinary experience that is being explored, but it is not the end of the whole campaign. We say that the invasion of the continent took place on D-Day, but the crossing of the channel and the securing of a number of bridge-heads on the coasts of France at the end of the first day which we call D-Day, did not end the invasion: it only represented the successful completion of one difficult stage. The total invasion only finished when the allies had reached some point decided upon by the High Command well inland, as, for example, the Rhine. Similarly St Thomas speaks of article 3 as dealing with the question 'does God exist?' but at its conclusion he has only successfully accomplished the first stage in the whole programme. Merely showing that there is some kind of cause for the effects we know in the universe, which is itself different from the things in the universe, and which men call God, is clearly not a final conclusion, but, as it were, the securing of some point at which to call a general pause in operations and from which to recommence later. Thus I come to the same conclusion as Professor Van Steenberghen: 'Aucune des cinq voies ne se suffit à élle-même et ne peut être présentée dans sa teneur littérale comme une preuve complète et rigoureuse de l'existence de Dieu'.[29] In other words we have not in the text of the Five Ways as given in article 3 the complete proof of St Thomas for the existence of God. Why, then, we may ask, did St Thomas handle the question of God's existence in a manner which is so much at variance with that to which he was accustomed?

\*    \*    \*

I feel quite certain that some of my readers are objecting that I am only somewhat perversely and stupidly creating a number of imaginary difficulties, for St Thomas quite clearly meant his readers to understand that the being whose existence he establishes at the end of each Way and whom he says all men call God, really is the one true God. They will tell me to take a glance at chapter 13 of the *Contra Gentes* once more: here the first Way ends: 'et hoc dicimus Deum', like the third and fourth, but the second Way finishes: 'quae est Deus'. Furthermore towards the end of the passage in chapter 15 in which St Thomas is proving the eternity of God (which so many Thomists regard as a variant of the third Way), St Thomas concludes that there must be a being which is *per se* necessary, and he adds 'et hoc Deus est; cum sit causa prima, ut ostensum est (cap 13)'. Furthermore in chapter 3 of the *Contra Gentes* St Thomas writes of the truths concerning God which reason is able to know unaided by faith 'sicut est Deum esse, Deum esse unum, et alia hujusmodi; quae etiam philosophi demonstrative de Deo probaverunt, ducti naturalis lumine rationis'.

To this I reply that if we examine the structure of each of the Five Ways, and also the sequence of thought followed by St Thomas throughout questions 2, 3, 4 and on to 11, it will become clear that this third article does not, and is not meant to, give the complete proof, but only the first stages of the complete proof, which St Thomas had in mind. He has used the proofs of the philosophers, notably of Aris-

[29]F. Van Steenberghen: *Ontologie*, p. 163. cf. M. F. Sciacca: *L'Existence de Dieu*, p. 187.

totle, to establish that the things of this world, the universe itself, are effects in many different kinds of ways, and therefore that they have a cause which is itself uncaused. But he has not followed the arguments which the philosophers used any further in article 3, so that he leaves the reader without any precise knowledge about what kind of being, or beings stand to the world as its cause. The Five Ways only establish that there exists something corresponding to God as nominally defined for the purposes of beginning a discussion on the question of God's existence. In the previous article St Thomas had said: 'unde, demonstrando Deum esse per effectum, accipere possumus pro medio quid significat hoc nomen Deus'.[30] As article 3 links on to article 2, St Thomas takes his argument for God's existence in article 3 as far as he laid down in article 2. The expressions, 'quod omnes dicunt Deum esse', at the end of each of the Five Ways, then, refer to what all taking part in the discussion have agreed at the beginning of the investigation to call God. The Five Ways only prove that God exists as defined in an initial nominal definition acceptable to everyone, Christian and non-Christian alike; that is to say, St Thomas has only proved that there is a being, whatever it might be, which is the cause of the universe, which is personal in some kind of way, and itself not an effect.[31] But once we have proved that there is a God *in the sense just defined* there is evidently much hard thinking still to be done before we can conclude that this being is the God who has revealed Himself to us as the God of Abraham, Isaac and Jacob, and later in Jesus Christ. Thus, as Professor Van Steenberghen justly remarks: 'De toute façon, isoler le texte des "quinque Viae" de leur contexte et surtout des questions suivantes de la "Somme Théologique", c'est commettre une mutilation injustifiable et dangereuse.'[32] The final stages, in which we will find in the most unmistakable form what we are all looking for and some are so disappointed on failing to find, viz. the personal contributions of the angelic doctor, appears in the Quaestiones which follow article 3.

[30]'[whence, in demonstrating that God exists from effects, we are able to take for the medium of demonstration what the name "God", means]'. Qu. 2, art 2, ad. 2. cf. Victor White: 'Prelude to the Five Ways', in *God the Unknown*, p. 57ff.

[31]cf. F. Van Steenberghen: *Le Problème Philosophique de l'Existence de Dieu* (*op. cit.*), pp. 5–20 for an admirable account of the role of the Nominal Definition in the proofs for God's existence.

[32]F. Van Steenberghen: *Ontologie,* p. 163.

Hence the puzzling little expressions, 'quod omnes dicunt Deum esse', with which each Way ends are not a final conclusion terminating the whole discussion, but only a kind of provisional resting point at which to pause in the course of the complete argument arranged on set purpose. What this purpose is we will discuss in due course.

It is, I submit, surprising that Thomist philosophers have not been forward in recognizing the incompleteness of the Five Ways as proofs for God's existence seeing that this incompleteness has so often been pointed out. It was clearly noted long ago by no less an authority than Cardinal Cajetan, but unfortunately he tried to gloss the position over without examining the situation which led St Thomas to present the Five Ways in a separate article on their own. He says:

> Omnia enim haec praedicata, scilicet movens immobile, primum efficiens, necessarium non ex alio, maxime ens, et primum gubernans intelligendo, sunt secundum veritatem propria Deo: et ideo, concludendo haec inveniri in rerum natura, concluditur directe, quasi per accidens, quod Deus est, idest Deus, non ut Deus, sed ut habens talem conditionem, est; et consequenter ipsum substratum, scilicet Deus ut Deus, est.[33]

But since St Thomas is writing as a theologian he is writing about *Deus ut Deus,* not about *Deus ut habens talem conditionem,* and therefore he is trying to establish the existence of *Deus ut Deus.* There is no point in his proving *quasi per accidens* that *Deus ut Deus* exists. Unless he proves decisively that the one true God exists, there is no point in him introducing the arguments for the existence of God as a means of studying the theology of the divine essence. As Van Steenberghen says, in the complete proof for God's existence it is not sufficient to establish that there is a being with some attribute or the other which is proper to

[33]We can translate this extract from Cajetan as follows: '[All the above-mentioned expressions, namely the unmoved mover, the first efficient cause, the intrinsically necessary being, the being which is the greatest in being, the first intelligent being who directs all things to their end, pertain truly and really to God: and thus, in showing that such perfections exist in some being, we have shown directly, but, as it were incidently (per accidens) that God exists; we have in fact only shown that God as possessed of these qualities exists, and not that God in his divinity as such exists. The existence of God in his divinity as such has to be shown as the ultimate ground of these qualities]'. Cajetan: *Commentary on the Summa Theologica,* on art. 3. Also N. del Prado, O.P., *De Veritate Fundamentali Philsophiae Christianiae,* pp. 236–9.

God. It is necessary to show that it must belong exclusively to the being whose existence is proved, and that this attribute belongs to this being because he is God.[34] Dr Ronald Hepburn has recently raised once more the old criticism which, it seems, if justified is unanswerable, and it is the same as that which a Christian theologian might well make against Aristotle's argument. Talking about the problem of halting the series of causes regressing to infinity, he says, like Dr Mascall:

> The God at whom we have arrived by tracing back the causal regress would be a God far too closely tied to his creation to satisfy Christian demands for his 'otherness' or transcendence. Whatever inaugurated the causal sequence would be part and parcel of the natural world in which it is causally operative. . . . Paul Tillich is perfectly right when he says that the cosmological argument degrades God to the level of the world itself.[35]

Indeed, though St Thomas composed article 3 writing as a theologian, it is impossible to find in the body of the article any trace of an idea of God coming from the Bible, though the *Sed contra* mentions the capital text of Ex. iii 14. As far as the Five Ways go the unmoved mover, the uncaused cause, and the being which is *per se* necessary, might well be, for all we can tell, immanent to the world of experience as a kind of soul of the world, for the arguments themselves do not establish the existence of a being who is, simply speaking, not of the world of nature, but transcendent to and other than nature. The fourth Way alone argues to some kind of being which, because supreme and not limited, is presumably transcendent. But it is absolutely impossible to hold that the proof for the existence of God has come within sight of the completeness envisaged by the text of the *Sed Contra* till it has established the transcendence of God *vis-à-vis* all created and creatable things.

Finally, as Van Steenberghen is so often insisting, not one of the Five Ways save the fourth, establishes the existence of just one cause of the world. As far as the other Ways go we might conclude that there are more than one unmoved movers, or uncaused causes or necessary beings, and there is no argument provided by St Thomas to

[34]F. Van Steenberghen: *Acta III Congressus*, p. 239.
[35]R. Hepburn: *Christianity and Paradox*, pp. 166–7. The reference to Tillich is to his *Systematic Theology*, vol. 1, p. 205 in the edition of the University of Chicago Press (1951).

show that the unmoved mover, uncaused cause, the necessary and the supreme being are one and the same. They might be a number of equal partners with a common interest in keeping the universe going as we find it. It is true that in the first Way, as it is given in the *Contra Gentes*, St Thomas does claim to prove that there is only one Unmoved Mover, but he only does this because he follows Aristotle in admitting the existence of the heavenly spheres and therefore the idea of the one outermost sphere which is moved by the one Unmoved Mover 'whom all men call God'. But in the *Summa Theologica* he has done away with these heavenly spheres and so he cannot conclude directly that there is just one Unmoved Mover: he can prove that there is at least one, and no doubt that is all that St Thomas means by saying that there is need to come to 'aliquod primum movens'.[36] He leaves the question as to whether there are more than one such beings over for later treatment. Therefore, strictly speaking, the first three Ways ought to conclude that there may be many unmoved movers, uncaused causes, *per se* necessary beings, and one of these no doubt is the being men call God. Thus, once again, we must say that till St Thomas has managed to prove that there is but one being on whom all things we know depend, his proof for the existence of God has not come within sight of its natural finishing point. I submit, therefore, that I am not perversely making superfluous difficulties.

It is interesting to note that in his *Commentary on the Sentences,* while explaining that we come to know of God's existence discursively by reasoning, St Thomas gives in rough outline the sort of process by which we would establish that God exists. He says: 'Visis sensibilibus, non devenimus in Deum nisi procedendo, secundum quod ista causata sunt et quod omne causatum est ab aliqua causa agente et quod primum agens non potest esse corpus. . . .'[37] It is just significant enough to merit notice that in article 3 St Thomas may be said to argue that 'omne causatum est ab aliqua causa agente', but he only argues that 'primum agens non potest esse corpus' in Quaestio 3. And this, he says, is a part of the total proof that God is.

[36]F. Van Steenberghen: *Ontologie,* pp. 159–60.
[37]'[Starting from sensible things, we only come to God by stages, treating sensible things as caused, then arguing that all caused things are the effects of an active agent, and that the very first of all active causes cannot be material]'. *Sent.*, Dist. III, qu. 1, art. 2.

# 6

## FURTHER CONSIDERATIONS ON THE THEOLOGICAL SETTING OF THE FIVE WAYS

The basic programme inspiring the lifework of St Thomas, which he developed gradually from the early days at Paris commenting on the *Sentences* of Peter Lombard till he attained the full mastery with which we find him employing it in the *Summa Theologica,* consisted in the effort to think, and teach others to think, the Sacred Teaching (it was his duty to expound) as a science in the technical Aristotelian sense of the term. St Thomas aimed quite explicitly at finding a new way of presenting the Sacred Teaching of the Church. We would say nowadays that his aim was to construct and present to others a new way of theologizing. In the thirteenth century many theologians were beginning to interest themselves in Aristotle's idea that the most perfect and desirable knowledge, from the human point of view, is that which a man seeks by his own efforts and attains when he has appropriately reasoned and demonstrated from evident premises what he knows, and so come to understand it; when a man can explain not merely that such or such is the case, but why it is, and even why it must be the case, he has reached a knowledge that is as perfect as can be, and so dignified with the title, 'scientific'. For Aristotle science was a knowledge of a thing through its causes, or in terms of all that contributes in any way to the formation of a thing. Any man who observes what goes on around him may know that there has been an eclipse of the moon; the astronomer explains what brought the eclipse about, and what conditions conspired to make the eclipse necessary or inevitable. A number of theologians had been trying, before St Thomas had commenced his teaching career, to present the Sacred Teaching of the Church in this humanly satisfying form of a deductive science, but by the middle of the thirteenth century they had achieved little by way of constructing out of the truths of faith a science that would prove of lasting value.[1] From the beginning of his teaching career at Paris St Thomas evidently understood the importance of continuing the effort to construct the Sacred Teaching into a scientifically conceived theology. At the very beginning of his *Commentary on the Sentences,* in the Prologue, he discussed whether *Sacra Doctrina* is a science (it seems that he is here using the term in its technical Aristotelian sense), and whether its 'modus procedendi sit artificialis'.[2] In the *Summa Theologica* he discussed the same problem towards the end of Quaestio 1 when in article 8 he asked 'utrum haec doctrina sit argumentativa', and he constructed the whole of his *Summa* on his maturest ideas of what he conceived Sacred Teaching ought to be when thought in the manner of a science.

In order to understand how St Thomas was able to conceive the teaching of the Church in the manner of a science it is necessary to say something about what the doctrinal teaching of the Church really is in her own mind and that of her theologians, and then on Aristotle's conception of science. We can then show how St Thomas brought the two together.

The Church has always regarded her work of teaching men as one of her most sacred duties. She is a teaching Church by virtue of the charter of her institution, 'Go ye and teach all nations, teaching them to observe all things whatsoever I have commanded you',[3] and by reason of the very nature of her work which is to teach men to know, love and serve God. The Church holds that she has a message from God to impart to all men, so that she has the duty of instructing all men in God's name, even as they have an obligation to listen to her instruction and accept it as God's own word and message, for 'he that heareth you, heareth me'. This teaching is sacred both because it comes from God, and because it is about God and man's duties to Him. The Church has a right and a duty to teach men which is God-given, and her duty is to teach men the full truth that Christ taught while He lived on earth. With this duty of having to preach the entire Gospel of Christ goes the obligation of preserving Christ's teaching unaltered, without

---

[1] cf. M. D. Chenu, O.P.: *La Théologie comme Science au XIIIe Siècle.*
[2] *I Sent.,* Prologus, qu. 1, art. 3 and 5.
[3] Matt. xxviii,18–20; Mark xvi,15–16.

changing one jot or tittle of the message she has received from Jesus Christ, for by its nature a message has to be conveyed faithfully (i.e. completely and unimpaired in its integrity), by the messenger whose duty it is to transmit it as given to those for whom it is intended. The responsibility of a messenger, like that of an interpreter, lies in transmitting faithfully and effectively the contents of the message with which he is entrusted; he has to give the message in the most appropriate manner possible, and therefore in terms that will at once express its exact meaning and convey that meaning to the minds of the recipients as accurately as possible. Knowledge that is entrusted as a message to be conveyed to others must be treasured by the messenger as something inviolable because, for one reason, it belongs by right to the person who entrusted it to the messenger's safe-keeping, and, for another, those for whom the message is ultimately intended possess the right to be informed exactly of what the sender of the message wishes them to know. A messenger holds the information he has been sent to give to others on trust, so that he is answerable for the efficiency with which he carries out his task, both to the person who gave him the message and to the person or persons for whose benefit he has been sent to deliver it. In the mind of the Church her doctrine is a message and a doctrine which is intrinsically holy and sacred because it has been entrusted to her by God Himself. The Church teaches all men the word of God, Christ's own word. Her teaching is for her as sacred and inviolable as God Himself. In the eyes of the faithful the doctrine of the Church is likewise a treasure to be loved and sought for its own sake, for it is God's gift to their minds or knowledge estimable beyond all other knowledge. When we believe what the Church teaches us in Christ's name we believe because God has revealed what we are taught. But in believing what God has revealed we are believing what God Himself knows and understands perfectly, so that in believing we receive from God something of the knowledge He has of Himself. By accepting the teaching of the Church we thus become united with God, as something of His own knowledge of Himself is imparted to us,[4] and in so far as we know something of God which God knows of Himself we possess something of God's own mind.

We talk about the teaching of the Church and about the teaching

[4] cf. M. D. Chenu, O.P.: St Thomas d'Aquin et la Théologie, p. 37.

Church. In the ultimate analysis, however, we must look beyond the Church to God, for it is God, and not merely the Church, who gives us the knowledge of the truths which the Church is for ever putting before us.[5] The Church does not teach us instead of, or in the place of God. The Church teaches by means of the spoken word which we hear coming from the lips of those who speak on her behalf, but she is teaching us as a legate in God's name, or as an agent God uses in His work of imparting to us the supernatural truths about Himself He wishes us to know. Those who listen to the spoken word because they are seeking the knowledge God has given to us through his Church, are inwardly and supernaturally enlightened by God Who acts within the Church, assisting her in her work of spreading the knowledge He has revealed. It is God Who gives to each person the gift of divine faith raising and proportioning their minds to see the meaning and truth of the divine mysteries, and so enabling those hearing the spoken word preached to them to draw more benefit from whatever is authoritatively preached in God's name. Without this inward gift of faith no man would of himself be able to accept nor perceive the truth of the mysteries which the Church preaches, for they are supernatural. Thus for the mediaeval theologians Sacred Teaching meant, in the active sense of the term, the process of bringing something of God's knowledge of Himself into being in the minds of men, and therefore besides the external work of preaching by human teachers, it included the actual infusion into men's minds by God of powers issuing in the activities by which they believe and acquire knowledge of divine mysteries.[6] Normally this birth of divine knowledge in men's minds is the outcome of the Church's work of preaching through human agents fecundated by the action of God in the minds and souls of those who hear and believe. The Holy Teaching, then, comes to men from God through the Church, for God works through the agency of the Church even as the Church reaps the harvest of her labours by the aid of God's power. The Church labours at the works of sowing the seed and watering, but God alone gives the fruitful yield of the harvest, for without God's activity man's work of teaching such supra-natural truths could produce nothing. 'Therefore, neither he that planteth is any thing, nor he that watereth: but God

[5]cf. *Summa Theologica:* II–II, qu. 6, art. 1; qu. 1, art. 7, ad. 3.
[6]cf. G. Van Ackeren, S.J., *Sacra Doctrina,* p. 118.

that giveth the increase.'[7] The Apostles laboured at the nets from their fishing boats, but Christ alone gave the abundant catch.

In brief, then, the Holy Teaching is sacred or holy because it is from God and also because it is about God. It is a knowledge of God which rightfully and in the natural way of things belongs to God alone, for in God this knowledge is God. In Him being and truth are one identical reality. No created mind can possibly know God as He knows Himself: 'Who else can know a man's thoughts, except the man's own spirit that is within him? So no one else can know God's thoughts, but the Spirit of God.'[8] Thus the Holy Teaching gives a knowledge of God and of God's works which only God can know without being taught. In the ultimate analysis no one can possibly derive this knowledge from anyone but God Himself. The generation of the divine knowledge which God wishes all men to have is, therefore, properly speaking the work of God, but in the order of things ordained by Christ, it is a work administered by the Magisterium of the Church to whom Christ entrusted the human work of preaching the truths He has revealed to all men. The human teachers of the divine truths appointed by the Church work as instruments God uses in the accomplishment of His own ends. They must therefore preach faithfully the message Christ as God entrusted to the Church and preserve it throughout time exactly as Christ entrusted it to the Church while He was on earth. Human teachers may instruct, but they cannot themselves impart the gift of certitude about such truths to those whom they instruct; they can state what the truth is, but they cannot give the actual knowledge of the truth. Faith, as knowledge possessed with certitude by the mind, or as scientia,[9] comes from God alone, and Sacra Doctrina is as much the free gift of God to man as divine grace or any other divine favour. The idea that the teaching of the Church is a message is thus intimately linked with the idea that in teaching the Church acts solely as an instrument of God in teaching men.

*     *     *

When St Thomas thought of presenting the Holy Teaching as a

[7] I Cor. iii, 7.
[8] I Cor. i, 11.
[9] In the sense in which St Thomas uses 'scientia' in qu. 1, art. 2 of the *Summa Theologica*, cf. pp. 39–42.

science he had in mind the kind of thing that Aristotle visualized in writing about the 'unqualified scientific knowledge' we possess when we are able to show not only that something happens or is the case (e.g. that there is an eclipse of the moon), but why it is happening and must necessarily happen. Obviously, then, the premises from which we are going to demonstrate the necessity of an event taking place 'must be true, primary, immediate, better known than and prior to the conclusion, which is further related to them as effect to cause',[10] for a conclusion becomes known from the knowledge we have of the premises. St Thomas expresses this idea most concisely in saying that we have a science, that is to say a deductive as distinct from an inductive science, when from things already known we come to a knowledge of things that were less or only partially known, or in some respects quite unknown.[11] Scientia, then, is knowledge methodically acquired by reasoning from things or principles which are known to us by immediate evidence to other things which become known in virtue of the evidence furnished by a reasoning process. We have scientific knowledge when we have the evidence for what we know before us, so that we can see clearly not merely that something is true, but why it is, and why in the conditions before us it must, or cannot not, be true. Knowledge becomes 'unqualified scientific knowledge' in the measure that we are constrained by the necessity of the evidence to see that the conclusion must follow, and thus 'unqualified scientific knowledge' gives us understanding and insight. Knowledge attains the dignity of science when we have the intrinsic evidence for what we know before us. Certitude is that quality of perfect knowledge which is engendered in the mind from the perception of evidence. Some certitudes are based on intuitive perception of intrinsic evidence, as, for example, the certainty I have of existing within the physical world with other men, the certainty I have of my present sensations, or of the truth of the first basic principles of all thinking, such as those of contradiction and of excluded middle. I have the evidence for these certainties immediately before me as soon as I use my mind and senses. I can only doubt these certainties by having recourse to some artificial stratagem, such as Descartes employed in his famous method of universal doubt com-

---

[10]Aristotle: *Posterior Analytics*, Book 1, ch. 2, 71b, 19–24.
[11]cf. St Thomas: *In Boetii de Trinitate*, Prooem., qu. 2, art. 2.

bined with the artifice of the supposed evil genius; but if I do attempt some such stratagem to justify my basic natural certainties, I only justify them artificially. I could just as well say that I must invent some other stratagem to test whether I can really justify anything by the first, and so on *ad infinitum*. In fact it is more logical to doubt of the validity and use of all such stratagems, and examine the evidence I have all the time for my natural certainties, seeing that I have the evidence for their truth accessible to me. Thus, Aristotle maintained, it is only if we have certain self-evident ultimate premises before us that we can construct a science at all, for without them as foundations we would have to demonstrate everything, and then we could not succeed in demonstrating anything.[12] A science is thus formally a knowledge of conclusions as conclusions, i.e. as reasoned from premises of which we are certain because we have the evidence for their truth before us. It is something built up piece by piece, stage by stage, gradually and in a reasoned manner.

To apply this idea of science to *Sacra Doctrina,* St Thomas would have to say that the science of theology he hoped to construct is a knowledge of the things of God which we acquire not from God by faith, but by our own study and thinking, and which is based on certain facts and truths as on first undemonstrable principles accepted somehow as evident, so that it is rooted on certainties that are absolute and unshakeable. How did St Thomas set about building such a science of the truths of faith?

\*     \*     \*

It might well seem at first sight that Holy Teaching and science, as visualized by Aristotle, are simply speaking incompatible with each other. Granted that God gives us genuine knowledge in his Holy Teaching, the knowledge He gives is none the less of a totally different order to any we can consider scientific, so that faith and science ought to be treated as incommensurate with each other. Sacred knowledge is supernatural and so supra-rational, or essentially mysterious in the sense that though we can know and up to a point think about what God has said, we can never understand the mysteries He has revealed by coming to see the intrinsic evidence of their truth. We may know,

[12]cf. for example, Aristotle: *Posterior Analytics,* Book I, ch. I.

for example, that there are three persons in God, each person being one and the same identical God, but none the less each person being distinct from the other two persons; but we can never possibly see how there must be three persons in God as God Himself sees the necessity, and as the blessed in heaven see in the measure given to them. Sacred knowledge is simply speaking, knowledge reserved to God alone to understand, and this being the case, it would seem that sacred knowledge cannot be presented as a science at all. Scientific knowledge is understanding or insight into reality attainable by man by the use of reason; but such a knowledge of the divine mysteries is utterly unattainable by any human efforts, and beyond the reach of reason ever to attain on earth. God gives us a knowledge of Himself but He does not give us to see the intrinsic evidence for the truths He teaches us so that their inner necessity, their entire inward reason of being, is simply speaking not known to us. We accept the truths taught by the Church on the sole authority of the word of God, and we know that what we believe on God's authority is and must be true, for God could not teach anything unless it was true. But we cannot aspire to understand what we believe. By faith we know 'as in a glass darkly',[13] not merely because we happen to be unable to understand what we are given to know, but also because we are positively incapable of understanding truths so far exceeding anything proportioned to our powers.[14] In other words, instead of having the intrinsic evidence before us for the truths we accept, from which (if we needed) we might possibly be able to construct a science of theology, we have only the extrinsic evidence of the word of God, the evidence of authority, supported by the testimony of the miracles Christ worked as signs of His supreme authority to teach all men as God Himself.

St Thomas was always at pains to emphasize that there are two different orders of truth. First, we have the truth that is natural to, or commensurate with the knowing powers of the human mind. This is attained, or in principle attainable, by reason working on its own and it is such that in principle we can aspire to seeing the intrinsic evidence for the truth the mind knows. When we attain this perfect kind of knowledge we have knowledge which is pre-eminently scientific.

[13] I Cor. xiii,12.
[14] cf. *Summa Theologica*, II–II, qu. 7, art. 2, ad. 3.

Second, we have truth that is supernatural or divine and this exceeds not the powers of the mind to know, but its powers to understand or to comprehend fully. The mind finds these truths intelligible, but it does not perceive their own intrinsic intelligibility. This knowledge is given as a free gift from God in the gift of faith. It gives the firmest possible certitude, for the motive of faith is the authority of God revealing.[15] None the less this kind of knowledge, superior to all others as it is by reason of its certitude and the Being it enables us to know, is a knowledge which as knowledge is imperfect because we know without understanding. Faith is necessarily an obscure knowledge for we cannot account for what we know as we can when we are really certain of something of which we can attain certitude by natural means. The imperfection lies in the manner, the obscure manner, in which we know, and not in the nature of what we know. Faith cannot give us that perfect manner of knowing by understanding enabling us to explain what we know as it really is; it can only give us an incomplete and fragmentary way of knowing which may be compared to the dark vision we have when we look down a vast building at night time lighted by a solitary flickering lamp. We see dimly this and that, something or the other here and there, but we know that it is utterly beyond the power of our eyes to see all that is there to be seen in the daylight. Thus we cannot explain what we do see in the sense that we can account for the necessity of its being there, and its appearing as it does. There is thus an essential disparity between the knowledge which we attain naturally and which in principle may always become scientific, and that which we are given supernaturally to know by faith, which, it seems, can never become scientific because lost in obscurity, not for lack of light but for our lack of intellectual powers to understand.[16]

Though there is an essential diversity between faith and science in that faith is an imperfect and science a perfect way of knowing, St Thomas is adamant in holding, as is the Church herself, that there is no essential heterogeneity or incompatibility between faith and reason, nor is there any possible conflict between them, for reason knows and faith is a knowing.[17] All knowledge comes ultimately

[15]cf. qu. I, art. 5.
[16]cf. M. D. Chenu, O.P.: *Is Theology a Science?*, pp. 18–22.
[17]cf. *Contra Gentes*, I, ch. 7.

from God, and God, as the source of all truth, is as much the author of faith as He is of reason; as God cannot possibly contradict Himself, so faith and reason must ultimately be in harmony one with the other. Thus the mysteries of faith, though they surpass, do not violate, the basic principles of reason; there is nothing self-contradictory nor unthinkable about the mysteries of faith. Though we cannot understand, we can bring our minds to think about the truths of faith, and we can examine them in the light of the fundamental principles of reason and metaphysics, and we can employ truths that are naturally accessible to reason in our efforts to think, as best we can, the truths of faith. By so doing we can come to some knowledge, humble though it be, of divine truths.

But even granted that there is no essential heterogeneity between natural and supernatural knowledge in that for St Thomas all knowledge is of being, and even granted that divine mysteries are intelligible truths about which we are able to think and reason, this does not advance us very far towards showing that *Sacra Doctrina* can be presented as a science, if by science we mean what Aristotle meant by 'unqualified scientific knowledge'. Aristotle's 'science' seems to be quite incompatible with divine faith on several further scores. Science, as Aristotle conceives it, is acquired knowledge, and many of the thinking processes involved in our acquiring knowledge enter into the nature of any science: faith, on the other hand, by which we know divine truth, is infused as the free gift of God, and not acquired by our own activities of thinking. Not all the study of a lifetime will ever enable a man to accept as absolutely certain the truth, for example, of the Blessed Trinity unless he receives the gift of faith from God. Again, science, as Aristotle conceives it, is concerned solely with the necessary and universal, and not with the contingent or particular, so that science is not concerned with the narration of events which go on in the world and contribute to the making of its history; God's revelation to man, on the contrary, is essentially the manifestation of a plan He works out in time, comprising events which unfold as time goes on as the fulfilment of prophecies, and which make up a history of God's dealings with men; though God reveals truths to us, He does so only within the pattern of unfolding events through which we can trace the finger of God in the history of the world. Holy Teaching, then, is necessarily, at least in part, the narrative of the story of what God has done for us in history, and because it is intrinsically historical, it cannot be treated as a science. We cannot afford to fashion a science of theology concentrated on the necessary and universal, and jettison the historical narratives given to us in the Bible. Finally, Aristotle's science, as we have explained, is based on intrinsic evidence, but faith is of its nature a knowing which is devoid of intrinsic evidence. Science begins with the self evident, and the perfectly known and thus with truth of which the knower is fully the master; it progresses towards what is less perfectly known so as to make it more perfectly known at the conclusion of a reasoning process. But in faith we have the opposite, for faith begins with what reason does not know, and with that of which the human mind has no mastery whatever. 'Scientia procedit ex principiis per se notis; fides autem est ex auditu'.[18] There is then, it seems, no sure foundation in *Sacra Doctrina* for such a human invention as a 'science'.

\*    \*    \*

The key theme of St Thomas's solution to the problem of whether Holy Teaching can be treated as a science lies in his theory of subalternate sciences, and in the way he conceived all the knowledge that we are given of God as He is in Himself as being a knowledge derived immediately from, and dependent wholly on God's own knowledge of Himself. There are, St Thomas reasons, two kinds of science. One kind is based on principles which are *per se* evident to the mind which itself possesses the science; such is the science the mathematician has of geometry. The mathematician builds his science on principles which are evident to him. These sciences are autonomous and self-sufficient sciences for they stand securely on their own feet. No other science or form of knowledge has anything to contribute to them to make them what they are. The other kind of science is based, at least partially, on principles which it borrows from some higher science, the borrowed principles being evident to the masters of the higher science, but not necessarily to those borrowing them to construct a subalternate science. These subalternate sciences 'procedunt ex principiis notis lumine superioris scientiae: sicut perspectiva procedit ex principiis notificatis per geometriam, et musica ex principiis per arithmeticam

[18]cf. Chenu: *La Théologie comme Science au XIIIe Siècle*, pp. 68-69.

notis'.[19] The architect believes the geometrical principles he borrows from geometry, and the musician believes those he borrows from arithmetic, so that these subalternate sciences are, to a certain extent, dependent for their welfare on the security of the higher mathematical sciences. The architect and musician believe the principles they accept from the mathematicians, convinced that the mathematicians know perfectly that they are true and why they must be true. The master of the subalternate or applied science just accepts the mathematical principles he requires for his work as true and gets straight on with his own work of seeing how he can use them for his own purposes, or, in other words, what conclusions he can draw from them as premises he accepts as evident because he knows they are evident to a mathematician.

Applying this conception of the dependence of a subalternate science on knowledge perfectly or intuitively possessed by the master of a higher science to the case of *Sacra Doctrina*, St Thomas argues that all knowledge of God as He is in Himself that we can possess is knowledge which we receive from God Himself who alone understands Himself. Thus in God alone are we to find perfect knowledge or understanding of Himself. For God is 'evident' to Himself alone. But God gives us to know Himself as He does, and we can only accept this knowledge from Him as a gift without having any understanding of it. Thus the knowledge we possess of God by faith, and which the saints in heaven possess of Him by vision, is subalternate to the perfect knowledge God has of Himself. It is God's knowledge of Himself which makes our knowledge of Him by faith what it is and which gives it its absolute certainty. Thus St Thomas writes: 'Sacra doctrina propriissime determinat de Deo secundum quod est altissima causa: quia non solum quantum ad illud quod est per creaturas cognoscibile, . . . sed etiam quantum ad id quod notum est sibi soli de seipso, et aliis per revelationem communicatum.'[20] Holy Teaching is thus a reflection or im-

---

[19]These subalternate sciences '[are built on principles provided by a higher kind of knowledge, as the knowledge of perspectives is based on a knowledge of certain principles of geometry, and a knowledge of music presupposes a knowledge of principles of arithmetic].' Art. 2.

[20]['Sacred Teaching gives us a knowledge about God in so far as He is the highest of all causes: for it considers God not merely in so far as He can be known from creatures . . . but also as He is known only to Himself and as He has revealed the knowledge He has of Himself to others.'] Qu. 1, art. 6.

pression in our minds of God's own knowledge of Himself: 'Sacra doctrina sit velut quaedam impressio divinae scientiae, quae est una et simplex omnium.'[21]

Our knowledge of God received from Him by faith can, in St Thomas's view, be regarded and treated as a science in Aristotle's sense of the term on condition that it is put as subalternate to God's own knowledge of Himself and so as a knowledge deriving from and dependent upon the knowledge God has of Himself. The principles of this science of theology will be the truths we receive from God which are self-evident to Him, but no to us who accept them from God by belief. The science of theology does not therefore try to prove by reason the truths of faith, nor even to establish their possibility: the theologian accepts the truths of faith as first principles, and then, by applying reason to them, he sees what he can deduce as necessarily true from these revealed principles. The theologian also investigates how he can by the aid of reason express these revealed truths in such a way et to enable the mind to think them ever more and more fruitfully: 'as hoc modo sacra doctrina est scientia, quia procedit ex principiis notis lumine superioris scientiae, quae scilicet est Dei et beatorum'.[22]

The articles of faith, then, are the first principles of a subalternate science of theology, which as subalternate is necessarily a purely deductive science built on principles we accept on faith from the mind of God, and which God Himself implants within our minds by the infused virtue of faith. 'Theological science can only come to birth and grow to maturity *within* the faith',[23] for the articles of faith are 'the very rudiments of his (the theologian's) knowledge'.[24] We build up the science of theology by ordering the revealed articles of faith systematically, linking them logically one with the other in a coherent sequence,[25] and by drawing from them the conclusions which we must draw if our profession of the faith is to be reasonable. Theology as a science is thus a science of conclusions in the sense that the activity of the theologian is directed to the drawing of the conclusions faith

[21]'[Thus sacred teaching is, as it were, a kind of impression of God's own knowledge, which is one and simple though inclusive of all things]'. Qu. I, art. 3.
[22]Qu. I, art. 2.
[23]M. D. Chenu, O.P.: *Is Theology a Science?*, p. 22.
[24]M. D. Chenu, O.P.: *Is Theology a Science?*, p. 23.
[25]cf. *Summa Theologica*, II–II, qu. I, art. 7 and 8.

sooner or later enforces on reason. Thus the divine light of faith is to theology what the natural light of the understanding is to any of the natural sciences. The use of reason does not drag faith down to its own level; faith rather raises reason up to its divine level. As St Thomas replied to his critics who accused him of polluting the purity of faith with the alloy of reason, and working the debasing miracle of changing the wine of faith into the water of reason, the speculative theologian, in making *Holy Teaching* a science, is not polluting anything nor debasing anything: he is interpreting the faith to reason and teaching the believer to think his faith; he is ennobling reason, converting the water of reason into the wine of faith. The theologian is indirectly enriching reason and showing how in fact, far from having anything to fear from faith, as from some kind of divine irrationalism, it has much to gain by becoming steeped in thought about God. As grace perfects nature so faith perfects reason. Reason has nothing to fear from knowing of God what the blessed in heaven and what God Himself knows of Himself; it has nothing to fear from the articles of faith reflecting in our minds the perfect knowledge of God.

This conception of St Thomas of the science of theology as subalternate to the knowledge God has of Himself casts much light on the ideas we mentioned in chapter 4 about *Sacra Doctrina,* and especially on St Thomas's insistence that its sole subject is God, so that all other things are considered solely in the relation they have to God. It is *one* science, because it is a human thinking about the knowledge God has of Himself and the many truths and facts which are revealed and learned, for example, from the Bible 'communicant in una ratione formali objecti hujus scientiae'.[26] Clearly theology does not deal with God and creatures 'ex aequis', but 'de Deo principaliter, et de creaturis secundum quod referunter ad Deum',[27] for God knows Himself, and only knows creatures in knowing Himself.

*       *       *

St Thomas takes architecture and music as examples of subalternate sciences, and just observes that theology is another subalternate science. Theology is not, however, a subalternate science of the kind he thought

[26]Qu. I, art. 3.
[27]Qu. I, art. 3, ad. I.

architecture and music to be, for these are something like what we call applied sciences. The modern physicist, for example, applies mathematics to material things, using it to attain a knowledge, not of mathematics, but of material things. The theologian, however, receives knowledge from God, not in order to apply this knowledge to something else, but rather to apply something else, namely reason to it, and to apply reason so as to make the revealed truths themselves the more clear to our minds. Reason is used by the theologian not to prove the truths of faith, nor to add anything to them, nor to change them in any way, but to manifest these truths to the mind.[28]

Reason manifests the supernatural truths of faith first by showing how we can think of the truths of revelation so that they may present themselves to the mind in the most intelligible manner. The earlier professors of theology had been *Magistri in Sacra Pagina,* and their work had been devoted to commenting on the text of Scripture. They thought of the Holy Teaching as fitting into the historical order of the events recorded in the Bible as into its rightful framework, and so as comprised in the narratives of the Old Testament histories from the creation of the world to the Birth of Christ, and then passing on to the New Testament narratives of the story of Christ's birth, life and work of effecting our redemption in His passion, death, resurrection and ascension, and finally leading up, through the period of the life of the Church, to the end of the world as envisaged by St John in the Apocalypse. The classical exponent of this historical conception of the Holy Teaching had been Hugh of St Victor in the twelfth century, for whom the work of the commentator in *Sacra Pagina* was to show how the whole of the history of God's dealings with man centred on the divine economy of Christ's redemptive work, and thus on the mystery of the Incarnation: 'Primus liber a principio mundi usque ad incarnationem Verbi narrationis seriem deducit; secundus liber ab incarnatione Verbi usque ad finem et consummationem omnium ordine procedit.'[29] For this purely historical order of biblical exegesis St

---

[28]Qu. 1, art. 8, ad. 2.

[29]'[The first book follows the development of the narrative from the beginning of the world up to the incarnation of the Word; the second book begins with the incarnation of the Word and continues to the end of the world].' Hugh of St Victor: *De Sacramentis,* Prol. (PL CLXXVI, col. 173). cf. Chenu. *Introduction à l'Etude de St Thomas d'Aquin,* pp. 258-9.

Thomas substituted the scientific arrangement of the speculative theologian which, in brief, requires the introduction of the all-important distinction between the material and the formal object proper to Aristotle's theory of science. All the events recorded in Scripture, all the events of Christ's life and work enter within the material object considered by the theologian, and they are brought together under the distinctive view-point or formal object characteristic of theology so that they are considered not for themselves but as referred to the formal object. The formal object of the science of theology is God, and thus the theologian orders everything that God has revealed in relation to God, and thinks of everything as having its theological meaning from this relation it has to God. For the theologian, then, all the events that are recorded in the Bible narrative have their real meaning not as events taking place in time, but as events that manifest God to men, for these events are the works of God, and as events which God brought about ultimately to lead all men to Him through His Church. Thus for St Thomas the theologian uses reason first to order all that is comprised within the material object of revelation to God, so that he may begin correctly by thinking of all that God has revealed and done in relation to God, as God Himself knows them.

In making the Holy Teaching a science St Thomas brought faith and reason together as into a dialogue, but the kind of dialogue in which reason is lodged fully within revelation and put at its disposal, so that the mind can imbibe ever more and more from the truths which God has graciously given it. The theologian does not use reason in order to attain a knowledge of the things of this world which he desires to know simply because they strike him with a sense of wonder; he is not even concerned with explaining the things of this world as the work of God. The theologian uses reason in order to attain such knowledge as he can of the truths God has revealed about Himself, simply because God has spoken in order that He might be heard and that His message or teaching should be understood. God gives us the gift of faith in order that we may know Him and therefore that we may think about what He has given us to know to the best of our human ability. Thinking about God and about what He has revealed of Himself is just a part, and a most important part, of our service of Him. The science of theology, therefore, is the study of the truths of revelation undertaken by reason for the purpose of attaining as comprehensive a way of thinking about God as we can attain by our own efforts acting in response to God's teaching. Hence reason begins to order all that is recorded in the Bible, and all that the Church teaches us so that all God's teaching may be seen as manifesting God Himself. The theologian uses reason, not that he may rejoice in its work and findings for their own sake, following reason to its own pasturage amongst the things of this world where it naturally lives, but that he may benefit the more fully from the supernatural gifts God has bestowed upon him; he lets reason be led to the pasturage to which God raises his mind that he may rejoice the more in knowing God as God gives Himself to us to be known. The truths of faith are given to us as a nourishment for the rational activities of our minds, not however that the mind may, as it were, absorb and empty the truths it contemplates of their contents, but that, with the contemplation of these truths, the mind may find ever more and more in them as it rises to an ever deeper knowledge of God and finds therein fulfilment which is but an anticipation of the vision of God after death. Chenu, mindful of the famous definition in the Epistle to the Hebrews of faith as 'argumentum non apparentium', states that 'la foi comporte non seulement une "conviction" religieuse, mais une capacité d'élaboration rationelle, de manifestation, de probation, selon le sens philosophique du mot *argumentum*'.[30] This is accurately expressed. The theologian's use of reason corresponds to a capacity for receiving a reasoned expression which is inherent in revelation itself, so that in applying reason to revealed truths the theologian, so far from doing any violence to faith, is but thinking his faith in a way that faith itself suggests the believer should think it for his own spiritual good. Clearly, the use of reason is not meant to supply for any imperfections in the divine truths themselves, nor to serve as a remedy for any imperfections or shortcomings in their revelation, but solely as a remedy for the imperfections and weaknesses in the human mind, for its faintness of vision, to enable it to see as clearly as possible at least as much as it can be naturally trained up to see of the truths revealed by God. Revelation does not itself just give a rational or intelligent appreciation of divine truth: it is itself just a Teaching, which requires the personal reasoning response of those taught if they are to

[30]M. D. Chenu, O.P.: *La Théologie comme Science au XIIIe Siècle*, p. 85.

assimilate as best they can what they are taught. St Thomas sees theology as a dialogue between revelation (that is to say God revealing) and reason, in which on the one hand God instructs men in divine truth, and on the other men, using their reason as best they can, collaborate with God in an effort to assimilate and appropriate to themselves the more intimately by thinking the truths God teaches them. Reason serves faith, and collaborates with faith as an instrument in God's work of the Holy Teaching. This is clearly the teaching of St Thomas:

> Utitur tamen sacra doctrina etiam ratione humana: non quidem ad probandum fidem, quia per hoc tolleretur meritum fidei; sed ad manifestandum aliqua quae traduntur in hac doctrina. Cum igitur gratia non tollat naturam, sed perficiat, oportet quod naturalis ratio subserviat fidei; sicut et naturalis inclinatio voluntatis obsequitur charitati. . . . Et inde est quod etiam auctoritatibus philosophorum sacra doctrina utitur, ubi per rationem naturalem veritatem cognoscere potuerunt. . . .[31]

And again St Thomas writes:

> Haec scientia accipere potest aliquid a philosophicis disciplinis, non quasi ex necessario eis indigeat, sed ad majorem manifestationem eorum quae in hac scientia traduntur. Non enim accipit sua principia ab aliis scientiis, sed immediate a Deo per revelationem. Et ideo non accipit ab aliis scientiis tamquam a superioribus, sed utitur eis tamquam inferioribus et ancillis; . . . Et hoc ipsum quod sic utitur eis, non est propter defectum vel insufficientiam ejus, sed propter defectum intellectus nostri; qui ex eis quae per naturalem rationem ex qua procedunt aliae scientiae cognoscuntur, facilius manuducitur in ea quae sunt supra rationem, quae in hac scientia traduntur.[32]

[31]'[Sacred Teaching, however, makes use of human reason, though not to prove the truths of faith. If reason could prove the truths we believe, belief would be deprived of its merit. It uses reason to manifest clearly the conclusions which are contained in holy teaching because they are contained in revealed truths. Since grace perfects, and does not suppress nature, human reason must be used in the service of faith, even as the natural inclinations of the will are to be put at the service of charity. . . . And so it is that holy teaching makes use of the authority of philosophers wherever reason can know the truth]'. Qu. 1, art. 8, ad. 2.

[32]'[This revealed knowledge may borrow from the philosophical sciences, not because it has a natural and intrinsic need for them, but merely for purpose of

Reason has, then, two works to perform for the theologian. One is to undertake the defence of the articles of the faith; it is for reason to meet the adversaries of the Holy Teaching and expose the emptiness of the reasons they bring against it. This work of reason is, however, extrinsic to faith and its doctrines themselves, so that we need not consider it here. The other, its noblest work, goes on within faith, and in this work reason has a real causal role to play, albeit in full dependence on faith itself in that it is our effort to accept, by raising our minds up to God's own knowledge.

Such, in brief, is St Thomas's doctrine in the first Quaestio of the *Summa Theologica*. Though he says much about reason and its uses, he says nothing directly about philosophy and the philosopher's use of reason, nor is he interested with the philosopher's knowledge of God. The whole discussion is on the theological level, about what God has revealed to us of Himself and how we can mentally assimilate this revelation.

*      *      *

We can now return to article 3, and, with these ideas about the science of theology in mind, ask ourselves, what exactly is St Thomas doing in this article?

He is selecting a number of arguments advanced mainly by Aristotle in order to stress, for the benefit of the Augustinian theologians, whose opinions he was opposing and who were so shy of reason which they positively distrusted, the genuine accord existing between faith and reason, between revelation and philosophy even when deprived of the direction of faith. He commences the *Summa* by trying to strike a balance between faith and reason from the very beginning while he is treating of God, Who is the proper subject of theology, and he

explaining more clearly the truths it imparts to us. It does not derive any of its principles from these sciences, but solely from God through revelation. Thus it does not borrow from any human science as from a higher kind of knowledge; it merely employs these sciences as lower and ancillary forms of knowledge; . . . Moreover, holy teaching does not use these sciences on account of any defect and insufficiency of its own, but on account of the weakness of the human mind, which is the more easily led from those objects which are known by the natural light of reason, from which the philosophical sciences proceed, to those which are above reason, with which holy teaching is concerned].' Qu. 1, art. 5, ad. 2; cf. also II-II , qu. 1, art. 5, ad. 2; qu. 2, art. 10, ad. 2.

devotes the whole of Quaestio 2 to saying as much as he can on reason and its knowledge of God. His first preoccupation was to reject the ideas of those theologians whose views put too close a relation between God and the human mind, saying that the mind just knows of God's existence without reasoning; he denies this theory that God is just naturally known, or more naturally known than are the things of this world, or the elementary principles of thinking. If he thus from the start strikes out against the current opinions of his brother theologians, and puts a certain distance between the mind and God, this is ultimately to ensure that we have a sound conception of reason, and equally that we have a proper conception of the transcendence and tremendous mystery of God. Thus Quaestio 2 which is entitled 'De Deo: an Deus sit' is also to a certain extent 'De Ratione et de Habitudine Rationis ad Cognoscendum Deum'.

St Thomas seems to have thought that the best way he could show the Augustinian theologians that, though man has no direct and immediate knowledge of God, reason and faith can be harmonized with each other, was to point out that, despite the distance between God and our minds, it is still natural for man to attain some knowledge of God by reason. To do this he has but to remind them that quite a normal part of the non-Christian philosopher's work was devoted to proving the existence of God, and that in fact they often came closer to a knowledge of Him than they ever realized. Therefore, instead of giving his own arguments he proceeds as he had said in article 8 a theologian should when he is using reason: he has recourse to the authority of philosophers to show what they have managed to do without the aid of divine faith towards establishing God's existence. Human reason can attain some knowledge of God, he is saying in article 3, though it has no direct perception of God, and we know this to be true from our knowledge of the history of non-Christian philosophy: 'Et inde est quod etiam auctoritatibus philosophorum sacra doctrina utitur, ubi per rationem naturalem veritatem cognoscere potuerunt, sicut Paulus inducit verbum Arati, dicens: "sicut et quidam poetarum vestrorum dixerunt: genus Dei sumus".'[33] As he argued elsewhere in the *Summa*, even if a man has not any intuitive knowledge of God's existence making the *Esse Dei per se notum* to him, he has a

[33]Qu. 1, art. 8, ad. 2.

natural inclination towards the good that is conformable to his nature as a rational being, and so he has a natural inclination to come to a knowledge of the truth about God even as he has a natural inclination to live in the society of other men: 'tertio modo inest homini inclinatio ad bonum secundum naturam rationis, quae est sibi propria: sicut homo habet naturalem inclinationem ad hoc quod veritatem cognoscat de Deo, et ad hoc quod in societate vivat'.[34] St Thomas wrote this article 3 of the *Summa,* to introduce reason, especially Aristotle, who in those days almost stood for reason, but also indirectly the Arab and Jewish philosophers who were the pioneers in Aristotelian studies during the Middle Ages, to Christian theology. He is trying to reassure the timorous Augustinian theologians that the philosophers who had not the faith were not really the menace to their Christian acquaintances they were held to be, for they knew *something* about the existence and nature of God. By reason the ablest of them attained some knowledge of God, and thus they used their reason in a way that was basically good and salutary. No doubt their arguments left much to be desired, not because they were necessarily defective, but because they were incomplete, or in so far as on solid foundations they built unsound theories. There is thus still a real need for revelation that all men may come to know God more truly and surely than mere reason can know Him; revelation brings home to the philosopher both the warning that their quest for knowledge of God is a quest for knowledge of a Being far exceeding their understanding, and the assurance that they can receive a more perfect knowledge of Him than any they ever could acquire for themselves by reason. But, St Thomas argues, the arguments of the philosophers for the existence of God are sound *as far as they go.* It is, therefore, possible for the Christian theologian to meet the philosophers, for revelation to be bought into a dialogue or conversation with reason, on some common ground. It is possible for the theologian to build upon and complete what the philosophers have ably commenced. The very first question the theologian considers, our knowledge of God, is one in which the theologian can build upon and complete what the philosophers have certainly ably commenced. Thus in article 3 of Quaestio 2 St Thomas definitely lets the philosophers speak for themselves; in article 3 he, as it were, introduces them in a

[34] I-II, qu. 94, art. 2.

body in the person of their leader, Aristotle, to the theologians of the day, and, in order to do so effectively, he intentionally and deliberately put himself on one side, and took his seat in the audience of theologians. St Thomas is clearly writing the *Summa Theologica,* or at least these opening Quaestiones, not for our benefit or to meet the kind of problems we might have in mind, but with his mind riveted to the problems set for him by the theologians of his own time, and by the circumstances created by the sudden invasion of Europe by the newly discovered writings of Aristotle. All his tactics of composition are designed to enable him to get inside the minds of contemporary theologians, and to a large extent to get the philosophy of Aristotle inside their minds, so that he might present the Holy Teaching as a science. In this famous article he has let the philosophers speak for themselves that they may have every chance of securing a good hearing in the schools of theology. St Thomas considers that proofs of reason for the existence of God are necessary and that, as the proofs of the philosophers are valid as far as they go, he may just as well allow them to claim before their theological audience that the absolute being which they prove to exist can be called God. It seems unquestionably clear from the context that the 'omnes' of the concluding sentence of each of the Five Ways means 'all we philosophers presenting our proofs and represented by our spokesman, Aristotle', and thus each Way terminates with the claim 'and this is the being we philosophers call God'.[35] There can be no gainsaying the truth of this statement, as there can the truth of the claim that any of the beings they prove to exist really is God, or that any of them is the Being all men, including all Christians, call God. St Thomas as a theologian allows their claim to stand for it is not untrue; it is correct as far as it goes, and it will provide a satisfactory basis for further discussion and reflection. But satisfied as he was with the reasonings of the philosophers, he did not mean his readers to understand that the entire proof is complete as the philosophers have left it. He has in fact followed them up to the point where they have shown that our universe is caused, that it has been produced as an effect by some being or beings unlike it in that this being (or these beings) is uncaused, and not limited. But here he stops; he lets the philosophers go no farther on their own. He omits, for example, all

[35]cf. pp. 61ff; 72ff.

that Aristotle had to say about the kind of being his Unmoved Mover is, for when the philosophers went on, guided by reason alone, to say what they considered God's essence to be, they proved to be unreliable in their way of reasoning. Because St Thomas does not permit them to go beyond this fixed point in expounding their own arguments for God's existence, each of the Five Ways seems, as we said (p. 72ff) to break off so abruptly. None the less, the philosophers genuinely raised the question 'Utrum Deus sit?' and they managed to go a good deal of the way towards answering it, and so article 3 goes into Quaestio 3.

When he has finished article 3, therefore, St Thomas has only gone as far as to show what reason has in fact successfully been able to establish working on its own, independently of faith. Article 3 represents what reason has been able to discover without going astray. But St Thomas does not continue the work of the philosophers for them in Quaestio 3. Instead, in this and the following Quaestiones he brings the theologians into the discussion; he himself enters the chair and he brings his own theological teaching to bear on the question of what God has revealed Himself to be. If Aristotle represents the philosophers, Aquinas himself is the spokesman of the theologians. Obviously he has a great deal more to add, for simply speaking much more is required before the theologians can possibly be satisfied that the existence of the one true God Who fills heaven and earth, Who is the infinite ocean of Being, and Who alone interests theologians has been established. So far we have only seen how far reason in fact has been able to progress on its own. In Quaestio 3 St Thomas begins to speak for the Christian theologians, and, using reason directed by faith, he considers how much further reason has to go till it reaches the kind of conclusion faith demands, namely, that 'He Who is' exists.[36] He thus adds a further stage to the total argument for the existence of God, which it seems ranges from Quaestiones 3–11 (all of which, remember, are on the same theme mentioned in the prologue—the divine essence), and in these Quaestiones he really speaks for himself and adds his own personal contribution to the total argument. St Thomas reaches the conclusion of the original query put at the beginning of article 3 'utrum Deus sit?' at the end of Quaestio 11, article 3 which establishes that there can only be

[36]cf. *Sed Contra* of art. 3, cf. also *Summa Theologica*: II–II, qu. 1, art. 8, ad.1; qu. 2, art. 3.

one Being who is necessarily and of Himself perfect, and, reverting
back to the *Maxime Ens* of the fourth Way, he concludes the whole
argument by saying: 'cum igitur id quod est primum, sit perfectissi-
mum et per se, non per accidens, oportet quod primum reducens
omnia in unum ordinem sit unum tantum. Et hoc est Deus'.[37] The fourth
and last article of the Quaestio clinches the matter by explaining that
the unity of God's Being is unsurpassable in perfection, for God is the
'maxime ens, inquantum est non aliquid esse determinatum per ali-
quam naturam cui adveniat, sed est ipsum esse subsistens, omnibus
modis indeterminatum', and 'est etiam maxime indivisum, inquantum
neque dividitur actu neque potentia secundum quemcumque modum
divisionis, cum sit omnibus modis simplex'.[38] The decisive words 'Et
hoc est Deus' are the words of a Christian theologian, and they contrast with the 'quod omnes dicunt Deum esse' of article 3 which are
those of various philosophers committed to nothing but reason.

\*     \*     \*

If the reader now works his way through the contents of Quaestiones 3–11 and traces the sequence of the argument as it develops, he
will see that a totally new conception of St Thomas's argument for
the existence of God is emerging in his mind, and once he has attained
this vantage point he can glance back at the enigmas we mentioned in
the previous chapter and see how their appearance has changed, and
how unenigmatic the Five Ways have now become.

For example, the grievance over the lack of originality of article 3,
which (as we have seen, p. 56ff) began to look less plausible on closer
examination of the sources of the Five Ways, is now seen to be quite
unfounded. What could be more original and more distinctive of
Thomas Aquinas than the whole sequence of thought traced out and
followed in detail from Quaestiones 1–11, with its overall conception
of theology as a science, its discussion of the existence of God on the

[37]['Since therefore that which is first is most perfect, and also *per se* and not
purely accidentally, the first, which accounts for all things being set within one
order, must itself be one. And this one is God].'
[38]['Absolutely supreme in being, inasmuch as his being is not determined by
any nature with which it is conjoined; he is subsistent being itself without any
kind of limitation whatsoever. And he is not merely undivided, but absolutely
indivisible by any kind of division whatsoever, for his being is altogether simple].'

basis of the relations holding between reason unaided by faith, and reason working under the guidance of faith, and the idea of making the argument for the existence of God identical with the theological study of God's essence? The whole originality of the plan running through Quaestiones 2–11 consists in the way St Thomas has brought the Aristotelian conception of being, formed from reflections on the nature of the universe, to its ultimate development in the third and fourth Ways, so that it could be integrated into Thomas's own metaphysics of being formed on the basis of the biblical revelation of God as 'Qui est', or 'He Who Is'. By bringing these two currents of thought together Aquinas has made one vast, total argument for the existence of God, the climax of which is reached when, in Quaestio 3, article 4, he develops his own metaphysics of being as denoting primarily the act or energy of *Esse,* and applies this to explain how God is the Maxime Ens.[39] It should be noted that in the *Sed Contra* of article 3 (of Quaestio 2) St Thomas mentions the famous text of Ex. iii.14, but in that article he never comes anywhere near to reaching the Being 'Who is'. Clearly the *Sed Contra* of article 3 looks beyond the end of the article on to article 4 of Quaestio 3. With article 1 of Quaestio 3 St Thomas takes up the argument where the philosophers had left off, and, expounding the words of St John that 'God is a spirit', he continues with arguments of reason to show that the kind of being the philosophers called God (the unmoved mover, etc.) must be immaterial. In article 2 he continues yet further to show by reason that their God cannot even be composed of matter and form, so that He cannot be regarded as of our material universe in any kind of way. But in article 3, and yet more in article 4, St Thomas develops the argument on his own, introducing his own metaphysical ideas, and quite plainly he is developing arguments from reason based on an idea of being enlarged and enriched beyond anything Aristotle conceived because framed to meet the requirements of the biblical teaching about God. In article 3 the *Sed Contra* is from John XIV 6, and in article 4 it is from St Hilary, but clearly echoes the *Sed Contra* of article 3, i.e. Exodus III, 14. Thus the argument for the existence of God is in the hands of the theologians, and of St Thomas himself, by the time we reach article 4, and he has taken over the discussion now to

[39]E. L. Mascall: *Existence and Analogy,* ch. 3, especially p. 52; also pp. 12ff.

expound the Christian theology of the divine essence while continuing the argument for God's existence. For St Thomas this coalescing is inevitable for in God essence and existence are one. We cannot prove that God is and omit considering what God has said He is. He explains that in God essence cannot be a principle of limitation at all: it just denotes the way in which God exists, and the perfections of Him Who is being without qualification of any kind. In the rest of the Quaestio he rounds off the discussion with the philosophers, and in Quaestio 4 he continues to show in what the perfection of the divine Being consists.

The difficulty over the brevity of the Thomist arguments for the existence of God are also fully met. Such a difficulty could only occur to one who reads the Five Ways wrenched out of their context, and who fails to see them as fitting in position within a vast line of reasoning, and fitting in just where we find them because they have been placed there for a strategical purpose of the first importance to St Thomas, that of dealing with difficulties raised by theologians with which he had to contend at the beginning. A study of the first eleven Quaestiones of the *Summa* will reveal to the reader how profoundly St Thomas considered both the numerous problems a theologian in his position had to envisage in denying the kind of distinction many theologians made between the way we know the *Esse Dei* and the *Essentia Dei* (cf. p. 57–59), and the strategy required in order to meet the theological difficulties the theologians were bound to raise against his use of reason in theology. If the line of argument he follows does not meet the kind of difficulties the modern philosopher has to consider and which we have mentioned in chapter 2, St Thomas need not be blamed, for there is no conceivable reason why anyone should expect him to anticipate or deal with them.

I have, I think, dealt with the other enigmas of the Five Ways in the earlier parts of this chapter; at least I trust that I have explained enough to show that, if the Five Ways are read as the first stages of a vast theological argument, most of the *prima facie* difficulties disappear.

To conclude this chapter it only remains to point out that St Thomas distinguishes three kinds of truth a theologian has to envisage when he is treating about God. (*a*) Truths revealed by God which reason can and did discover on its own without the help of revelation; (*b*) truths which reason could, in principle, have discovered on its own, but in fact did not do so, for we learned of them from the teaching of Christ and the Church; and (*c*) truths which reason could never possibly discover on its own even after they had been revealed to us, for they are in the strict sense of the term supernatural mysteries. Most theologians fail to distinguish revealed truths into these three kinds. Generally speaking they only mention the first and the third. These may be all that are required for many treatises on theology, but in questions about our knowledge of God they are not sufficient. It is clear that, at least implicitly, St Thomas made the threefold distinction in the way he planned his treatise on God in the *Summa,* but it is equally clear that he did not regard the distinctions between (*a*) and (*b*) as equivalent to hard and fast separations. In the *Summa Theologica* truths of the classes (*b*) and (*c*) overlap to a certain extent. Furthermore, St Thomas makes these distinctions, especially those between classes (*a*) and (*b*), not purely empirically, but on a scientific and strictly theological foundation. He included in class (*a*) those truths which reason actually discovered on its own without the aid of revelation, in a way that he judged was sufficiently securely reasoned to justify the theologian saying that they had attained the status of a genuine certainty. Those truths which before the coming of Christianity had not in fact been discovered by reason alone with sufficient exactitude of reasoning as to be considered genuinely certain, but which reason could in principle have demonstrated, or might in time have demonstrated even without guidance from faith, St Thomas puts under class (*b*). In the *Summa* we find truths of class (*a*) in our article 3, and those of class (*b*) in Quaestiones 3–26, though of course even in this section there are truths about God which reason can never demonstrate on its own even after they have been revealed, but which it can show to be perfectly intelligible. Thus, for example, our certitude that God loves all men and each man individually is plainly intelligible for one who believes in Jesus Christ and the story of the redemption, but certainty on such a truth seems beyond the reach of the non-believing philosopher. In fact, as the *Summa* is a *Summa Theologica* these Quaestiones 3–26 must of their nature consider all revealed truths about God which are accepted as certain by those who believe in the Christian revelation, even though some of them were vaguely known by philosophers by reason as well. Thus St Thomas puts the consideration of the pure spirituality of God in this class (b), no doubt because, though demonstrated by Aristotle and other philosophers, he still had qualms about the sufficiency of the arguments of the philosophers from the point of view of the strict and rigorous standards required for theological certainty. Revelation has, in any case, much to add to many of these sound ideas about God which certain philosophers had come to perceive in some way, and thus, having so much more to say about them than the philosophers, St Thomas placed in list (b) truths that may have been touched upon by the philosophers because he is writing about them as they have been revealed to us by God. The third kind of truth about God, which reason could never demonstrate at all, but only reflect upon in so far as they are intelligible, are considered not exclusively, but most especially in the treatise on the Trinity, in Quaestiones 27–43.

St Thomas has no fear that some theologians may retort that his Five Ways are of little value for the purpose of bringing home to the ordinary man the reality of God, for he grants fully that human reason alone is not going to be able to convince men of all that they need to know about God to accept the Christian revelation. The real necessity of revelation to give men an adequate understanding of God's Being and of His attributes, to give them a knowledge of God that will be so secure and certain that it need never fall away or become weakened by doubt in the way that all our own thinking about the ultimate mysteries of life and being may easily be, is something of which St Thomas never had any doubts. The ordinary man would in any case be incapable of embarking on the laborious intellectual task of establishing God's existence with complete finality.[40] All St Thomas is trying to show in the Five Ways is that reason is capable of attaining some minimum knowledge of God, that this knowledge is adequate enough as a foundation on which faith can build its fully developed teaching, and that faith must inevitably presuppose such a minimum knowledge of God as attained by reason, even as grace presupposes the existence of nature which it too perfects. St Thomas did not even consider the question which interests many philosophers and theologians

[40]cf. *Contra Gentes*, I, ch. 4; *Summa Theologica*, qu. 1, art. 1.

today, as to whether philosophers without the aid of faith can attain
a fuller knowledge of God than that minimum contained in the idea
of an uncaused cause, of a necessary being, or even the Maxime Ens.
All that he was concerned to show was that men can attain by reason
some knowledge of God that is perfectly sound, by arguing to His
existence as the cause of the world. He evidently considered that the
best way to establish this capacity of reason was to show that philosophers had in fact succeeded in attaining this knowledge, though paradoxically enough they had learned rather more of the world as an
effect than of the God Who is its cause. They might in fact have succeeded in attaining this knowledge of God more readily than they
themselves realized, and to show this St Thomas took two of his Five
Ways from Aristotle and, as we have shown (p. 61–63), made them what
Aristotle never made them—arguments for God's existence, by just
adding the conclusion 'quod omnes dicunt Deum esse'. From Quaestio
3 onwards St Thomas ceases to be interested in the philosophers, even
though some of the ideas of God he deals with in this Quaestio may
have been known to them. In Quaestio 3 he is concerned with God's
simplicity and with the biblical teaching about the simplicity of God's
Being, and he rises to the exalted heights (to which no philosopher had
before or has since come near), of thinking of God as *Ipsum esse subsistens*. The fourth Quaestio, on the perfection of God, definitely takes
us beyond anything that reason had been able to attain by its own
unaided powers. From now onwards St Thomas takes us deeper and
deeper into the theology of the unity of God's Being. No pagan
philosopher had ever conceived of the goodness, the infinity, the transcendence and immanence of God to creation, nor of the immutability
and eternity of God as these are presented to us by reasoned argument
in Quaestiones 5–10. No doubt St Thomas deliberately delayed treating of the Divine Unity in Quaestio 11 till he had treated of all these
other matters so as not to conclude his total argument about God's
existence till he has said all that a Christian theologian must say about
God's essence or being. There are many ways of expressing the same
idea describing the strategy guiding St Thomas's method of arranging
the different Quaestiones which enter into the latter part of his argument for the existence of God. We might say that St Thomas begins
with what is easiest (but not for that reason easy) to reason in the Five

Ways, and then in Quaestio 3 he moves on to stages which are more difficult but none the less not altogether inaccessible to non-believing philosophers, till in Quaestio 4 and onwards he leaves ground which is reachable by philosophers on their own to explore what reason can come to know under the positive guidance of faith. Christian revelation thus opens up a much fuller understanding of the nature of God than mere reason had attained before the time of Christ, and it also shows how much more has to be attempted and accomplished before we can be said to have proved the existence of God than those without the faith ever realize. It is far more difficult for the Christian to prove the existence of the God in Whom he believes in a way that is intellectually satisfying than for any non-Christian to demonstrate the existence of a necessary being or uncaused cause which he takes as God for lack of anything better.

Would it be better to say, then, that the Five Ways do not give St Thomas's proofs for the existence of God at all? No! because they do give the important commencement of his total proof, which he clearly considered to be valid as far as it goes, and which reaches a point at which it is possible for the Christian theologian to meet the non-Christian philosopher on common ground. St Thomas deliberately put the text of Exodus at the beginning of the Five Ways to show that he was using the philosophers to supply a stage in his own theological argument which he would have had to supply himself if philosophers like Aristotle had not been at hand to supply it for him. In so far as he agreed that the necessary being, uncaused cause, etc, are not incorrectly called God St Thomas at least adopted the Five Ways as his own.

Can we say that St Thomas distinguishes between a 'God of Reason' whom he considers in the Five Ways, and the 'God of Revelation' Whom he presents in the subsequent questions of the total argument? To this, in full agreement with Fr Victor White, I must say categorically, no! The *Summa* treats of one, and not of two kinds of God. Fr White shows that already in the first article of the *Summa*, replying to the second objection, 'It is of one and the same God that reason and revelation speak to us'. In the *Summa* reason and faith are both thinking about the same God: the necessary being of reason is the perfect and infinite Being of the faith, and as Fr White says:

It is a vitally important preliminary to understand his (Thomas's) identification of the 'God of Reason' and the 'God of Revelation'. It will enable him to maintain that reason can establish the reality of the self same God who reveals, though it cannot establish *that* he reveals or *what* he reveals. On this account only have the *viae* any place in a *theological* work.[41]

Finally, we know that St Thomas held that one of the functions of reason is to prepare for faith by establishing the truth of the *praeambula fidei,* and one of these truths which reason can establish is that of the existence of God. There is no need to maintain, however, that the proof for the existence of God which is anterior to faith and amongst the *praeambula fidei* must be the full and entire proof that the dogmatic theologian might require. The text of the *Quinque Viae* can, perhaps, be understood as giving in part the kind of proof that St Thomas had in mind as required for the *praeambula fidei,* but there is no evidence to show that he wrote article 3 as a preamble to faith:[42] 'Deum esse, et alia hujusmodi quae per rationem naturalem nota possunt esse de Deo, ut dicitur Rom. i.19, non sunt articuli fidei, sed praeambula ad articulos; sic enim fides praesupponit cognitionem naturalem, sicut gratia naturam, et ut perfectio perfectibile.[43] Thus for St Thomas the *Esse Dei* can be established by reason; but so far from giving the complete arguments, the Five Ways give arguments which St Thomas considered sufficient to establish God's existence, in the sense that the kind of being whose existence they establish can ultimately be shown to be the Infinite God. But we must always remember that whatever reason unaided by faith can establish about the existence of God, reason illuminated subsequently by faith will learn a great deal that will serve to complete the proofs of mere reason. If, as St Thomas says, grace perfects nature, and faith perfects reason, the knowledge of God we have by faith will perfect the arguments of reason we had for the existence of God before we received the faith. The 'God of Faith' is not a different God from the 'God of Reason', but the divine manifestation of the God reason strives to think as it can.

[41]V. White, O.P.: 'Prelude to the Five Ways', in *God the Unknown,* p. 40.
[42]cf. p. 51.
[43]I, qu. 2, art. 2, ad. 1.

# 7

## ST THOMAS AND SOME MODERN CRITICS OF THE ARGUMENTS FOR GOD'S EXISTENCE

We now leave the mediaeval schools of theology, and return with lightning rapidity to our own times to pay a visit to an imaginary group of philosophers who have assembled together to discuss some problems in the philosophy of religion. On this occasion the group has met to welcome two special guests, who have returned to life on earth in response to an invitation to preside over this special meeting arranged to discuss the merits of the arguments for the existence of God. One of these guests is Kant who at the moment is engaged in earnest conversation with a number of the philosophers assembled in the hall, and who is to act as their spokesman for this occasion. His influence on those gathered in the hall is unquestionably deep for in questions about the philosophy of religion there is a widespread sympathy with his ideas, not so much because they subscribe in any large numbers to the principles of his philosophy, but because he inspires, and gives confidence to the general attitude of agnosticism which prevails amongst the members of the group. They are almost unanimous in accepting his refutation of the traditional arguments for God's existence, as well as his contention that we are incapable of proving by reason that God exists. We know, from what we have seen in chapter 2, the basic difficulties the philosophers in the group have against the arguments that they are now discussing with Kant. Kant criticized the very structure of what he called the cosmological argument for the existence of God by claiming to have shown that the argument comprises two entirely different stages, embodying two unrelated and unrelatable lines of reasoning artificially patched together to give the appearance of forming one argument. He considered that he had, and many philosophers still credit him with having, exposed once and for all the spurious unity of the structure of the traditional arguments; he claimed that he had done this so decisively as to have established at the same time that the speculative reason is incapable of proving that God exists, or indeed of coming to a knowledge of God in any manner. The assembly as a whole grants that he made good his claim, no matter how much its individual members may differ from him in their views about the basic principles of his philosophy. There is widespread agreement with his rejection of the pivotal idea of the traditional arguments, that God is the cause of the world; and his thesis that the human mind is limited to knowing phenomena, so that it is constitutionally incapable of thinking anything which is not phenomenally presentable to it, still glows in the minds of most contemporary English philosophers, especially of those in our group. The prevalent view is, then, that Kant's arguments for rejecting the traditional arguments have been definitely established and confirmed, for philosophy since his time has other and even more satisfactory reasons to support the position he established. In brief, the traditional arguments for the existence of God are no longer intellectually respectable.

The other guest speaker who is shortly to be received by the assembly of philosophers is, of course, St Thomas Aquinas himself. He, too, has returned to earth to accept the invitation of the group to defend his arguments for God's existence. At the moment, while Kant is conferring earnestly with the philosophers in the assembly hall, St Thomas is sitting quietly in the near-by visitor's room gathering his ideas together, and feeling no doubt as much a stranger now that he is back on earth amongst the philosophers as Aristotle had felt when he had been summoned by St Thomas in the middle of the thirteenth century to confront a body of theologians before whom he had to plead the cause of reason. He is busy trying to recollect the way he had conceived the structure of the argument for the existence of God in the far off days when he was so heavily worked in the schools of theology. He recalls how the argument he presented in his *Summa Theologica* developed from a first stage based on processes of reasoning he took from Aristotle, which he had placed in the famous article 3 of Quaestio 2, to reach its full completion in the course of a long dialogue that passed between faith and reason from which he had formed the second stage of the argument, and which he had put in Quaestiones

3–11. The formation of the total argument from these two stages had been inspired by his conception of Holy Teaching, or theology, as a science dealing with the great truths God had revealed to us about His own being or essence. In those days the argument had been framed for the purposes of constructing a system of theology; he, in his capacity as a theologian, had interviewed important philosophers from the ancient and contemporary non-Christian worlds, notably Aristotle, in order to give them an opportunity of convincing his fellow theologians that reason can attain some knowledge of God, and that, as it is theologically respectable, reason can be profitably employed by the theologian in his work of thinking, and thence presenting scientifically, the truths of faith. St Thomas realizes, however, that the situation he has now to face is of a very different kind, and that it calls for a complete change of outlook on his part. For one thing, it is he who is to be interviewed, and it is the philosophers who are going to conduct the interview; this time it is he who has to give an account both of the faith which he, like all Catholics, insists is a gift of genuine knowledge from God, and also of theology which he holds is a science showing us how to think about God and the great truths He has revealed to us about Himself. This time, furthermore, he has to account for the knowledge he professes we have of God before an assembly which will judge him and all that he says by its own standards of reason. The mediaeval scene is thus reversed so completely as to be turned all but inside out, and for the moment St Thomas is trying hard to acclimatize himself to the transformation that this will demand in the way he presents his ideas to his new audience.

St Thomas realizes that this reversal of the scene involves far more than a mere transposing of the roles of host and guest, in that it is now he, the theologian, who for a change is being interviewed, and the philosophers who are conducting the interview in their own halls and on their own terms. The most disturbing factor involved in the change-over, as far as he is concerned, arises from the fact that he has now to confront an assembly of philosophers of a very different intellectual character from those whom he had invited for interview when he was preparing his *Summa Theologica*. The philosophers who had influenced the thinkers of the thirteenth century, especially those whom he had invited from the ancient world, may have been men who knew noth-

ing of Christian theology, but at least they were not unfavourably disposed towards it by their philosophies; they had not adopted such a
position in philosophy that they would have been set against the faith
from the start as intellectually unacceptable. On the contrary he had
always considered, though the theologians of his day had not always
agreed, that, so far as their philosophy enables us to judge them, many
of the great philosophers of antiquity would have had no reason to
be anything but intellectually well disposed towards Christian theology,
and that men who studied and thought like Aristotle in particular
could be treated as thinkers whose minds would be more or less open
to receive knowledge from God (should He grant them such a gift),
for their thinking would lead them to consider seriously the idea of an
uncaused being beyond our universe who is in some way the ground
of the universe. In those days it was perfectly feasible for him to argue,
even if many theologians disagreed with him, that philosophers could
be welcomed by theologians as constructive thinkers, for Aristotle,
who was recognized at the time as their master, was at least thinking
on lines that would have suggested that a philosopher might well consider not merely what reason on its own could come to know of God,
but what Christian theologians held God had revealed to us that we
might know Him more perfectly than mere reason can know Him. The
leading philosophers of the ancient world were prepared to receive
knowledge coming from a non-philosophical source, and especially
from on High (if and when they had reason to think it had really
come), so that the philosophies they bequeathed to mankind were
capable of being developed and enriched even as philosophies by
Christian theologians in ways quite unimaginable to themselves now
that this knowledge from God really has come. I had always insisted,
he continues thinking to himself, that God's gifts of grace and of faith
logically presuppose the natural man who lives and thinks as best he can
on his own and who receives the gifts that God graciously gives him.
The idea that faith is received by and perfects reason, even as grace is
received by and perfects human nature, did not present formidable
difficulties in the thirteenth century from the side of reason. I had
argued that Aristotle who stood for and represented reason, and a
reason which could be perfected by faith, would not have found any
difficulty in the idea, even if some theologians could not see in what

way faith was to be received by reason without more or less corrupting faith. But the philosophers with whom I am now to be confronted are of a very different intellectual character. Their philosophies are open enough to outside influences so long as these come from the empirical sciences. After all, he reflects, since I left the world these sciences have developed to such an extent that they have considerably reduced the former empire of the philosophers. There are some philosophers who go as far as to consider that the sciences have suppressed their empire altogether, and set up in its place the new empire of the sciences. These philosophers are content with a modest but quite respectable place in this empire of knowledge; though they have had to renounce any claim to be able to give us a knowledge of existent realities, they fulfil an important role by dealing with many difficult problems connected with the logic of science. This is, admittedly, an extremist position. None the less philosophers who nowadays do claim a kingdom of their own which maintains friendly relations with all the domains of the sciences, are not open to any influence claiming to come from on High in the form of a divine teaching or imparting of knowledge. However beneficent such an influence might be or might claim to be, it is not envisaged as an influence having anything to contribute to the mind, or to the vast store of knowledge which men have succeeded in acquiring for themselves during the past few hundred years, and still less as an influence which, once felt by the mind, has any right to take first place within all minds and establish itself as a knowledge above, because of a higher order than, the knowledge of modern science. Kant had ushered in the new unmetaphysical age which now thrives exclusively on the wealth of the empirical knowledge man has acquired for himself. His critical philosophy had been formed under the positive influence of non-philosophical ideas provided by the most reliable of human sources known to him, the idea of science he found in the Newtonian physics, and as he had conceived the human mind to be supreme in knowledge and of its nature closed to any order of things beyond the phenomenal, Kant's philosophy could not be anything but closed, even absolutely unopenable, to a divine revelation claiming to give us a knowledge of God. Man's mind, thus firmly closed by Kant to thought about God, has remained as firmly closed for many philosophers ever since. After Kant's death philosophy became dominated more and more by science, to such an extent that many of the classical philosophical terms, particularly that of cause and effect with which I am concerned in the argument for the existence of God, have lost their original philosophical meaning and acquired for philosophers the kind of meanings they have for contemporary scientists.[1] Many of the difficulties I will be confronted with shortly have their origin in this domination of modern philosophy by the scientific meaning of terms.

Thus St Thomas, almost as soon as he is back on earth, realizes that in a moment he is to face an audience which rejects in principle his whole conception of the elevation of reason to the supernatural order of faith considered as a supernatural knowledge, the whole idea of the perfectibility of reason by revelation and the Catholic idea of dogma and a dogmatic theology. He is to be confronted, in other words, by philosophers with various conceptions of human reason which for the moment he cannot do otherwise than classify *en masse* as 'unaristotelian', and which in the measure that they resemble Kant's idea of human reason are a real danger to faith as the Church has always presented it to men. He has to admit that, perhaps to his surprise, he is now to be confronted with the kind of thing his brother theologians of old had warned him reason really is, or at least must inevitably become when it appears in its true colours. Perhaps they are smiling at him from their places in heaven now that he is at last, and out of due time, confronted with the monster he professed to be a myth during his life on earth! The task of converting theologians to reason as he had seen it did not prove in the event too difficult. But now he has either to confront contemporary philosophers with a conception of reason which will strike them as being some kind of mediaeval super-reason, or convince them

[1]Thus Hume considered that the relation of cause and effect only holds between events which are constantly linked in the same temporal sequence, the first being called the 'cause' the second the 'effect'. Similarly Kant conceived causality as a category ordering phenomena, and as functioning solely within the Newtonian universe. He argued that because causality as a category for ordering phenomena cannot be used 'transcendentally', the theologian uses causality illegitimately in regarding God as the cause of the world. Many contemporary philosophers hold that causality involves determination in a sequence of events, and therefore whenever we have causal sequence of events, we must be able to predict effects. For this reason they object that Heisenberg's principle has disproved the validity of the principle of causality (cf. pp. 159-71).

that human reason really is more metaphysical than the modern critical and scientific philosophies admit. This may well turn out to be a task of Herculean magnitude in comparison with that of converting mediaeval theologians to reason. If now he can do something to defend what he considers to be the lawful claims of reason, it may be he will be able to make some philosophers see what he means by the truths of faith, and how reason is able to know God by reasoning to His existence.

However, these ruminations must stop for the door of the visitor's room is opening, and Kant is entering to conduct him to his place on the rostrum from which he is to speak to the assembly. But one last thought flashes across his mind as he and Kant exchange salutations. It may well be that few of the philosophers present in the hall have studied, or even glanced at the *ipsissima verba* of his article 3 and chapter 13 ! They were written so long ago before what is now called 'modern philosophy' was born. Again the haunting thought returns: philosophy and science (especially astronomy and physics) have changed beyond recognition since the innocent days of Aristotle and Ptolemy ! It may be just as well as if they have not tried to read what I wrote about demonstrating the existence of God in these two extracts of my works which I am told are so much admired in the contemporary schools of scholastic philosophy. But I had better get comfortably settled in this huge chair, and listen attentively to Kant, for having generously eulogized my work (which I know *he* never read !) by way of introducing me to my audience, he has now started to present me with every item that you, gentle reader, studied some time ago when you read chapter 2.

*          *          *

Within a few moments Kant settled down to serious business and recapitulated for St Thomas's benefit his demonstration of the impossibility of a cosmological argument for the existence of God, and goes over other arguments which contemporary philosophers asked him to raise on their behalf. St Thomas realized at once that the assembly is not likely to make much of the reasonings of the ancient philosophers as he embodied them in the Five Ways, for these ways take too much for granted that is open to question for most present-day philosophers. Instead of giving once again the old arguments of the

*Summa Theologica,* he sees that he will have to take another line. He will have to outline the strategy directing the whole of the operation of thinking about God which he followed in the *Summa.* He must explain certain fundamental points he took for granted as evident in the Middle Ages, and amongst these the way he conceived the two stages of the whole operation of reasoning about God's existence and being, fitting together to form one vast argument of reason working now on its own, and now under the guidance of faith. When he has traced the basic principles of the structure of the argument, the course of the discussion will no doubt reveal certain changes of emphasis which he will have to make now that he is discussing his ideas with philosophers and concerned especially with meeting their difficulties. By following this line of thinking he may have a better chance of reaching an agreement with some philosophers on certain common principles essential to the very nature of theistic argument before even attempting to formulate any particular argument, for so long as he and the philosophers disagree on the very principles proper to the nature and structure of theistic argument, discussion of particular arguments cannot get anyone anywhere. When he had defended reason against the Augustinian theologians of old his problem had been to show that God and the human mind are not to be so closely related as to justify the view that all men just know the *Esse Dei* intuitively. Now that he has to defend reason against Kant's critical philosophy and those influenced by his critical estimate of reason (not to mention modern positivist theories of reason such as we have them, for example, in philosophies expounding the verification principle), he has to show that the human mind and God are not to be regarded as so far apart from each other that one cannot have anything to do with the other, that (in other words) we cannot have any knowledge of God and God cannot reveal Himself truthfully to our minds. Again he sees that his problem now is the opposite to that he had had to face during his lifetime, but he has still to maintain the same kind of balance between faith and reason as of old. Of old he had had to explain what the Church means by faith in order to make room for reason in theology, but now he has to explain what the philosopher must understand by reason if he is to see what divine revelation of truth is and what the science of theology is. The crux of the problem appears the same as it did a moment ago, that for those to whom he is about to speak reason will mean almost exclusively modern scientific reason whereas for him it may mean this, but it must mean much more. Thus, instead of spending all his time giving arguments to show that God exists, he must give his time to explaining the overall strategy which must be followed in arguing successfully for the existence of God. This will be the only effective way of showing that Kant's idea of the structure of the cosmological argument is at fault, and of preparing the way to meet the other difficulties of which Kant is speaking.

Kant finished his introductory address, and St Thomas rose to speak. He began with an introductory move from which he could not very well fail to emerge successfully and thereby secure for himself a foothold from which to attack other misunderstandings which he had to clear away in order to make any headway at all. He said straight away that the kind of arguments Kant had just criticized and which he had presented as giving the scheme of the traditional cosmological arguments for the existence of God, bear only a superficial likeness to the arguments that he had used in the Middle Ages. Kant had criticized the kind of arguments that Leibniz and Wolff had popularized amongst philosophers, and St Thomas agreed that in the second stage their arguments do reason from necessary to infinite being on the imagined strength of a positive idea of necessary being we are supposed to have, enabling us to understand its intrinsic possibility and the attributes that its nature involves. Baumgarten made this argument famous in his textbooks of philosophy which were well known during the eighteenth century, and by the end of that century they had become accepted in rationalist circles on the Continent as the 'classical' or 'traditional' arguments for the existence of God. It was from Baumgarten in particular, he said, not from me nor any of my confrères, that Kant derived his knowledge of the arguments which he examined in his *Critique of Pure Reason*.[2] It may well be only too true that the rationalist philosophers of the *Aufklärung* did run into one argument lines of reasoning based on what they conceived to be our experience of the universe with other lines of reasoning stemming from a purely *a priori* idea of necessary or perfect being. I have no quarrel with Kant

[2]cf. A. D. Lindsay: *Kant*, pp. 17–23; F. C. Copleston, S.J., *A History of Philosophy*, vol. VI, pp. 192, 294ff.

for rejecting these arguments, but only for his assuming that these arguments are typical of all arguments for God's existence. Kant made the mistake of thinking that these arguments must be the 'traditional' arguments because they had gained notoriety in the eighteenth century, but they can only be said to be traditional within a rationalist system of philosophy, and I reject such a philosophy as whole heartedly as he rejects its arguments for the existence of God.

By establishing this point of agreement at the very start St Thomas gave the discussion a turn unexpected by the vast majority of those whom he was addressing. By professing to regard Kant's onslaught on theistic argument as destructive of nothing more than the arguments in vogue amongst a minority of theistic philosophers of modern times who happened to have been well known to Kant, and by declaring that he himself was content to see them demolished, St Thomas showed that he intended to defend a position many of his critics had not fully envisaged. St Thomas continued without delay to drive home his first point by coming to his first major theme and explaining that he, in common with other mediaeval theologians, never professed to have an idea *of* God in the proper sense of the expression 'having an idea of', which for example Descartes employed when he spoke of the idea of the perfect being which presented itself to his mind.[3] In the proper sense of the term, 'having an idea of', I have, he said, no idea of God, nor of necessary being, nor of perfect, nor of infinite being. In fact I am prepared to grant that the use of the expression 'my idea of God, or of necessary being' might be taken as a good example of what Professor Ryle calls 'a systematically misleading expression'.[4] The ideas that we have *of* things when we say, in the proper sense of the term, that we have ideas of this and that, are derived *from* those things, and, as a means of knowing, they are more or less adequate to the things they enable us to know and which they positively express to our minds. Hence in the proper sense of the term we only have ideas of objects known from experience. I have, for example, an idea of human nature and an idea of gravitation because I have experience of men and of certain physical forces from which or through which I have derived

[3]Descartes: *Discours de la Méthode*, Part IV; also *Meditations*, V.
[4]G. Ryle: in the First Series of *Logic and Language*, pp. 11–36 (edited by A. G. N. Flew).

my ideas of these realities. If anyone asks me to show from where I obtained my ideas of realities like these, I can show him easily enough. Now we can also form ideas of objects which we have been told exist, or have existed, or may one day exist of which we have had no experience whatever, so we have not obtained these ideas from the objects of which they are the ideas. We fashion these ideas for ourselves from *other* objects connected in some way with these unexperienced objects of which we later try to think and so form such ideas of them as we can. For example, I can form an idea of dying, of being lost in space, or of an angel; I will no doubt say that I have an idea of myself dying, or of myself being lost in space, but these ideas are *of* their respective objects and give me knowledge of these objects in a very different way to that in which my idea of human nature is an idea *of* human nature and in which it gives me knowledge of human nature. These ideas are not derived from, nor are they positive ideas of the objects of which we say they are the ideas; I have never died nor been lost in space. They are rather ideas constructed by each person for himself as he takes and manipulates various ideas derived from experience of *other things* and adjusts them as best he can to the conditions characteristic of the object he is trying to envisage without knowing it exactly as it is. Though he can, no doubt, make some of the adjustments he needs to make in the ideas which he has already acquired (and has still to work on to fit them to serve as a kind of idea for the object about which he is trying to think), he realizes that he can never hope to make all the adjustments that are required to attain the positive understanding he might wish to have of whatever it is that interests him. For example my ideas of myself dying, or of myself being lost in space, or of myself in other contingencies beyond my experience, must be predominantly negative in that I form them from positive ideas I already have of other happenings experienced in my life (as I do, for example, when I think of myself dying as though it was in some way something like myself falling asleep from physical exhaustion); I manipulate these ideas by introducing various negations in order to make them fit as best I can what my reason tells me these other conditions must be like. Thus I think of myself dying by taking the ideas I have already of myself sleeping and then manipulating these ideas as I judge, for example, that my dying, though in some ways like my falling asleep, will be without certain characteristics found in merely falling asleep. My dying may be like falling asleep, but it is *not* just falling asleep. No doubt there is much lacking to the idea I form in this way of myself dying, but I can none the less attain *some* understanding of this unexperienced ultimate event of my life from the ideas I construct not from immediate experience, but from my judgements on analogous ideas; and such limited understanding as I can attain in this way, being satisfactory as far as it goes, is well worth holding on to for lack of anything better. It would be wrong to reject the ideas I have formed in my efforts to think of myself dying (for example) as utterly false because they are not adequate, or precise, or because they are incapable of giving me the positive insight I would like to have; it would be equally foolish to pretend that we ought to be able to understand as much about the realities of which we say we have ideas (merely because we have constructed something to serve in the place of a genuine idea), as we can from positive ideas we have derived from our actual experience of the objects they enable us to understand clearly. Obviously in the literal sense of the term 'idea of', I have no positive idea of myself dying, but I have a way of thinking about it by analogy, yielding an idea that is predominantly negative because it consists largely of negations correcting *something* in every statement I positively make without negating the entire statement.

Now, St Thomas continued, I have *no* idea of God which I have derived from an experience of Him; what I call my idea of God, or *of* necessary being, or of infinite being, is really only an idea I have constructed for myself as best I can in the course of time, while thinking about the beings I know from experience and manipulating some of the ideas I have attained from them to think as best I can of the Transcendent Being whom I realize must exist, but of Whom I cannot have an idea in the proper sense of the term. My so-called idea of God may be fantastically distorted as a result of my faulty thinking. The one decisive point Kant made against Leibniz and Baumgarten, and, going farther back to the source of the trouble, against Descartes, when he criticized the second stage of the argument he took as traditional, was that we have no positive idea giving us an insight into the nature of necessary or perfect being. Leibniz seems to have thought that our idea of necessary being is an idea in the proper sense of the term showing us positively and adequately what necessary being is. In so far as Kant holds that our ideas in the proper sense of the term are ideas of material things which we have derived from our experience of them, I agree with all that he said in criticizing the second stage of the rationalist form of argument for the existence of God. My idea of God is not an idea of Him in the sense that my idea of man can be regarded as an idea of individual men. I disagree with Kant, however, when he added that we cannot possibly think of a non-material reality because we only have experience of phenomena, and equally that we cannot form the kind of ideas which scholastic philosophers call transcendental as distinct from generic or specific ideas. What I call my idea of God expresses not what I have experienced of God, but what I have come to think about Him while thinking in terms of the transcendental ideas I have derived not from God but from the world of experience (which I maintain is an effect produced by God), even as my idea of being lost in space expresses what I have come to think this kind of calamity would be in terms of what I know about being lost, for example, in the wide open spaces of the Sahara. This is the only means I have of thinking of what being lost in space would be like. Thus my idea of God is not an idea of Him in the same sense that my idea of man is an idea I may use to think of you or other men. We can never establish that God exists if by this we mean that we can be led to form an adequate idea of what God is at some stage of the argument which will inevitably compel our minds to assent to His eternal existence. The kind of proof I advocate is 'not a proof in the rationalist metaphysician's sense'.[5] In my view establishing the existence of God can only mean that we have to show that the proposition 'God Is' is a true proposition: it does not mean demonstrating by making evident the real necessity inherent in God's own Being. To set about showing that this proposition is true I do not need to have an adequate idea of God's Being at all: all I need to know is how the term God is to be understood, and especially how it is that all men, Christians and non-Christians, think of God in terms of ideas they have derived from this world and as somehow or the other the cause or creator of the world.[6] This is sufficient to begin, even

[5] cf. Alasdair MacIntyre: *Difficulties in Christian Belief*, p. 81, ch. 8 entitled, 'Proof and Trust', is especially interesting on this point.
[6] *Summa Theologica*, I, qu. 3, art. 4, ad. 2.

if more is required to complete the discussion. This is what in my *Summa Theologica* I called a nominal definition of God.[7] I hold, then, that our ideas of necessary and infinite being are likewise derived from what we learn of things familiar to us from experience, and thence constructed by ourselves for the purpose of thinking about God Who is not like the things we know because He is more perfect than they are. As we do not experience Being which is necessary nor Being which is infinite, our ideas of God as necessary or infinite Being cannot be purely positive ideas for we do not know what necessity and infinity really are in the Being of God. None the less I can attain *some* knowledge of what it means to think and talk about necessary and infinite Being, and this is satisfactory as far as it goes and worth holding on to for lack of anything better. In fact, I will try to show how the second stage of the argument gives us something better. But reflection shows that it would be erroneous either to reject these ideas as utterly empty because they are not as fruitful as we would wish them to be, or at the other extreme to regard them as positively intelligible in the rationalist manner.

I hope that I have now shown to everyone's satisfaction that I would never have argued from the idea of necessary to that of infinite being, as Kant considered all theists must do, in virtue of what we understand positively of the intrinsic nature of necessary being, in the kind of way that the ontological argument reasons from what we are supposed positively to understand perfect Being must be. All I am prepared to claim is that reason can know something *of* what is to be understood by the words 'God', 'necessary being', and 'infinite being', by thinking of certain perfections, which scholastics call 'open' or 'transcendental',[8] and which we discover in every contingent, finite or limited being we know from the world of experience, being found in a Being without any of the contingentness, finiteness or limitation we find with these perfections in the world of experience. Thus for me our ideas of necessary and infinite being are predominantly negative—as I wrote so often, I understand what they do not mean more clearly than

[7] cf. I, qu. 2, art. 2, ad. 2.
[8] cf. D. J. B. Hawkins: *Being and Becoming*, ch. III. cf. L. de Raeymaeker: 'Le Caractère Spécial de la Preuve de Dieu', from *Studi Filosofici interno all' Esistenza, al Mondo, al Transcendente*, pp. 243–56.

what they do mean. We have some positive understanding of what such transcendental perfections as unity, existing, goodness, truth etc, mean, though we have no positive idea of what they would be in the Being of God Which is totally different from any that we know from experience. We must then come to think of God 'ex effectibus ejus' in order to attain a knowledge of the perfections in terms of which alone we can think about God at all. As we never experience the way in which these perfections are in God, and as we have to justify our conviction that they are indeed to be found in unsurpassable splendour in God, we can never get beyond showing that the being we think God to be, and state that He is, does exist without our being able to understand how these perfections are His.

In brief, then, I reject the theory that we have any intuitive perception of God's Being of any kind, even in the mitigated sense that we perceive Him indirectly as the background on which we somehow realize the contingency of the universe,[9] or in the rationalist sense that we have a clear, distinct, adequate or positive idea of God as necessary being, or in any other aspect of His Being. I hold that we think of God in the judgements we make about the transcendental perfections we find in the universe, and in the judgements by which we say both that God is, that He is one, perfect and infinite etc, and that He is not, that He is not one, nor any other perfection in the manner of the objects we know. God is, but His existence is uncaused; He is one, but He is absolutely indivisible in His Being; He is perfect, but without having to acquire, or being able to lose the perfection of His Being; He is infinite, not in the sense that material things can be said to be infinite, in that they are indeterminately vast, but in the sense that He is the plenitude of all being. Thus we have to think negatively, or affirm negatively of Him, whatever we think God positively is, affirming a perfection of Him and in the same breath denying that God is that perfection as the things we know. We thus form our ideas of God from the complex judgements we make in reasoning to His existence, and not from any knowledge we may have of being (necessary) itself in real ideas of God. I hold that God gave being to the things of the world, but the only knowledge we can have of Him is that which we eke out of the things of the world and from the ideas we can derive from these things. We

[9] cf. E. L. Mascall: *Existence and Analogy*, pp. 76–79.

cannot have, and at no point in the argument for the existence of God do we find ourselves with, a positive idea of God Himself.

I therefore deny that I ever conceived the second stage of the argument as deducing God's infinity *a priori* from an idea of necessary being, and I deny that Kant's analysis of the cosmological argument has any relevance to the arguments I sponsored in my *Contra Gentes* or *Summa Theologica*.

\* \* \*

St Thomas paused for a few moments to give himself a chance to decide how he would develop his next point, and his audience time to reflect on what he had said so far. Then he resumed his talk, by saying that, having first rejected Kant's analysis of the second stage of what he conceived to be the nature of the argument for the existence of God, he would now tackle Kant's thesis that the cosmological argument of its very nature must have two stages, artificially patched together, the first or cosmological stage arguing from contingent to necessary being, and the second or metaphysical stage from necessary to infinite Being.

To start with, he said, I agree with Kant that all arguments for the existence of God must comply with certain principles of structure, no matter what particular forms each one may take. But I reject the analysis of the main principles of the structure of their two stages proposed by Kant, and his analysis of the way the two stages are linked together to form one complete argument. I will, therefore, outline the structure of the argument as I conceived it when I wrote my *Summa Theologica,* and for the sake of clarity I will deal with the two stages which I presented as distinctive of the arguments under two headings A and B. I am not, please let me add, trying to justify any particular arguments in this conference, nor what I wrote about each stage in my *Summa;* I am only trying to explain what in principle has to be done by anyone arguing for the existence of God, to see if we can come to some agreement about the structure of the arguments we must try to construct. After all we ought to be clear about what we are trying to do, before we start doing anything.

A. *The First Stage of the Argument:* It would have been better from my point of view if I had said that actually I conceive the total argument, if it is fully laid out, as comprising three stages, but for the purposes of this discussion with Kant I can run the first two together and treat them as subdivisions of the first stage A, which corresponds roughly with what Kant called the cosmological stage of the argument. I will subdivide stage A then into the two subdivisions (i) and (ii).

(i) I hold that, first of all, it is necessary to establish that the universe is an effect, that is to say, that in certain ways its whole reality depends on some other being (or possibly beings), as any thing we know of (no matter what it is, one particular thing or a whole system of things united together as parts to form one complete whole or system) depends on something quite distinct from itself for being produced and sometimes for being kept in being. Quite obviously I hold that the entire argument for the existence of God, from the very beginning of the first stage is a metaphysical argument, and though it may be useful to speak of the arguments as cosmological inasmuch as they are based on the universe, I deny that the first major stage is cosmological in the sense that it is some kind of argument about the physical nature of the cosmos, and not a metaphysical argument about the being of the cosmos. Thus when I begin to reason about the things of the universe, I am not considering them as a modern scientist would consider them, and when I say that I am arguing from the cosmos to show that there is a necessary being I am not arguing to the existence of anything that a physicist, or any scientist could conceive scientifically. I am arguing to the existence of a Being which can only be thought of with the aid of a sound metaphysics. I deprecate Kant's way of referring to the first stage as cosmological and the second as metaphysical: the entire argument is metaphysical in character, and it is specially important to realize that 'necessary being' is not a cosmological idea.

We must establish that the universe is an effect, then, by metaphysical arguments. We do this by showing that a universe like ours, which consists solely and entirely of changing things, and in which changes of countless kinds are found to be (not necessarily always but certainly generally speaking, in a vast number of cases, or *ut in pluribus*) intelligible because expressible in intelligible ways (such as they are expressed in the laws and theories of the sciences), a universe in which change is everywhere present, and in which the change processes are found to be not necessarily perfectly nor easily intelligible, but still intelligible, is quite certainly an effect of some being other than itself on which it depends for being the changing and intelligible universe it is. The next step is to show that a universe of this kind demands an explanation, not in the scientific sense of the term 'explanation', but in the sense that being an effect, and therefore dependent, it leads the mind to think beyond it to some other reality in terms of which it can be understood as an effect. The intelligible and vast organization of its numerous change processes is certainly no more self-explanatory, least of all in terms of some *Deus ex machina* such as an irrational evolutionary theory explaining all law and order in terms of mere 'survival value', than is a prolonged correspondence existing on paper apart from the authors.[10]

Again, a universe which consists solely and entirely of things which are limited in their being, and of things which, so far as they themselves are concerned, might or might not exist, and which are certainly not the causes of their own existence, nor of the manner of their existence, nor of the time of their existence, must also be an effect of some being (or beings) other than itself, for it is of its very nature dependent, or suspended, in existence. It cannot possibly be said to depend on the things of which it is composed for it cannot be suspended on itself. Such a universe is as dependent, in its entire being, or as much an effect as the suspension of an object in mid-air is an effect of certain forces acting upon it against the forces of gravity and so keeping it suspended in mid-air. Dependence in being means literally being suspended from and therefore dependent on another as an effect on a cause.

I can summarize these different lines of thought concisely by saying that in every aspect of its being the universe is contingent. Thus, as I understand the term, 'contingent' means not merely that a thing or the universe just happens to be in some odd way, though as far as it is concerned it might just as well not be; but rather both that it exists without being in any way able to account for its existence, and that in its being, in what I know of its overall structure, it is changeable and

---

[10]I say *irrational* evolutionary theory, as a rational evolutionary theory is perfectly compatible with theism. If God orders change processes, why not also those change processes which result in evolution?

intelligible;[11] but though it is intelligible, we cannot possibly or reasonably hold that its intelligibility as we find it in experience just belongs to it for no reason whatever. In a similar way we cannot say that because we understand the meaning of some lengthy correspondence on reading it carefully, therefore it is intelligible in itself without worrying ourselves about its authors. A universe comprising nothing but limited and changing things, the existence of which is not self-necessitated, and which is intelligible in its structure, is an effect which points beyond itself to a cause responsible for its entire being. Those of you who have studied my Five Ways will recognize that in what I have just said I have mentioned the outstanding characteristics of our universe which I used as the basis of the arguments I gave to show that God exists, but not everyone seems to realize that in the Five Ways I was arguing first of all that these characteristics establish that the universe is an effect. My first objective in those Five Ways was to show in five different but complementary ways how the universe is to be recognized as an effect, and having done this, to show that we can come by reason to some knowledge about the character of its cause.[12] The full force of the argument of the Five Ways can only be appreciated if we take them, not as five different and independent arguments, but as five complementary expressions of one and the same way of thinking about the universe, and if, furthermore, we take the term 'contingent' to denote the composite idea of the universe as an effect obtained by taking the Five Ways together, like five different ways of viewing one scenery. The term 'contingent' then means not just that the universe happens to be whereas it might just as well not be (which was the meaning Leibniz gave it, and which may be read into my third Way if it is separated from all the others), but that for some reason the universe consists solely of changing things, that for some reason it is intelligible in its change processes, that in its structure it comprises nothing but things which are limited in their being, this limitation being the condition necessary for the existence of things subject to change, and that the universe exists, though no reason for its existence

[11]As I have said, the more we come to know the universe, the more we are in fact able to understand it, and the more astonishing we find its intelligible make-up to be.

[12]cf. E. L. Mascall: *Existence and Analogy*, pp. 71, 79–79.

is to be found within the universe itself: none the less, as the being of the universe is intelligible, its existence must be as well, for existing is the most vital factor in the being of things.[13] Leibniz diluted the idea of contingency I intended to convey in my Five Ways, and so shortened and weakened the argument.

Some of you may object that, in what I have just said, I did not follow the sequence of thought that is implicit in the order in which I arranged my Five Ways, and that I have omitted to say anything about the argument from design. But I would like to say that I do not see anything sacrosanct about the order in which I arranged my Five Ways, and that for the time being I do not wish to discuss the merits of the arguments from design. In any case I am uneasy about the wisdom of putting the argument showing that there is law and order in the universe (whether this is to be understood teleologically or not) in the fifth and last place; I think it ought to be closely linked with the argument from change, for these two lines of reasoning are very closely inter-related. For present purposes I can show that the universe is intelligibly produced by using as the basis of the argument other and, for many nowadays, more acceptable forms of intelligibility, such as those on which the whole of modern science is based, and which the whole of modern science logically presupposes, for these are accepted universally. We are all quite certain that the fundamental laws of physics, for example, are permanent laws which will not turn out to have vanished after a year or two. Had the modern scientific conceptions of law and order been established in the thirteenth century as strikingly as they are now, I would most certainly have used them to prove that the universe is intelligible as a vast system of changing things. All I am concerned with establishing for the time being is that the universe is what it is because things take place in ways that are ordered according to fixed laws, and the common use of the word 'universe' is justified by the overall unity resulting from the prevalence of the same laws everywhere within it. The laws of physics apply universally for all material things and manifest to our minds the unity of the system we call the 'universe'. In fact, in some ways, the universe is far more strikingly one system of material things than it used to be for us in the Middle Ages, when we thought of one kind of mechanics applying

[13] cf. E. Gilson: *Being and Some Philosophers*, especially chs. 5 and 6.

to the earth and another applying to the supra-lunary world. I am arguing, then, that it is absurd to say that such a 'thing' (I must beg you to take this word for the purpose of the argument to mean any kind of real unity, whether it is that of an individual existent like a man or a dog, or that of a number of existents taken as forming a whole, such as a university, the government, or the universe) as the universe just happens to be and to be intelligible as it is for no reason whatsoever; since that which just happens to be for no reason whatever is not intelligible, it is impossible to say that an intelligible universe just happens to be, and thus the universe cannot be anything but an effect produced by some kind of cause. Any and every intelligible system must ultimately be the effect of some intelligent cause, no matter how many intermediaries (such as forces of all kinds) may have played a part in the development of the system. In fact the greater the number and complexity of these intermediary forces (such as those of evolution) the more remarkable the system that emerges from them, and the more striking its character as an effect.

I will not pause here to discuss objections about my use of the terms 'cause and effect' as I am discussing the main principles of the structure of the argument for God's existence with special reference to the relations holding between the different stages of the entire argument. I will discuss difficulties about causality later after the interval. But I must add a word to say that by the word 'universe' or 'cosmos' (which some might use) I mean nothing but a sum total of real individual things, such as our earth, the stars, the planets, radiations, and all that contributes to make of the earth, the planets and stars the vast system of existent material things we call the 'universe'.[14] I do not mind how vast it is, nor for how long it has existed, or will exist, nor how much it has changed in the process of its development (or evolution): all the time it has existed as a material system, it has been becoming what it now is, and has been for millions of years the universe with the scientific laws which explain to us how changes go on within it. Thus I speak of the 'universe' or 'cosmos' even as you speak of the Government to denote the collective unity of the individual ministers who compose it, and at Oxford and Cambridge you speak of the University to denote the collective unity of the different colleges which exist within, and

[14]cf. F. C. Copleston: *Aquinas,* pp. 85–86.

work together as parts of, the university without losing the individual
rights and liberties which each holds from the university. Everyone
knows that Oxford and Cambridge are two different universities, or
two different and rival groupings of colleges; similarly everyone knows
that the 'universe' or 'cosmos' is one vast system formed by the organization of an astonishing complexity of myriads of parts, of which the
earth, with all that lives on it, the stars and planets are, as it were,
parts. Everyone knows that the dismissal of the ministers from office
brings about the dissolution of the government, and vice versa the
dissolution of the government involves loss of office for each minister;
again everyone knows that if the university of Oxford was to be declared dissolved, the separate colleges would not be colleges any more,
and vice versa if each of the colleges were to be closed and turned into
factories the university would cease to exist. Likewise, without or
apart from the particular things in the world there would be no
cosmos or universe, and the destruction of everything in the universe
would mean the end of the universe itself, even as the formation of
the things within it into an ordered system was the formation of the
universe. The question which is of fundamental interest to the philosopher, then, is that concerning the cause of the universe as such, for the
answer to this question provides a key to our understanding of the
being of all things within the universe.

(ii) Having shown first of all that the universe is an effect produced
by some other being (or beings), we have next to establish what we
can about the nature of this other being (or these other beings), so far
as we can from the fact that it is (or they are) the cause of the universe.

We have to explain how it has come about that there is a universe
of changing, limited and not self-necessitated existent things at all
and how it is that it is as intelligible as it is, for a contingent universe
is a question-raising kind of universe. I may explain why one thing
changes, comes to be or ceases to be, and is limited in some way or the
other, in terms of some other things which like it exist within the
universe, and this explanation may be the kind of explanation that is
needed for the purposes of science, but it does not get the philosopher
anywhere if he is looking for an answer to the question which, as I see
the matter, he ought to be asking as a philosopher. I am quite well
aware that many whose philosophies have been modelled too closely

on the pattern of modern science may not understand precisely the
nature of this question they ought to be asking, and this difficulty must
handicap those who experience it severely at this point in the argument.
Once again I must stress emphatically that this part of the argument
is thoroughly metaphysical in character, and it calls for an effort to
think metaphysically; it is of no use whatsoever seeking any help from
a modern science in this difficulty,[15] nor is it reasonable to dismiss the
question as unreal just because it is not the kind of question a modern
science investigates. The point that we have to get perfectly clear in
our minds is that the question, why there should be such things as
changing, limited, and not self-necessitated existent beings at all and
how it is that they co-exist to form a universe which is intelligible, is
different in kind from all scientific questions. To ask, what it is which
explains the existence or the being of the universe, and accounts for the
intelligibility it has, is to put to oneself the supreme question towards
which, in my view, the whole of philosophy converges, and without
which philosophy is something less than it ought to be. Quite obviously
the kind of intelligibility for which the philosopher is seeking, if he is
really asking the question he ought to be asking, is not that which the
scientist is seeking, for the philosopher is not trying to explain this or
that particular thing and its behaviour by showing how it is related to
other things in their behaviour. In other words the relationship between contingent and necessary being will be very different in kind
from any relationships holding between two or more beings within
the cosmos, and therefore the proof of the existence of God as the
necessary being must inevitably be a very different kind of proof to
that we would give of the existence of anything within the cosmos.
However, it may be that some of you do not quite understand the real
nature of this question, or perhaps do not see that it is a real question,
so I will give an example in the hope that it will bring out the crucial
point I am trying to make about the character of a metaphysical
inquiry.

I have been fascinated, during my few hours back on the earth, by
the inquiry that is going on at the moment into a recent railway accident which happened some time ago in the course of some shunting

[15]cf. F. Van Steenberghen: 'Sciences Positives et Existence de Dieu', in the
*Revue Philosophique de Louvain*, August 1959, pp. 397–414.

operations on a siding near a main line. According to the morning
paper it was the duty of some experts to investigate how a wagon
became derailed and obstructed the main line just as an express train
was about to pass. The first question that had to be investigated was,
how this particular wagon came to be moving so fast that it was derailed. The experts concerned with the investigation of this question
found that it was pushed by some other wagon which came on to its
line over points which, by some oversight on the part of a shunter,
were so set as to let it on to that line. They then showed that this
wagon had itself been set moving with exceptional force by yet another
wagon which in its turn had been set moving by an engine driven by a
certain railwayman whose record as an engine driver had been thoroughly investigated. The driver of the engine had on this occasion mis-
calculated a distance and so started the wagons moving at undue
velocity. Everyone in court was satisfied with this explanation, and the
inquiry into the derailment of the wagon which obstructed and derailed the express seemed to be finished. But the judge presiding over
the inquiry caused no little stir yesterday, for so far from declaring the
inquiry finished and asking the jury to consider its verdict about the
conduct of the men engaged in the shunting operations at the time, he
declared that the inquiry had so far only dealt with one aspect of the
case, and that another of vital importance had yet to be investigated.
We need to know and we must inquire, he continued, why there was
any shunting going on at all on that day, seeing that none was sche-
duled, and whether, if there was to be any, it would have been pre-
ferable to have conducted it on a vaster scale than the very limited one
on which it was done at the time. The judge reminded the court that
for the conduct of this inquiry it was no good re-examining the
mechanical question of the movements of the wagons and engines,
for the question was not concerned with how anything moved or was
moved, but with why anything should have been moved at all. The
inquiry that the experts had made into what had happened just before
the accident revealed that the shunting had been done according to
certain rules which were perfectly intelligible, and the mistakes that
had been made, so far from showing that no rules were observed,
showed that an effort had been made to observe the shunting regula-
tions, that they were intelligible, even if we think they might have

been improved upon. Hence he could not accept the supposition that there was no reason at all for the shunting being done on that day, nor could he accept the declaration that the question why there was any shunting at all done on such a limited scale was no question to investigate because it was not about a matter of mechanics. It was one thing to ask how the shunting had been done, and another why it was being done at all. He reminded the court of the altercation between Alice and the footman at the entrance to the house of the duchess, in which Alice asked the footman how she was to enter the house, and the footman ended by reminding her that the real point to be decided was not how she was to enter, but whether she was to enter at all. The judge ended by announcing that he would appoint another body of experts to investigate this question, and the court would adjourn till they had completed their inquiries. In my old terminology, which I ask your pardon for using if you dislike it, I would say that the first inquiry showed beyond all possible doubt that the shunting operations were an effect, and an effect which must be explained in the way the judge demanded. Thus the question arose in the judge's mind as to who was responsible for ordering this shunting operation and for putting these men to do the shunting at that time. Was he in any way to be blamed for the accident as well as the railwaymen who were doing the shunting? If the committee appointed can answer these questions they will be answering the question as to why there was any shunting going on at all. I trust it is clear that no one can reasonably dismiss the question as to why there was any shunting going on as needing no explanation, or as no real question, just because it was not itself a particular mechanized event. The first question was purely scientific; the second is a metaphysical question.

As I see the situation, St Thomas continued, the philosopher is in a position similar to that of the judge insisting on the need of investigating the reason for the very existence of the shunting. The philosopher has not to investigate particular instances of change, nor account for the behaviour of this or that particular thing in this or that condition, for these are matters considered by the scientific experts. Their reports of these matters show without a shadow of doubt that the behaviour, to use the widest possible term, of the things in the universe, and what we can call the overall structure of the universe as a system, is intelligible. I am not claiming that things are, or have to be made perfectly intelligible, as some critics of theism imagine theists are always trying to do, but that they call for an explanation for being as intelligible as they are. Clearly enough, as he has not to investigate how particular things change, but why there should be a universe of changing, limited and non self-necessitated-existent things at all, the philosopher ought to begin his work by setting aside the methods of investigation used by the scientists, and the scientific way of using certain terms (such as causality), for the question he is investigating is not one that can be treated in the way we investigate empirical facts. It would be no good answering the judge's question, as to why there should have been any shunting at all on that day, by saying 'Why shouldn't there have been any?' If the movements of the individual wagons made no sense at all, and had just taken place without conforming to any kind of rule or law, then the question why there was any shunting at all on that day could be dismissed as meaningless because there would not have been any to account for; but because the movements of the individual wagons did conform to rules and laws, we know that there was shunting, and therefore we know that there must have been a reason for there being shunting movements going on. Thus we know that the retort, 'Why shouldn't there have been any?' must be ruled out by the judge as no proper reply. Similarly, to say in reply to the question, 'Why does the universe exist at all rather than not exist?' that it is no proper question, and so there is no proper answer to it, for after all 'why shouldn't it exist?'[16] ought to be ruled out by the philosopher as quite unjustified. As the universe is intelligible in the general lines of its structure, and as we spend a great part of our lives explaining it or having it explained to us, we know that its being and existence are intelligible, and that it is not meaningless to try to account for the intelligibility it has.

I am arguing on the principle that where we have law and order in the behaviour and structure of things, we have intelligibility of being as well; as, then, we have a universe the being of which is intelligible,

[16]cf. J. J. C. Smart: 'The Existence of God', in NEPT, p. 46. I cannot see how an *argument* like that for the existence of God which Mr Smart thinks is 'completely absurd', can be said none the less to 'appeal to something deep seated in our natures', or if it does that it should be allowed to do so.

we are intellectually compelled to look for the cause of the universe to account for its intelligibility. Dr Hepburn voices a common objection to this line of argument by saying that it follows the line 'this . . . would be vain, unless . . .'. He writes: 'This phrase contains an important supposition, namely that nothing in the world can be expected to be "vain", irrational, or unplanned.'[17] Not at all. I am perfectly aware that for all we can tell much happens in the world that is 'vain', and that there is some disorder. I am arguing that, whatever may be in vain, irrational or unplanned in the universe, we cannot logically hold that it is the universe itself. If Dr Hepburn will glance at the fifth Way as I gave it in article 3 he will find that I only argued that there is some law and order (remember I was arguing from design when I wrote) of some remarkable kinds, so that there must be some kind of mind responsible for it. It may be that the world is not *completely* explicable in all its details, and that we cannot make *perfect* sense of it, as Dr Hepburn maintains; after all there is evil and there is pain of all kinds, and so far as we can tell there is a great deal that happens by accident or chance. I have no desire to minimize the acuteness of the problem of evil.[18] Therefore I agree with the objection that is so often made nowadays against certain arguments for the existence of God, and which Hume and Kant made originally, that from the limited order and law we find in the world, we could only prove at the most that there is some mind who is responsible for it; we can never prove *from it alone* that it is the mind of the infinitely wise God. But all this means is that the full argument for the existence of the infinitely wise God does not end with the first major stage of the argument. Once again I would like to say that the problem in all the arguments is why, after all, there should be a *limited* universe, and a limited universe is one in which failures, accidents, disorder, and possibly moral evil are to be expected. A limited universe can only have a certain limited intelligibility of its own. There is no reason why it should be perfectly intelligible. But so far from concluding that just because it is limited we can take what we find to be rational and coherent, and cease to worry about its cause, as Earl Russell and Dr Hepburn hold we can reasonably

[17]R. W. Hepburn: *Paradox and Christianity*, p. 180.
[18]cf. Alasdair C. MacIntyre: *Difficulties in Christian Belief,* ch. 4 on 'Evil and Freedom' for a penetrating study of the problem of evil.

do, I am contending that we must ask, that we are logically compelled to ask, what is the cause of the universe, and of its being limited as we know it to be. I certainly hold that it is untrue that there is no more than just enough intelligibility in the universe 'for the maintenance of sanity, the setting before us of practical objectives, and even the radical manipulation of nature which is applied science'.[19] Unless the universe was intelligible and remarkably well ordered in the vast majority of its numerous laws we would be quite incapable of setting before ourselves the sort of practical objectives we do set before ourselves, nor would the radical manipulation of applied science be possible without the extensive understanding the speculative scientists have attained of the laws which hold throughout the universe. Our practical triumphs and our applied sciences imply the truth of the very point I am trying to make, that our universe is replete with law and order, that its being is as a consequence intelligible, and that the sanest of learned men seek a speculative knowledge of the world because of the wonder of its intelligibility.

But we must return to our main topic of the essential structure of the argument for the existence of God, and for the time being avoid discussing difficulties unless they bear directly on this topic.

What, then, we must ask, is the cause of the existence of our universe of changing, limited and non self-necessitated-existent things? What is the cause of the contingent universe? That is our question. Because the existence of the universe is inexplicable in terms of anything within the universe itself, and because we cannot reasonably just drop the question because we cannot explain the universe in terms of itself, the various arguments must show that we are logically compelled to accept the only conclusion left as an alternative, that ultimately it owes its existence and its entire being to a being (or possibly some beings) which is unlike the universe itself or anything in it in that it is un-changeable, non-limited, uncaused and non-contingent or necessary. Whatever we might mean by these terms, it is clear that an unchanging, non-limited, uncaused and necessary being is not of our universe, but a reality altogether different in kind from anything of the cosmos, the existence of which could not be established by a strictly cosmological argument, or by a process of reasoning resembling one by which we

[19]R. W. Hepburn: *op. cit.*, p. 180.

can reason from one to another thing in the cosmos. Once again, therefore, I deprecate the use of the word 'cosmological' to refer to this stage of the argument; we should name the argument not from the cosmos from which it commences to reason, but from the character of the reasoning by which we argue from the being of the cosmos to a non-cosmological reality, for it is the nature of the reasoning which makes the argument what it is, obviously metaphysical. Such, then, was the overall structure of the arguments which I found in several passages of Aristotle's works and in various writings of the philosophers of the Middle Ages. I took the arguments almost as they stood and made them into my Five Ways because at the time I had reason to consider them amongst the most remarkable contributions made by philosophers to the study of a supreme being which the Middle Ages possessed. You find them in my *Summa Theologica* presented in their distinctive Aristotelian mould and style, with all their Aristotelian doctrines, such as the theory of act and potency, and the emphasis on the impossibility of having an infinite regress in a series of essentially, as distinct from accidentally, subordinate causes,[20] and, of course, a pardonable failure to distinguish, as fully as you have learned to do in modern times, between scientific and philosophical questions about the universe.[21] The reasoning to be employed in arguing from contingent to necessary being needs to be worked out in more detail in strictly metaphysical arguments and some changes need to be made in the whole formulation of my Five Ways, especially in the third and fourth Ways, but as we are only concerned with the principles involved in the overall structure of the complete proof, I do not propose to say more about the first stage of the complete proof here. All I hope I have managed to do is to convince you of the reasonableness of what I suggest a theist has to do in proving that God exists.

This, St Thomas continued, was in fact as far as human reason, as I knew of its achievements from the writings of the ablest of the ancient philosophers of pre-Christian times, had been able to go without the aid of the Christian faith with any claim to intellectual security. This is

[20]cf. for example, E. L. Mascall's *He Who Is,* pp. 43–45, or any of the works of Thomist natural theology to which I referred above on p. 14.
[21]The distinction was made successfully enough in the first Way, but not in the third Way.

not as far as many Christian philosophers, especially those who regard themselves as my disciples, nowadays claim that reason is able to go, and, as I will explain shortly, it is not as far as I am prepared to go myself, but it is a good deal farther than many philosophers in these days hold that reason is able to go. I fear that it is a good deal farther than the majority of the philosophers present at this meeting are prepared to go. The general verdict of this assembly is, I fear, that none of the actual arguments framed according to the principles I have laid down is compelling, even if they admit that we are entitled to make the attempts I have described. I feel that some of you are already asking what they are to understand by unlimited being, by uncaused and necessary being, and until they can understand something about the meaning of these expressions, they cannot see the point of the arguments. However, I must ask them to listen patiently for the time being while I continue to outline the basic principles of the strategy in the operation of arguing to the existence of God, as I have something to say about these difficulties in what I have to say now concerning the second stage of the argument.

B. *The Second Stage of the Argument,* as I presented it of old in my *Summa Theologica* and *Contra Gentes,* did not consist in arguing by reason alone and unaided by faith directly from necessary to infinite Being, or at least it did not consist solely or essentially in this as it did for Leibniz. I must remind you once again that I conceived the argument for God's existence from the point of view of a theologian, and of the way I thought of theology as a science, and thus as a kind of dialogue between reason and faith. Thus I thought of the whole argument as being formed by bringing together, from the first stage, what reason had discovered on its own about God, with, in the second stage, what human reason can come to understand of the truths God has revealed about Himself. The argument is metaphysical in character throughout, but in the first stage it consists in reason arguing from the universe, and in the second stage in reason arguing from what God has revealed. The whole argument is formed, and derives its force, as the perfect harmony existing between what reason has been able to demonstrate on its own, and what God has revealed about Himself, strikes the reader's attention. Thus the second stage of the argument, as I conceived it, consists before all else in a carefully planned course of reasoning about the biblical teaching concerning God as from certain first principles. In the second stage of my proof, then, the theologian steps on to the scene to show that divine revelation provides us with the best possible, and indeed the only conceivable way of understanding what you were left asking at the end of the first stage of the argument, namely what are we to understand by necessary, uncaused, unlimited being. This was the reason why I left my Five Ways so unfinished with the enigmatic expressions with which each Way ends, and this was also the reason why I never intended to close the discussion of God's existence I raised in the notorious article 3 till I had finished showing how we are to think of God's Being (or essence). As a theologian I was primarily interested in the theological study of God's Being in the second stage, so I spread myself on this part of the argument; I delayed the conclusion for some time and did not write the decisive words 'et hoc est Deus' till I had reached article 3 of Quaestio 11. Thus the second stage of my argument for the existence of God consisted, not in arguing directly from necessary to infinite Being, but in showing how we are to think of the biblical revelation of God. From this theological study of the truths divinely revealed in the Bible about God's Being, it becomes perfectly clear, first, that there is, and can only be, one uncaused, non-limited and necessary Being, second, that the God of divine revelation is uncaused, non-limited and necessary Being, and third, what we are to understand by the terms uncaused, non-limited and necessary Being. Thus the total argument emerges from the dialogue between reason and faith, with reason ascending intellectually towards God as it thinks about the being of the universe, but getting lost in the ascent, and God stooping, as it were, to meet our efforts to find Him by speaking to us and accommodating His message to the level of our minds that we might come to realize something of the reality and mystery of His Being.

In the course of writing the second stage of my argument I introduced a new metaphysic of being, showing that being is not just an essence as the Greeks, and especially Aristotle had thought, but that in God being is the full positivity of existing and of what modern scholastics call the transcendental perfections, while with the things of this world being is this same positivity of existing rendered limited by the individual essence which makes each thing the changing and contingent being it is.[22] There is thus a real distinction between being and essence in all the things of the universe, but not in God for He is pure Being without any limiting essence. We use the expression 'the essence of God' to denote the perfections of His Being which we call His attributes, but these, so far from being what an essence is to a created thing (namely a principle of limitation of being), are really only manifestations of unlimited Being which we cannot but think of as different from unlimited Being itself.[23] As we think of God and each of His attributes we speak of God's essence as though His essence was distinct from His Being. I worked out this metaphysics of being for myself following the way in which the Bible presents God to us as the full positivity of perfection, as life at the highest intensity of unalterable and unchanging act, as the entirety of being so that God is not and cannot be a 'this' or a 'that' kind of being. I expressed this idea of God's transcendence in terms canonized by the Aristotelian logic by showing that God is not in any species, nor even in any genus.[24] I therefore argued that we must think of God as simple or unqualified Being, and therefore as the pure activity or limitless energy of existing (*ipsum esse subsistens*), so that His existing and Being are one and the same identical reality. Thus God is uncaused and un-causable in His Being.[25] God exists in the right of His own Being, and thus we cannot possibly think of anything causing God's existence, and least of all of God causing His own existence (in the enigmatic way that Spinoza talks of God as *Causa Sui*). I repudiate, therefore, Dr Paton's suggestion[26] that being in the desperate situation of having to find some positive meaning for the term 'neces ıry being', theists have been forced to do this by arguing by pure reason that necessary being is being whose essence is the ground of its existence, and that they have been forced back on to the ontological argument by having to say that a necessary being is a being whose non-existence is inconceivable.

---

[22]cf. E. Gilson: *Le Thomisme*, ch. 1–4, and *The Christian Philosophy of St Thomas Aquinas*, ch. 1–4; D. J. B. Hawkins: *Being and Becoming*, ch. 2 and 3, and *The Essentials of Theism*, pp. 69–76.

[23]cf. D. J. B. Hawkins: *Being and Becoming*, ch. 4, for a discussion of the various kinds of distinction.

[24]*Summa Theologica*, 1, qu. 3, art. 5.

[25]*Summa Theologica*, 1, qu. 3, art. 4.

[26]cf. pp. 22–23.

In my view the idea that an essence is the ground of an existence is meaningless. Theology teaches us that God *is* His own Being and existing, and that He cannot be the ground of what He is. God is being and existing in Himself and without ground. To ask why God exists, when we have reached this point in the argument, or who caused God, or what is the cause of God's existing, is meaningless. Those who say, with Russell and Dr Hepburn,[27] that we ought to ask what is the cause of God's existing if we ask the question of all other beings, fail to see that we only ask this question of all other beings because they are contingent and limited beings, and not because they are beings. God exists ultimately because He is Being, and ultimately being is self-existent reality. Theists have got over the difficulty raised by Dr Paton in quite a different way to the one he imagines.

God is one and utterly simple in His Being without any possibility of division of any kind or any internal multiplicity of parts or aspects, for division and multiplicity are the denial of the full positivity of being. God knows and loves the Being He is, and indeed His life, which is His Being, is the life of knowing and loving Himself in the splendour of His Being, for knowing and loving are the life activities of spirit. God is unchanging activity because He is pure spirit, the unchanging activity of knowing which is identical with and more than the mere possession of the being known, and of love rejoicing in the splendour of the Being He is. It is absolutely impossible, therefore, to say that for God love 'means just what we mean when we speak of love in human contexts',[28] or that for God knowledge means what it does in human contexts. I expressed all this in technical terms by saying that in God being and essence are identical, that being and act are unqualified so that God is to be thought of not so much as infinite Being (as Leibniz would insist) but as *Ipsum esse subsistens,* or as the Bible says, 'He Who Is'. God is transcendent in His Being, His life, His knowledge and His love. Such is the way we ought to understand the sublime truth of Ex. iii.14, of which I wrote in chapter 23 of the first book of my *Contra Gentes.*[29]

[27]cf. pp. 12–14.
[28]A. MacIntyre: in *Metaphysical Beliefs,* p. 181; cf. ch. I and the 'Theology of Falsification'.
[29]cf. *Summa Theologica:* II–II, qu. 174, art. 6.

As I have said, in constructing my argument in the *Summa Theologica* in two stages in the way I did, my purpose was to show that reason recognizes readily that the God Who presents Himself to us in Revelation and commands our belief, the God Who has told us of His own Being and thus given us the secret of thinking about Him in terms of existing and the pure act of being, is the one and only Being who enables us to understand the little that we can come to understand of what we mean by uncaused, unlimited and non-contingent or necessary being. The total proof for the existence of God, of the God Who is worshipped by the Christian Church, and on Whom the Christian theologian centres all his belief and thoughts, is therefore to be obtained by combining into one whole argument the truths that can be attained by unaided reason with those that reason can come to know with the aid of what the Bible teaches us of the living God of Abraham, Isaac and Jacob, Who spoke to Moses and the prophets, and revealed Himself Incarnate in Jesus Christ. It seems that when discussing the problems of theism with philosophers who are thinking on the lines of those who are caught in the meshes of the problem of the falsification of theological statements, it is essential to put them on their guard against judging truths about God which all Christians only know as certainly true because God has revealed them to us, as, for example, that God loves us and each living creature, by purely human standards, and not by the standards God Himself has given us to judge of Him and His love, namely the works He has revealed to us in the life, death and resurrection of Jesus Christ, which we must take into consideration especially when we are thinking of what the love of God really is. 'God so loved the world as to give His only begotten Son'. The statement that God loves us might have been falsified had God refused to redeem us from the evils of sin and hell. As things are He has shown His love for us by deeds which can never fail to witness to the love of God no matter what misfortunes may befall us in this short life. The statement that God loves us is so true that it cannot be falsified now that God has revealed His love for us, no matter what might befall us in life. Miseries like terrible cancers surely bring home the evil of human sin more readily than they falsify a statement about God's love for us: they certainly resemble the sinful deeds of men in the indiscriminate way in which both bring suffering to all men, even innocent children.

There is much that reason needs to learn from faith even in establishing that God exists, and philosophers who have not learnt anything from faith must be handicapped in philosophizing about God. The unity of God, which reason can demonstrate on its own, and which I might well have gone on to demonstrate at the beginning of Quaestio 3 immediately after finishing my Five Ways, shines forth in all its majesty in the revealed doctrine of the absolute simplicity, eternity and immutability of God's Being, and so I thought that my best plan was to delay the completion of my entire argument for the existence of the one God till I had covered all the ground necessary to reveal that the Five Ways do in fact establish something as true about various attributes of the Being who is the one true God worshipped by all Christians. Once the second stage of the argument has shown something of the Being of the God of the Bible, it is clear that the uncaused, unlimited and necessary being of article 3 is the God of the Bible; once I had done this, I could complete my entire argument by treating of God's unity, which I did eventually in Quaestio 11.

Before I finish I feel that I ought to say a word, seeing that I am talking to philosophers, on the nature of a purely philosophical argument for the existence of God which I always considered to be possible, though in fact I never had occasion to formulate a complete one myself. In brief, I think that a purely philosophical argument would have to consist of at least two major stages (the first one being subdivided into two parts as I have described), and that the first of these two stages would be the same as that we have just outlined, reasoning from contingent to necessary being. The objection that, whatever philosophers of the past may have thought about it, the modern mind finds no force in this kind of argument,[30] will not bear serious examination, for however difficult the reasoning embodied in any particular argument may be, the reasoning reposes on objective principles which are as timeless as the principles of logic or mathematics. One can understand some philosophers finding no force in the argument because, for philosophical reasons of their own, they cannot accept some of the principles intrinsic to its structure, but it is plainly unreasonable to reject them because of what 'the modern mind' feels about them. After

[30]cf. J. N. Findlay: 'Can God's Existence be Disproved?' in NEPT, pp. 47 and 54.

all there have always been some philosophers who have rejected the arguments for philosophical reasons of their own. It may, of course, be true that the arguments fail to convince those whose ways of thinking have been so conditioned that they have become unable to appreciate any argument but one which conforms to the pattern of a scientific argument, with the result that they have become blind to the force of non-scientific ways of thinking. But this in no way proves that the metaphysical arguments for God's existence are invalid, but only that it is no good offering them to those who know nothing about metaphysics, or who identify metaphysics with some form of idealism such as that of Bradley. If the objection means that nowadays many philosophers have a deep-rooted antipathy for non-scientific ways of thinking, it may be I must concede some force to the objection, but then I would reply that this only shows that the modern age is not a golden age for philosophy.

To drive home the force of the first stage of the argument, the philosopher ought to conclude his reasoning by showing that contingent and necessary, changing and unchangeable, limited and non-limited being are opposed as contradictories, so that there is no possibility of there being a third alternative, or some kind of being which is neither one nor the other. As all the beings we know from experience are contingent, and we cannot rest with them alone, there must be necessary, unlimited and unchanging, or rather unchangeable being. To meet the objection which some philosophers will inevitably raise that, having finished this stage of the argument, they are as lost men because they have no means of attaining any genuine understanding of what necessary and unchangeable being is, I would still say that, even as philosophers and perhaps philosophers who are not Christians, they ought to consider what theologians can explain to them of the Being of God as the Bible reveals this to us, for if studied thoughtfully the Bible can still be a source of philosophical ideas as it was to thinkers in my day. Some such study of theology might well help them in philosophy. During the past few hundred years philosophy has become more and more estranged from Biblical theology, as it has come more and more under the sway of the empirical sciences. I do sincerely suggest that modern philosophy would be immensely enriched if it would strive to regain and maintain its independence from the sciences (without, of course, ceasing to take cognizance of their work and progress), and also turn inquiringly once more towards theology as towards a divine relevation giving men knowledge of God and therefore enabling us genuinely to think of the truths God has revealed (without, of course, becoming subservient to theology). Nowadays you constantly hear the wail that the fires of theological interest have died down and that there is little chance of rekindling them for the time Being.[31] I can only speak for myself, but I would say that this only shows once again that the present age is not a golden age for philosophy, and that the so-called revolution in philosophy, which we are supposed to have witnessed, is not necessarily the one and only way to intellectual prosperity that their leaders imagine. Other reforms may be urgently required.

If, however, I am talking with a philosopher who has no insuperable difficulties with the first stage of the argument, nor against the ideas of uncaused, unlimited and necessary being, then I would be fully prepared to forget that I am a theologian and become a pure philosopher. I would thus approach the second stage of the argument without calling in the aid of revelation. But, as I have mentioned, the second stage of the argument does not reason from necessary to infinite Being, but from necessary to self subsistent Being by showing that in all contingent being there is a real distinction between being and essence, whereas necessary being is self-subsistent because it is pure Being, the full positivity of all perfection, and therefore necessary being is uncaused and without any limitation whatsoever. Thus, as it is a purely philosophical matter not intrinsically linked with theology, I would develop my metaphysics of being in the second stage of the argument in order to cast as much light as is humanly possible on the meaning of the terms with which the argument finishes at the end of the first stage.

I realize that many philosophers will object, as Kant did, that in so arguing I will be forced back to a kind of cryptic use of the ontological argument. As, however, my metaphysics are not based on *a priori* ideas, nor on any *a priori* ways of reasoning, I reject this very common opinion as quite unfounded. What is nowadays called the

[31]cf. for example, Gilbert Ryle: *The Nature of Metaphysics*, edited by D. F. Pears, p. 160.

Thomist metaphysics is a metaphysic of existence which, like Aristotle's, is based on experience, and it is a metaphysics which, I am glad to say, foresaw all the snares which are supposed to have bedevilled metaphysical systems as, for example, that existence is not a predicate which Kant made famous, or that it is not a 'proper concept' which Wittgenstein accused metaphysicians of making it. I claim that I realized all these points and still had much to say about what existence is, instead of stopping short by showing what it is not. I am happy to say that one of my present audience, Mr J. J. C. Smart, with whom I have already found more than one occasion to differ, has come to our defence this time against Kant in a manner that strikes me as being admirable. He points out that in Kant's opinion the second stage of the argument reasons that 'All necessary beings are infinitely perfect beings'. But this conclusion implies that 'some infinitely perfect beings are necessary beings' by a simple conversion, which of course must be accepted as true if the proposition from which it is derived is true. But since there can only be one infinitely perfect being, this implied proposition becomes 'All infinitely perfect beings are necessary beings', which is the principle of the ontological argument. Kant, therefore, rejected the second stage of the argument as invalid. To this I reply that Kant's reasoning is logically as fallacious as, to quote Mr Smart's example, the reasoning of a person who argued from the statement that 'All trespassers will be prosecuted' to the converse that 'some prosecuted people will be trespassers', and then, on entering a court of law and seeing a number of people being prosecuted, said that some, or one, of those being prosecuted was a trespasser. His conversion of the statement that 'All trespassers will be prosecuted' is sound enough, but his application of this converted proposition to the people in the court is unjustified unless he has first of all ascertained that there have been some trespassers. If, on the other hand, there have been some trespassers, and he has ascertained the fact of their trespassing, then (assuming there is only one court in the neighbourhood) he might conclude that some of those now being prosecuted are trespassers. Similarly in the argument of Leibniz that Kant was criticizing, the conclusion is that 'all necessary beings are infinitely perfect', but this only means 'if there are such beings as necessary beings, they are infinitely perfect'. Now Leibniz only converted this proposition after first

establishing (at least to his own satisfaction) that there really is a
necessary being; he did not convert the proposition he was proving
*without first of all assuring himself that there is a necessary being,* as Kant
accuses him and all theists of doing. Thus the conversion of the statement 'all necessary beings are infinitely perfect beings' rested in no way
on any form of the ontological argument.[32] If the second stage of
Leibniz's argument had been formed on its own, independently of the
first stage, and then added on to, instead of presupposing and developing from the first stage, then Kant's objection might hold. Presumably
this is what he considered theists always do, and he expressed his
criticism of their way of thinking by calling the first stage of the
argument 'cosmological' and the second something quite alien in his
mind to cosmology, namely 'metaphysical'. Kant's objection against
Leibniz's version of the second stage of the argument is of even less
use against my position, which in the second stage, is radically different
from that of Leibniz. I also reject as false the charge made against the
purely philosophical argument by Professor Paton,[33] and all he says
about the necessity theists were under of inventing the ontological
argument to escape from the impasse in which they found themselves
at the end of the first stage.

Having established, then, that there exists uncaused and necessary
being, I can safely continue to prove that such being is self-subsistent,
intelligent, immaterial and eternal without committing any error in
logic destroying the structure of the argument, but I might as well
add that I fail to see how anyone is going to make much progress in
this last stage of the argument unless he has a metaphysics of being of
the kind I thought out after the many years of reflection which I
devoted to it. I do not think that the cut and dried argument of
Leibniz, stripped of all genuine metaphysics, will get anyone very far,
and I certainly subscribe to the criticisms of all forms of *a priori* or
rationalist metaphysics made by Kant and many of you listening to me
now. It is a sound metaphysics of being which makes my argument, as I
developed it in Quaestio 3 and the following Quaestiones, so different

[32]cf. NEPT, pp. 36–37, also D. J. B. Hawkins: *The Essentials of Theism,* pp.
67–70, and A. E. Taylor's article on 'Theism' in *Hastings' Encyclopaedia of Religion
and Ethics,* pp. 274–81.
[33]Pp. 18–20.

from that of Leibniz. I hold, then, that the metaphysics which I developed with the aid of the Bible can be presented on its own merits as a pure philosophy without having recourse to biblical theology at all, and with such a metaphysics we can complete the second stage of the argument and establish that God exists. I would like to take this opportunity of saying that many of the disagreements amongst contemporary Thomist philosophers could be settled if they would but recognize that I never intended the Five Ways as they stand in article 3 of the *Summa* to be regarded as complete, and that I certainly intended a further, a second stage to be added to the Five Ways, both by theologians and by philosophers. Further, I never intended my actual formulation of the Five Ways, as you have them in article 3, to be regarded as so perfect as to be irreformable. I only presented the Five Ways as you have them in the text because, writing as a theologian, and anxious to befriend Aristotle as a philosopher, I handed this stage of the argument over to him, and within certain limits, virtually allowed him to formulate the arguments for himself, knowing perfectly well that such a policy was in place in the thirteenth century. But I never intended an article I wrote in this unusual manner in the thirteenth century to remain as it stands for all subsequent centuries! I do think that these Five Ways need rethinking nowadays by my disciples, considering the enormous changes that have taken place in philosophy and science since my time. None the less I remain adamant in defending the main structure of the total argument for the existence of God which, of course, cannot change, no matter how much philosophy may change, and I trust that I have done enough this morning to convince everyone that I never thought of trying to produce five arguments for God's existence in a few lines. I doubt if I could produce five arguments in an entire book! I really have only one entire argument for the existence of God, which begins with Five Ways of establishing that the universe is an effect, and that, as it is contingent, there must be a necessary being. My argument thus proceeds first from contingent being to necessary being, and then from necessary to self-subsistent Being.

Here St Thomas paused for a moment and then sat down. When the applause had died down, Kant announced that the meeting would now adjourn for everyone to take refreshments, and that after an hour's interval St Thomas would continue his talk to consider the objections which the assembly had raised.

*    *    *

After the interval everyone returned to the hall and St Thomas resumed his place on the platform. He spent a few moments running over some notes he had before him and, on rising to speak, began to state very concisely the difficulties which Kant had given him at the beginning of the meeting.[34] He then continued:

I do not think there is any need for me to add anything more to what I have said about the major difficulty, originally raised by Kant himself, concerning the structure of a theistic argument in two stages, nor with modern variants on this difficulty as we find them, for example, in the work of Dr Paton. As for Dr Paton's own difficulty, that if the cosmological argument is valid at all, it must be valid for any world in which objects are the effects of causes, so that it would have to be valid for those whose only world is hell itself,[35] I think that, taken on its own and apart from the context to which it belongs, it scarcely calls for comment as it is a purely fictitious kind of difficulty. Speaking as a theologian, who alone has any right to speak about the problems of heaven and hell, I would say that the difficulty overlooks the fact that the damned in hell have no need of reasoned argument to know of God's existence. After death everyone knows of God in some manner, and, though they do not see Him, the damned know of Him. They also know that, though they were created by God to enjoy the vision of Him for ever in heaven, they have, by their own deeds and of set purpose, rejected Him. They know of God in some way in the knowledge they have of themselves; they know that their misery consists essentially in the pain of the eternal loss of Him from Whom alone they can receive the happiness they desire. But they remain so set against God, for all that they know of Him, that they would rather remain what they have chosen to be, namely Godless, than choose Him and His Ways. Paradoxically, it is the knowledge they have of God, Whom they realize they will never see though they were made for no other end but to see Him, that is at the root of their misery, which, so

[34]cf. ch. 2.
[35]cf. p. 20.

far as this consists in the loss of God, is theirs in virtue of their own choice. Thus I deny the whole analogy between our status on earth and that of the damned in hell on which Dr Paton based his difficulty.

We have something much more serious in the difficulty raised by Kant on behalf of many philosophers present today, that it is meaningless or absurd to conceive God as necessary being, for the notion of necessary being is either fictitious or contradictory and impossible.

Before replying I would like to say that this difficulty cuts against a fundamental point not merely in my argument for God's existence, but also in my idea of theology as a science which depends to a large extent on my argument for God's existence. I trust you will pardon me if I say here that I thought of my argument for the existence of God as contributing, not only to the formation of a speculative theology about the divine being or essence,[36] but also to the formation of this science of theology. The vital objective I set out to secure in my Five Ways was the conclusion that reason by itself can see that, as the universe is contingent, there is a being which is *per se* necessary, which the theologian can identify as the one true God of the Christian Revelation. This objective was vital because, as you may remember, I followed Aristotle in his view that science is always of the universal and necessary, and not of particular or non-necessary events. Thus I had to show that God is the one and only being who is necessary *per se* in Himself in order to justify my view that theology is a genuine science treating of God as He is in Himself, and only of other things in so far as they are related to Him in some way. I certainly thought of unchangeable and unlimited being as identical with *per se* necessary being: in fact I thought that a being could only be unchangeable and unlimited because it is *per se* necessary. That is why the first stage of my argument reasoned from contingent to necessary being in the way I have already described. You can see, then, that my whole conception of theology as a science, to which I gave years of thought, depended on the success I had in completing the first stage of the argument. As I have explained, once I had completed this stage, which in fact (perhaps somewhat rashly) I handed over to be done for me by the philosophers I most admired to do for me, I could then continue in dialogue form to show what the theologian is to understand by necessary being,

[36]cf. pp. 42–47.

knowing quite well that God has revealed Himself to us as the one and only being who is *per se* necessary in His very Being. The objections you have raised do, therefore, attack one of the key points not only of my argument for the existence of God, but also of my idea of theology as a science.

I have already said that our idea of necessary being, derived as it is from contingent being, is, and is bound to be, predominantly negative, for it is really our idea of non-contingent being under a different name. But I do not see that this, of itself, is any difficulty peculiar to the idea of necessary being for all our ideas of God must be predominantly nega-tive. I used to say so often in the lecture room that we know what God is not rather than what He is. I agree with Dr Paton that one of the things we mean when we speak of God as necessary being is that God does not exist in space nor in time, and that He is not to be likened to anything we know within the universe. We also mean that He has no cause, no condition, and no ground. As we have seen it is absurd to say that God's essence is the ground or the cause of His own Existence. Spinoza's idea of God as *Causa Sui,* sponsored by some rationalist metaphysicians, is repugnant to Christian theism. Quite obviously, then, Dr Paton is correct when he says that, in speaking of God as necessary being, we are not using the word 'necessary' in the sense in which we would use it of anything we know within the universe, so that as applied to God it must mean 'necessary subject to no condition', and not just 'necessary subject to a condition'.[37] God is indeed necessary in His Being, absolutely. He is not necessary on some condition or the other, or purely hypothetically. Though the idea we fashion as best we can of necessary being must be predominantly negative, in that we do not know positively in what the necessity of God's Being con-sists, we are not for that matter playing with words, as Dr Paton thinks, for though we do not know positively what necessary being is, we can understand enough of what necessity of being means to see that it is different from and excludes all forms of existing which are conditioned. This should not cause any surprise for the idea takes shape in the pro-cess of reasoning the first stage of the argument from contingent being. The argument shows that, in so far as it involves an affirmation of being and existence, the idea of necessary being is positive; the idea is

[37]cf. p. 22.

negative in so far as it involves a denial of the contingency distinctive of all created things, but the denial of contingency does not suppress the affirmation of being. The idea is only negative in denying of God privations of being and perfection, or to assure that we affirm the fullness of being that we show is to be affirmed of God. So far from being wholly negative the idea of necessary being is basically positive in intent inasmuch as it assures that we affirm fullness of being in God. The difficulty with these negative-positive ideas of God arises from the nature of the causal argument for the existence of God, in that we find ourselves forced to affirm perfections of God which we know we cannot positively understand as uncaused or as perfections of God. Thus it is with the idea of necessary being. Though we do not positively understand what necessity of being is for God Himself, we can attain some understanding of what we mean when we say that God is necessary in His Being by reasoning to what He must be so as not to be contingent in any way. Ultimately it must mean that God is the self-subsistent act of Being, and the inexhaustible plenitude of the immanent life of pure spirit. This elucidation of the meaning of necessary being is the work of the second stage of the argument, the existence of which Dr Paton never seems to have suspected. I venture to suggest that the idea of self-subsistent Being we reach gives us some positive idea of necessary being, or at least as positive an idea as we can possibly attain, and that it is far more helpful than the purely negative idea of God as infinite (i.e. not-finite) Being which became prominent after the time of Scotus, and pre-eminent after that of Leibniz for whom it formed the climax of the whole argument for God's existence.

A metaphysical argument for the existence of God must show that, as the cause of contingent being, God is himself *per se* necessary Being. But in speaking of God as necessary being, the theist is not (as, for example, Mr Smart seems to think),[38] presenting God as the logically necessary being. The argument establishes that God is necessary in His own Being, that necessity is objectively the characteristic of His Being. It is true that this necessity of God's Being becomes known to us as the result of a process of reasoning which we are logically compelled to follow step by step so that there is logical necessity in the reasoning we follow. But the necessity of God's Being is not to be identified with this

[38]J. J. C. Smart: NEPT, p. 38–39.

logical necessity of our reasoning. We are forced by the necessity of certain laws to affirm as the conclusion of a process of reasoning that there is a being which exists necessarily. It is, however, not God's esistence which is *logically* necessary, but our eventual affirmation of His existence as really necessary. We must not confuse 'the necessity of God's Being with the necessity of our thinking about it'.[39]

It is well known to everyone here that Earl Russell and Wittgenstein drew a constrast, which is often driven to quite unjustified extremes, between the informative statements we make about facts and the tautologous statements we make about logical and mathematical laws. A statement of fact, for example, the air in the room is warm, and a statement affirming the existence of something, as it is raining, are synthetic statements for they state something about a subject not necessarily included in our idea of that subject. To be told that the air in the room is warm really adds to my knowledge, for the air in the room might not be warm; to be told that it is raining gives me knowledge of the weather I might not have had at all. Such statements cannot be necessary as the facts they report might well have been different from what they are; in stating that such or such is the case we know quite well that there are many conditions which might well have prevailed to falsify these statements had anyone made them. I know that I cannot always and no matter what happens say that the air in the room is warm, nor that it is raining. A statement of fact cannot be necessary: it only conveys knowledge that is probable, but never absolutely certain. By contrast laws of logic and mathematics are necessary, and they are necessary because they are analytic or tautologous. They do not give any information about real things; they merely state how we think and so they manifest certain formal conditions of human knowledge which hold good no matter what we might happen to know of the real world of things. The laws of logic and mathematics are necessary, but their necessity is purely logical. Necessity, then, pertains not to facts but to thinking: it is a purely logical category, a property of judgements or propositions. To talk about real necessity is simply to confuse logical with real categories. Hence we cannot talk meaningfully of God as the necessary being, but at the best of the necessity of the judgements that we can make saying that 'God exists'. But neither

[39]A. C. A. Rainer: NEPT, p. 68.

way of speaking gets us anywhere, for if it is fallacious to think that
God is the necessary being, it is idle to say that 'God exists' is a necessary proposition, seeing that necessary propositions do not give any
information about real beings. To say that 'God exists' is a necessary
proposition is merely to say how we might decide to use the term
'God', namely always in connexion with the word 'exists', it is not to
have any knowledge of God.

There is a great deal that might be said by way of commenting on
these theories if we had unlimited time. To start with, this hard and
fast division of propositions into merely probable, synthetic, informative statements of fact on the one hand, and uninformative, tautologous,
necessary propositions on the other, may be a useful division as far as
we may be concerned with contrasting mathematical or certain logical
laws with purely empirical statements of fact, but there is no justification whatsoever in just asserting that it is valid when taken as a universal
and necessary law, or as a kind of metaphysical law outlawing metaphysics. If it is so extended and treated as a universal, necessary law,
then surely it, too, becomes uninformative and tautologous; if on the
other hand it is taken as a synthetic, informative assertion, it is only a
more or less probable statement about certain facts, or a more or less
improbable statement about other facts. In my view metaphysical
statements are necessary statements about real things, but they are
necessary in a way that is quite different from that distinctive of a
tautology. I am asserting that God's existence is necessary in a way that
is informative, for I hold that God is necessary in a sense that is quite
different from that which makes certain mathematical and logical
propositions tautologous. Of course, the statement that 'God exists'
would be tautologous if one began by saying that by the word God
we mean the Being who exists of Himself, or the Being, the very idea
of Whom includes His existing. But as we have no proper concept of
God's Being from which to begin reasoning we cannot begin our
reflections by defining what God is in this way. In my view the statement that 'God exists', which we establish as true by argument, is both
necessary and informative because we come to understand that God
necessarily exists in a conclusion necessarily drawn from the argument
about the being of contingent things. That God necessarily exists is a
truth about God's Being which we may genuinely discover, or the

meaning of which we may come to discover by arguing to it from contingent being, so that we have gained both some new knowledge about God, and a new way of looking at the universe, namely as the work of God. To restrict the term 'necessary' solely to judgements or propositions on the ground that necessity belongs exclusively to the logical order, to assert that it cannot apply to a reality of any kind merely because statements of fact about the particular things of this world may or may not be true, constitutes a *petitio principii* when used to support the objection that 'necessary being' must be written off as an impossibility. If this restriction is enforced by philosophers as a kind of universal law, which as I have argued it cannot logically become, rather than noted as a statement about certain laws of mathematics and logic which does not hold in other fields of knowledge, we are given as perfect an example as can be obtained of a philosophy formed entirely to the shape of a modern science. A philosophy formed in this way is a kind of mongrel-philosophy; it is bad philosophy and poor science. The whole point of the discussion about the existence of God, or about the cause of the world of things (or of facts), is to ask whether or not there is a being who is not just a fact, but a reality of a different kind to any of the contingencies which make up the world of mere facts. Obviously the real necessity of God's Being is different from any kind of logical necessity, and I deny that in talking of both logical and real necessities in the argument I have confused in any way, or that I was ignorant of the differences between logical and real categories.

So far from being the only kind of necessity, I should have thought that logical necessity stands in need of some kind of support or justification which it would have if it is admitted that there are necessities of various kinds in being; without such justification it looks too much like some will o' the wisp which might well be explained away in time as the product of mere arbitrary convention. As knowledge is relative to being, logical necessity must in some way or the other be founded in, and rooted on real necessity. The modern theory sets up a purely artificial dichotomy between minds and things, between logic and knowledge. The theory that propositions must be either analytic, tautologous and necessary, or synthetic, factual and probable strikes me as a dangerously incomplete disjunction. I fear that when I am told that Hume established once and for all that from one fact we can only form a probable opinion about some other fact, I am no more impressed than when I am told that Kant established once and for all the impossibility of proving the existence of God.

I trust that Mr Smart can now see the difference between what he wrote, and what I hold about the conclusion of the first stage of the argument. Mr Smart wrote:

> If we cast our minds back, we recall that the argument was as follows: that if we explain why something exists and is what it is, we must explain it by reference to something else, and we must explain that thing's being what it is by reference to yet another thing, and so on, back and back. It is then suggested that unless we can go back to a logically necessary first cause we shall remain intellectually unsatisfied.[40]

I would re-write the last sentence as follows:

> We therefore conclude that unless we abandon the process of referring continually back and back as leading nowhere and explaining nothing, and argue not from particular things, but from the contingent being of the entire universe to the necessity of admitting a non-contingent or necessary being, we shall remain intellectually frustrated because confronted with an intelligible universe which we must write off as unintelligible in its being. This, however, is impossible because it is a contradictory position. Hence we must conclude that there is really necessary being.

Dr Hepburn raised difficulties similar to those of Mr Smart, but he is himself guilty of confusing logical and real necessity in a way, it would seem, to which the critics of the idea of necessary being are more liable than are its proponents. For example, he says if we wish to keep the logical use of the words 'necessary' and 'contingent', we might rephrase the argument as follows: 'The proposition "God exists" is necessary. That is it would be contradictory to deny God's existence.'[41] To this I reply that I have no wish to adopt the modern uses of the terms 'necessary' and 'contingent' and still less the idea that the proposition 'God exists' is necessary in the sense that it would be

[40] J. J. C. Smart: NEPT, p. 39.
[41] R. W. Hepburn: op. cit., p. 171.

self-contradictory to deny it. It is just this kind of logical necessity that the argument for the existence of God excludes. It is not the proposition, but the line of reasoning, which makes us affirm the proposition 'God exists', which is necessary.[42] The proposition we are led to affirm is that God's existence is objectively necessary in itself. As, however, we do not understand the real necessity of the divine Being, the proposition we make about the necessity of God existing can still be denied without the kind of contradiction Dr Hepburn mentions. Though God's existence is absolutely necessary, with the necessity of pure Being, our statement 'God exists' is only hypothetically necessary, i.e. on the supposition that we accept certain premises about the nature of the universe and that we follow the line of the argument. It may well be a logical absurdity to argue, as Dr Hepburn thinks we do, 'from beings whose non-existence is conceivable to a being whose non-existence is *inconceivable*',[43] but it is not a logical absurdity to argue from beings which are contingent to a being which is necessary in itself, though its necessity, like its being, is beyond our powers of conceiving. To confuse these two ways of reasoning, as Dr Hepburn does, is to confuse logical with real necessity. Dr Hepburn has missed the whole point of the distinctions I took pains to make in my *Summa Theologica*,[44] between what is evident and necessary objectively or in itself to a mind capable of understanding it, but not to us, and what is necessary or evident to us though not of itself. The things of this world are more evident and intelligible to us that the Being of God, though in Himself God is more intelligible than the things of this world. God's non-existence is unthinkable to God, because it is an impossibility, but it is conceivable to us because the evidence we have for this most evident of all truths is quite different from the evidence God has of Himself (if we may so speak): we have nothing but the evidence of contingent beings.

I find that the idea of God as necessary being is far less difficult to accept than the modern theory that necessity is exclusively a logical property of judgements, and though I cannot prove positively that necessary being is intrinsically possible, I fail to see any force in any of

[42]cf. F. C. Copleston: *op. cit.,* pp. 114–5.
[43]R. W. Hepburn: *op. cit.,* p. 172.
[44]I, qu. 2, art. 1. cf. also G. E. Hughes: in NEPT, pp. 62–63.

the objections trying to show that it is impossible. I submit, then, that my conviction that necessary being exists is perfectly reasonable.

\*     \*     \*

We come now to difficulties raised against the use to which the idea of cause is put in the argument for the existence of God, and against the way in which the argument sets the universe before us as an effect. Earl Russell, with many other philosophers, raised the difficulty that, even if we grant that we can speak of one particular thing as the cause of another, or of one particular thing as the effect produced by another, and therefore even if we think of causality as holding extensively between things and events within the universe, we must hold firmly that 'the concept of cause is not applicable to the total', that is to say, to the universe itself as the effect of some transcendent being. Russell expressed this contention in his well-known radio debate on the existence of God with Father Copleston during the course of which he argued that, though it is true, for example, that every man who exists has a mother, it does not follow that therefore the human race must have a mother as well, for individual men and the human race belong to different logical spheres.[45] Even if, then, particular things in the universe are effects, we cannot regard the universe itself as a real effect demanding a transcendent cause, any more than we can regard the human race as a real effect demanding a real mother. We have seen how, in a similar kind of way, Dr Hepburn challenged the defenders of the argument for God's existence to establish precisely what they can say without any absurdity or even difficulty about the totality of things we call the universe as a whole, that we also say with safety about particular things within it.[46] There are many statements we make about the limited and particular things within the universe which we cannot make about the universe itself; we cannot say, for example, that the universe is 'above' or 'below', that it is 'in time' or situated 'in a certain place' as we say of the things within it. It seems, then, that it might well be impossible to think of the whole universe with any of the ideas we use to think of the particular things within it, and if we transfer the ideas of cause and effect from their natural context within the universe

[45]cf. B. Russell: *Why I am not a Christian*, p. 152.
[46]cf. pp. 25–26.

and force them into use by speaking of the universe itself as an effect
and God as its cause, we are probably only spinning words, or vainly
trying to persuade ourselves that we are thinking the unthinkable.
Many philosophers are quite convinced that we cannot conclude, from
the fact that particular things within the universe have their causes, that
therefore the sum total of things we call the universe must have *its*
cause. The fallacy involved in reasoning to this conclusion consists in
treating as identical the logical principles governing the uses of the
words 'part' and 'whole'; as the differences between these principles
are irreducible, we can never affirm of a 'whole' what we can of a
'part'. Granted, then, that particular things are caused, we cannot
conclude that therefore the universe itself is also caused.

We often find these objections about the logical fallacy of the
theist's use of the ideas of cause and effect associated with some general
philosophical position: some associate it with one or another form of
Humean phenomenalism, others with the Kantian idea of causality as a
mental category applicable solely to sensible phenomena; for some it
follows immediately from Russell's theory of Logical Types, for others
it is connected with Wittgenstein's theory of Limits, or his later ideas
about Language Games. But with whatever kind of general philosophical position it may be associated, those who urge the difficulty
seem to regard it as evidently fatal on purely logical grounds to the
theist's use of the ideas of cause and effect. Thus Dr Hepburn considers
as evident to all that the word 'cause' applies to particular things only,
and that it just cannot be wrested from this, its natural context, to be
forcefully applied to a 'cosmic setting', as it must be if it is to be trans-
ferred to God as the cause of the universe.

I should like to begin my reply to this extensive difficulty by saying
that I will concentrate my remarks on the charge of the logical fallacy
brought against us, and try to show, while meeting this charge, that
the use of the ideas of cause and effect in the argument for God's
existence are grounded on a realist metaphysics of existent being.

I agree that, as far as we are concerned, the idea of causality belongs
first and foremost to the world of particular things, for we derive our
ideas of 'cause' and 'effect', as we derive all other ideas, from experience, that is to say, from our observation of the production of one
particular thing by another. I agree, therefore, that there is need of care

in extending the idea of causality from particular things to the universe as a whole, for obviously the universe is not an effect of God's causality in the same restricted sense that one thing in the universe is the effect of another we regard as its cause. But let me, too, work with the aid of an example to show how I conceive a theist has to use the idea of causality both with regard to particular things and on 'a cosmic setting'.

If I return to my room after going out for a walk, and, on opening the door, find things scattered everywhere in confusion, the safe forced open and emptied, the drawers of the desk broken and their contents strewn over the floor, I realize at once (to put things mildly!) that something has happened in my absence, that this state of affairs has come about, not by an odd chance, but as the effect of some careful planning and skilful manoeuvring on the part of one or more house-breakers. Without more ado I call for the police in the hope that they will be able to discover the rogue or rogues responsible for this deed, and as many of my belongings as possible. It makes perfect sense to ask who was the person responsible for, or who caused the damage to my property on this occasion, and equally it makes perfect sense to extend the question, and ask who caused the damage done in the course of any other robbery that may take place. No one is likely to doubt that people responsible for recent robberies exist somewhere, nor that the police may be able to catch them. But if anyone tries to extend the question about robberies yet further, and ask what is the cause of robberies as a whole, he would clearly be asking a question devoid of all meaning, for robberies as a whole are neither events nor realities, and only events or realities have causes bringing them about. Robberies as a whole do not happen; only individual robberies happen and each is independent of all others, and must be investigated on its own. Even if a gang is responsible for a series of robberies, no gang causes robberies as a whole. I may form an idea of robberies in general and then begin to talk about them, but in doing so I am talking about something be-longing exclusively to the logical and not to the real order. Now Russell's theory of Logical Types exposes the fallacy of arguing, as in this example, from particular robberies, or from particular instances of causality, to an imagined cause of a *logical* whole, such as robberies in general, and the example he gives (arguing that as individual men have mothers, so, too, the human race has its mother) is an example of the same kind of fallacy that involved in extending the idea of causality from particular robberies to robberies in general. I can agree that, because each man has a mother, we cannot argue that therefore the human race, or humanity as such, must have a mother as well, for, like robberies as a whole, humanity as a whole does not exist. But there is no logical parity between asking who is the mother of humanity as such, and asking who or what is the cause of there existing rather than not existing such creatures as men, or of there being a universe of particular, limited things rather than there not being one at all, for, unlike humanity as such, men and the order of things we call the universe do exist. There is a world of difference between asking what is the cause of humanity as a whole, or speaking of the mother of the human race, and asking what is the cause of men existing at all, or what is the cause of the existing things we call the universe. Thus I can extend the question about the cause of this or that thing within the universe to ask about the cause responsible for there being such a reality as the universe at all, because the universe is as much a reality as any particular thing within it, but in extending the question to the sum total of things I call 'the universe' I must, of course, avoid thinking that the cause of the universe will be just some kind of cause (for example a mother) like the causes we find within the universe itself. If I put the question about the cause of the very existence of the universe in this way, my question is not equivalent to putting the absurd question about the cause of the human race, or about robberies as a whole, because I am not extending the question about the cause of some existent thing to raise an altogether different question about the cause of some (non-existent) abstraction. Hence I am not offending against the theory of different Logical Types, nor am I extending my question from particular things to purely logical wholes, nor am I confusing, as modern logicians say, second with first order questions. A question about the cause of this or that existent thing is of the same logical type as a question about the existent universe or about all existent things, for both are looking for the real causes of real effects: in other words, both are metaphysical questions. Russell's likening of this extending of the ideas of cause and effect to that involved in extending the idea of mother from particular men to mankind as a whole shows, that, either he considers that all wholes must be purely logical (which, of course, can be as freely denied as asserted), or that he has himself fallen a victim to his own theory in confusing real and logical wholes. The existent universe is, as I have argued earlier in this talk,[47] a real 'whole', and it needs a cause not just because it is a whole, but because it is a contingent universe or whole. The argument goes not from part to whole, but from contingent things to the equally contingent universe, on the score that whatever is contingent in its being (be this a 'whole' or a 'part') is an effect, and therefore dependent on a cause. I trust you will give me credit for having seen clearly the difference Earl Russell had in mind and which you often refer to nowadays as a difference between first and second order questions. I only need remind you that, like the schoolmen of my time, I distinguished between first and second intentions, or statements (and questions) about things and about our ways of thinking about things,[48] and I certainly took all the precautions necessary to frame my metaphysical questions about the cause of the universe so as to avoid the elementary logical fallacies into which some philosophers imagine all metaphysicians blindly fall.

Let me now take another example to explain how we are to conceive the extension of the idea of cause to God Himself, and the extension of the idea of effect to the universe as a whole.

A visitor to Oxford may ask the name of the founder of each of the colleges as he visits them one by one, and, assuming that each has one founder, he will be given a name each time he puts his question. But in the course of his visits he may put another question and ask who was the founder of the university itself, and if he does, he will be given a different name, and on listening to the story of its foundation he will notice that founding the university was quite a different process from that of founding the different colleges within it. Special authority was needed in the founder of the university which was not necessary for the founders of the different colleges. But it was quite obvious to our visitor that both the particular colleges and the university itself were founded; they were both effects, real effects, and therefore they must both have had real founders. In asking questions about the origin of the university our visitor is not offending any logical law, nor wresting

---

[47]cf. pp. 130ff.
[48]cf. for example, St Thomas's Commentary on the First Book of Aristotle *Posterior Analytics,* lectio 1.

the term 'founder' from its natural context of particular colleges to fit it by force where it does not belong. The only question he could not reasonably put would be one about the founder or cause, not of this or that college, nor of the university itself, but of colleges as a whole.

I trust that from this example you can see that the questions about the cause of some particular thing (such as a college) within a 'whole' (such as a university), and about the cause of the 'whole' to which it belongs, so far from being independent from each other, are closely connected. There is not much point in asking the cause solely of this or that particular 'part' unless we have some knowledge about the origin and nature of the 'whole' to which the 'part' belongs, for if we know nothing at all about the 'whole' we cannot explain much about its 'parts'. To come straight to my main point, we cannot raise the philosophical question about the cause of the existence of particular things apart from the question about the existence of all contingent things, or the universe itself. To ask, for example, why it is that I should exist at all rather than not exist, I must ask why it is that other men exist rather than not exist, and to ask this question about all other men demands that I ask why it is that the universe, in which we all exist, itself exists. This, of course, may be one reason why some philosophers are so anxious to remove *all* questions about causes of being from philosophy, but their attempt to do so by arguing that questions about the existence of particular things and those about the existence of the universe itself are logically different and independent, so that we cannot go from one to the other, is quite erroneous. A question about the existence of particular things leads of its nature to the question as to how it is that any contingent things whatsoever exist, and to answer the question about the being of particular things, I must first of all answer that about the being of the universe itself.

This is the point our visitor to Oxford comes to see as he learns more and more about the origin of each college. He soon realizes that he needs to know all he can about the origin of the university itself if he is to understand how it was that so many people began to found colleges within the university at a certain period of history. After learning about the foundation of the university, he will be able to understand much more of what he has learned about the foundations of each of the colleges, and he is not likely to hold that he can dismiss as point-less what he has been told about the founding of the university just because it is a question about a 'whole' and not about a 'part'. I trust that this example will help you to see that, in my view, we are not merely entitled to argue that particular things within the universe have their particular causes, and then begin to ask questions about the cause of the universe itself, but that we *must* extend our question about the causes of particular things existing to the whole universe, not because the particular things are 'parts' of the 'whole' we call the universe, but because particular things and the universe are alike contingent as realities. There is thus no reason whatsoever for saying that the ideas of cause and effect apply only to particular things, and not to real 'wholes'. A contingent 'whole' can be as much an effect as any con-tingent thing it contains, and it is as contingent, not just as a 'part', or as a 'whole', that things require a cause. I see no reason whatsoever why the universe itself cannot be an effect, even though as far as our know-ledge goes, the idea of effect belongs first and foremost to the parti-cular things within the universe we spontaneously recognize as effects. It may be true that, in a sense which needs determining, the universe is, as Dr Hepburn says,[49] the *theatre* in which we find the interplay between things as causes and effects of various kinds, but it does not follow from this (unless one imagines the universe itself to be a reality on its own different from the things it comprises) that the universe is not an effect itself, even if we grant that it is an effect of a very different kind to any we find within the universe. We have argued that a universe made up solely of contingent things must itself be contingent; because it is contingent, we conclude that it is an effect; as it is an effect, it must have a cause of some kind. The rest of the argument for God's existence con-sists in establishing what kind of being this cause is. Dr Hepburn's objection does no damage to the argument because, as it stands without any explanation as to how we are to regard the universe as 'a theatre', it is too vague to convey any real meaning. I should have thought that he is wresting the word 'theatre' out of its natural context, if ever anyone misused words by wresting them in this way! If he holds that the universe is a 'theatre' in the sense that it is an existent, independent reality on its own containing particular things, I deny that the universe

[49]cf. p. 25–26.

is a 'theatre' in this sense of the word; if, on the other hand, he holds that the universe is just the overall unity in the organization of the things which exist, I deny that we are unable to prove that it is an effect.

I can quite understand that in one sense the 'natural habitat' of 'cause words' must be the things we know from experience and observation, but this is no special peculiarity of 'cause words'. It is a characteristic of all the words we employ to express ideas, in so far as they refer us primarily to the objects of experience from which we derive all the ideas we have. In this sense the 'natural habitat' of all the words we use must be the things of this world. What, then, does Dr Hepburn mean when he speaks of the 'natural habitat' of cause words? If he means that the world of particular events can be called the 'natural habitat' for the terms 'cause' and 'effect' because we think most easily in terms of particular things, I understand what he means and agree with what he says, but I see no reason to say that on this score alone 'natural habitat' must mean 'exclusive habitat', nor has Dr Hepburn explicitly provided a reason, as Kant did, for saying why we should have to restrict it to mean 'exclusive habitat'. But if we study what he says about the scientific uses of 'cause words', we will find the secret of why he is so anxious to make the 'natural habitat' of 'cause words' mean 'exclusive habitat'. Dr Hepburn would agree, I imagine, that we speak of things as effects and causes in numerous different senses, without marking any one of them out as the 'natural' or 'proper' sense. It is common knowledge, however, that physicists have come to use the word 'cause' in a highly technical sense for the purposes of their work, to mean not the production of some new thing by some other, but rather the unvarying or constant temporal sequence in the order of the appearance of events, so that an event is said to be the cause of another if it precedes it in time, or one event is said to be an effect of another if it follows on after a prior event. When this sequence of events is found to be invariable in our experience, we are able to presume that it will continue in the future as we have experienced it in the past, and so to predict the effects which will follow the appearance of known causes. Taken in this sense the word 'cause' means not the production of one thing by another (e.g. of this one book by this author), but invariability of temporal succession between events (e.g. the change of the traffic lights from green to red is followed by the halting of cars; as a thermometer reads 100°C all water begins to boil). For the specialized purposes of their work, many scientists use the word 'cause' in this technical sense. As a result they are led to deny that we can speak of 'causes' in cases in which a sequence of events turns out to be variable, and therefore undetermined and so unpredictable. Many modern philosophers, unduly impressed by this technical use of the term 'cause', have actually taken this specialized meaning of the word as its 'natural' and exclusive meaning, and so they deny that we can speak about causality in many cases in which most people and many metaphysicians would have no hesitation in so doing. This procedure can be likened to that of fervent devotees of rugby-football who, let us imagine, decide to use and restrict the use of the word 'ball' to the kind they use for their game, and therefore deny that balls are or can ever be though of as round, or made of any other material than leather! They would say that the 'natural habitat' of the word 'ball' is the game of rugby-football, and the wresting of the word ball to denote golf balls or billiard balls is to be reprobated as a serious abuse. Hume was the first to introduce this phenomenal or scientific idea of causality into philosophy, and under his influence causality came to mean for many philosophers not an objectively necessary link between an event produced and the cause producing it (between, for example, the act of drinking this poison and the instantaneous death resulting from this act), but an invariable temporal sequence in a number of observed events. Thus Dr Hepburn, taking this Humean and highly technical meaning of causality as its only natural meaning, objects that in the cosmological argument we are not reasoning to God as the cause of the universe, for:

> We are not in this case recording some observed concomitance of events, or stating a causal law according to which certain sets of events vary reciprocally. . . . It is not the case that every time we have observed a universe, we have noticed a First Cause causing it, and that therefore we feel justified in saying, 'No universes without First Causes'.[50]

In other words, in using the idea of causality in the argument for God's existence we are uprooting it from its habitat in the language, and

[50]cf. p. 26.

therefore only playing with words. In like manner Mr Alasdair MacIntyre writes:

> The important point about such expressions (as 'is the cause of') was made by Hume. Hume argued that when we say that one event A is the cause of another event B what we mean is that event A has always been followed by event B in our experience, and event B has never occurred without event A preceding it. In other words to say that one event is the cause of another is to say that events of the former kind and events of the latter kind are constantly conjoined in our experience.[51]

As a metaphysician I should say that one event A is rightly said to be the cause of another event B when event B is in fact produced by event A, and that in principle we may know that event A is the cause of event B even if we have had but one experience of their causal connexion. If event B regularly follows event A, A is said to be the cause of B not because of the regularity of the temporal sequence of the events (for if this were all that causality involved we ought to say that the dawn is the cause of the day, not that it just heralds the day), but because in each case event A produces event B. To say that one event is the cause of another is to say that in the future they may be constantly conjoined together, and even that they will be, provided the cause operates under the same conditions, but this prevision of the future linking of events is not required that I may recognize the causal relations existing between the events I have witnessed or am now witnessing. It does not seem to occur to Mr MacIntyre that the exclusive meaning he gives to the idea of cause is just one of its many possible meanings, and only one it has acquired in comparatively recent times; nor does it seem to occur either to Mr MacIntyre or to Dr Hepburn that this meaning is justified on the sole condition that it is used within the restricted domain of its 'natural habitat', i.e. as a technical term coined by scientists for their own scientific requirements. There is certainly no justification for assuming that this one meaning is the only, nor that it is a natural, meaning of the term. I deny that, because I am not using it in one of its highly technical and specialized forms, I am not using the idea of causality in a perfectly

[51]A. MacIntyre: *Difficulties in Christian Belief*, p. 59.

normal and natural sense, for I deny that its natural sense is to be found in its purity in, or to be restricted to, some one determinate kind of relationship between events which is of special interest to science.

In a metaphysics of existent being cause, i.e. efficient cause, means that which, by one or more actions, produces either the being, or something contributing towards the being of an effect, and in this sense of the term the universe can truly be said to be an effect for its entire being is produced by God Himself, though obviously there is no sense in which we could say that 'every time we have observed a universe, we have noticed a First Cause causing it'. In the same way I hold that by the one act of sacrifice by which He died for us on Mount Calvary, Christ merited for all men, as a universal cause, redemption from sin and the grace of eternal life. In saying that Christ's death on the cross caused the remission of sins, I do not have to say that 'every time we have observed a sinner repenting of his sins, we have noticed Christ dying on the cross'. I would suggest that we are only entitled to extend the use of the idea of causality to an observed regularity in the sequence of events if we preserve this fundamental characteristic of the term 'cause' as that which produces something new, for this is the one vital characteristic of all real causes. I do not even need to know *how* a cause operates (I freely admit that I have no positive idea of how God's creative causality is operative), nor do I need to know what a cause will effect in the future to know that it is operative here and now. If men started to drop down dead for no apparent reason, we would not presume that there was no cause for their death at all just because we had no positive idea of the nature of the evil causing them to die suddenly, or because we could not predict how many more people would die; we would search for the cause till we had learned all we could about it, convinced that there was one to be discovered, and, even if it turned out to be some rare and almost unknown germ, we would not deny its reality just because it might prove next to impossible to discover the secrets of its deadly influence. In the first stage of the argument for God's existence we prove that the universe is an effect, though we have no positive idea as to how it depends on its cause, nor of the nature of its cause. It is this lack of knowledge about the nature of the cause which finally sets us on the path of trying to reason to God's existence. I admit that even when we have reasoned to God's existence, and reflected on the Christian Dogma of Creation, we still cannot have a positive idea of what kind of causality creation is; but we know enough about God's creative causality to realize that it is unlike any form of causality we are acquainted with from experience, and to see that this is causality in a superlative sense of the term. This is all that the arguments for God's existence can ever claim to do, and I fail to see that any of the objections raised show that our claim to do this is unjustified.

Before finishing this section on the use of causality in the argument for the existence of God, I had better mention another difficulty which is sometimes raised, namely, that the principle of causality is considered by metaphysicians to be so absolutely necessary and universal that it does not admit of one single exception. Were we to come across one single exception, we would have to scrap the principle altogether as a metaphysical statement about things coming to be, and then our proof for God's existence would collapse altogether.

I am quite prepared, with all the philosophers who share my views about metaphysics as the science of existent being, to stand by this requirement of the nature of the principle of causality as a metaphysical law, and to do so without any feelings of anxiety about shocks the future may have in store. Metaphysical laws are like mathematical laws in the absoluteness of their necessity and universality, and like mathematicians, a metaphysician need have no fear that some day an exception will be found to a definitely established law. Suppose someone were to argue that he cannot accept the proposition that the square on the hypotenuse of a right-angled triangle must equal the sum of the squares on the other two sides because it might turn out in the indefinite future that someone will come upon an instance in which the law will be untrue; a mathematician would merely try to show his objector that no such instance could ever be found in the indefinite future for the same reason that one has never been found in the past, namely, that the supposition about the indefinite future possibility is absurd and purely fictitious. Similarly I would challenge anyone presenting me with this difficulty against the principle of causality to give me one certain instance which might even suggest that a thing has come to be without a cause of any kind whatsoever, and, failing his accepting my challenge, I would ask that he should give full weight to the known evidence of the laws governing the way things come to be. I, too, would insist that the supposition about the future uncaused events is purely fictitious, so that it cannot constitute a serious philosophical difficulty. Hume's well-known argument that we can conceive distinct and separate ideas of a thing which we call a cause and of another thing we call an effect, and what can be conceived separately can exist separately, is a pure sophistry of *petitio principii*.[52] It is the fashion with some writers to say that Heisenberg's principle of indeterminacy has provided us at last with one instance of uncaused events, but in fact all that his principle says is that we cannot predict the occurrence of certain individual quantum-events. His principle does not show that those events are uncaused. Heisenberg's principle deals with our knowledge of individual quantum-events, not with those events themselves.[53]

In conclusion, then, I find that there is nothing of serious consequence in any of the objections raised by the critics against our use of causality in the arguments for God's existence. On the contrary, my basic reasons for arguing that God must be the cause of the world's being remain as they were in the Middle Ages. There is every reason for admitting the existence of God as the uncaused cause and absolutely necessary being. No matter how difficult this idea may be, it is far more intelligible than the idea that we ought just to accept the universe and ourselves as they are, that we just happen to be here in the world, and that things just happen to be as intelligible as they are for no reason whatever.

\* \* \*

Before I conclude this talk, which has been devoted as much to answering difficulties commonly raised against a reasoned theism as to outlining the structure of a metaphysical argument for the existence of God, I should like to mention, in a very summary fashion, a number of points which I must leave those of you who write about my arguments for the existence of God to discuss in detail amongst yourselves. Needless to say, I intend the following remarks for the special consideration of those who claim to be exponents of my proofs for the existence of

[52]cf. D. J. B. Hawkins: *Being and Becoming*, pp. 142–3.
[53]cf. G. Jauncy: *Modern Physics*, pp. 531–2.

God. Though they may not agree with some of the points I am going to make, I venture to suggest that they should consider each of them in their discussions of the Five Ways. If this had been done some years ago, I am sure that many disputes over the interpretation of my arguments[54] might have been avoided altogether, and Thomist philosophers might have something to offer that would strike the attention of all serious thinkers, of your own or of any other time.

1. I suggest that there is really only one complete argument for the existence of God in my *Summa Theologica* and *Contra Gentes,* and that this argument comprises the two distinct stages of which I have spoken. The first stage argues from contingent to necessary being, and the second shows that necessary being must be self-subsistent Being, and thence perfect, infinite, eternal, and one in Being.

2. The first stage of the argument is as metaphysical in character as the second. But whereas the first stage is purely philosophical in that it reasons from the data of experience, the second stage is theological, that is to say, it is a metaphysical interpretation of the biblical and revealed teaching about God offered by a theologian to show how God has revealed Himself to us, and how we can think the truths about Himself He has revealed to us. Following my idea of theology as a dialogue between faith and reason I wrote Quaestiones 3–11 of the *Summa* to show how by His revelation God answers the questions the philosopher comes to ask about uncaused, necessary and non-limited being.

3. I compressed the first stage of the argument within the narrow confines of article 3 giving the Five Ways. Here, as in chapter 13 of the *Contra Gentes,* I only intended to establish that the universe is an effect dependent on a being (or beings) which is (or are) uncaused, non-limited, necessary and intelligent. They are not, therefore, so much five complete or independent arguments for God's existence as five complementary ways into one complete argument. An example may make my point clearer. Let us imagine a number of men on a mountain-climbing expedition splitting into five different parties to commence the difficult first phase of their climb, and let us suppose that they all agree to meet, if possible, at five points not far distant from each other about one-third the way up; we would say that they planned to begin their

[54]cf. pp. 14–15; 30.

one expedition of climbing the mountain by commencing in five different ways along five different routes. We would not say that there were five independent expeditions of climbing the mountain, because, after completing the first third of their climb, the parties arranged to meet and complete their climb together. So it is with the Five Ways: they begin to converge together in Quaestio 3, but it is not till Quaestio 11 that they all finally arrive together at the top, or at the conclusion of the whole operation.

I took the Five Ways of set purpose mainly from the works of Aristotle, because I knew that they would appeal to the Aristotelian ways of thinking which I was doing my best to foster in the mediaeval schools, and because I wanted to make Aristotle better known to my brother theologians at the time. I cast the arguments into the succinct form in which you know them now, because I was writing the *Summa Theologica* for the benefit of students beginning their theology, and I only required them to have summaries of the full arguments which professional philosophers would need. I still regard the main intention of the Five Ways as sound, that is to say, I still hold that we can argue validly from changing to unchangeable being, from beings which happen to exist to being which must exist, from limited to non-limited being, from an intelligible universe to a mind responsible for its formation, though I would revise my judgement about the merits of the arguments as they are stated in the Five Ways. Had I realized when committing the Five Ways to writing that they were to become the focal point for discussion amongst philosophers for centuries to come, and that they were going to be paraded by many as the 'traditional' arguments for God's existence, I would never have presented them just as they are. I would never have imagined that I could let Aristotle plead the full case for Christian theism before the philosophers of the world, as I could allow him to plead the case I set him to plead on behalf of reason before the theologians of the thirteenth century. If, then, you wish to present the full reasoning of the first stage of the argument for the existence of God before philosophers today, I cannot see that any good is to be gained by adhering literally and exclusively to the text of the Five Ways. The Five Ways need to be rethought and re-argued in detail with contemporary thinkers, and they ought to be revised so as to make room for the study of the basic problems of modern philosophy which need to be studied with great care. The Five Ways do not need to be scrapped, but improved and enriched by being kept in contact with modern developments in philosophy. The whole way of thinking this stage of the argument needs to be freed from the rigid Aristotelian mould in which I considered it advisable to cast the Five Ways. There is no justification whatsoever for saying that anyone who criticizes the use at the present day of the Five Ways in their mediaeval format must be prejudiced against my whole treatment of the argument for God's existence, for the Five Ways as they stand were never intended to meet the requirements of serious philosophical discussion of the problems of theism in the present century.

4. In my view it is necessary to take all the Five Ways together as five parts of one whole argument designed to show that the universe is an effect. The example of the mountain-climbing expedition should make this point clear. We establish that the universe is an effect by showing that it is contingent, i.e. dependent or suspended in its being: there must therefore be a cause on which it depends. The Five Ways convert the question 'does God exist?' into the question 'who is the cause of the contingent universe?'[55] In the context of the argument for the existence of God contingent being is to be understood to mean, not just that which happens to exist whereas it might as well never have existed or, as I have expressed the idea in this talk, that which is not self-necessitated in its existence, but also that which changes and is changed in its being, is limited and intelligible in its being, though it is clearly not the source of its own intelligibility. We have to show that the universe is contingent not merely in the weaker sense associated exclusively with the third Way, but in the radical and fuller sense which results from combining the Five Ways together. I suggest that the whole strength of the first stage of the argument comes from understanding contingency in this full sense.

For those who take them separately, I must point out how little I actually claimed to have established at the end of each of the Five Ways.[56] Considering the caution and restraint with which I worded

[55]cf. F. C. Copleston: *Aquinas*, p. 42, Fr Copleston says neatly that 'we can say that for Aquinas the proposition affirming God's existence is not so much an answer to the question "Is there a God?" as an answer to the question "What are things considered simply as beings?" '

[56]cf. F. C. Copleston: *op. cit.*, pp. 112–3.

the conclusion of each Way, I deplore the unaccountable persistency with which many Thomist writers regard the Five Ways as providing five independent and complete arguments for God's existence. I chose the little expression 'quod omnes dicunt Deum esse' with which each Way finishes because I expected everyone to understand that I used the word 'God' each time to refer, not to the God of the Christian faith whose existence I was trying to establish, nor to God as He has revealed Himself to us, but to God as we had to define Him nominally at the beginning of the argument. The *Deus* mentioned at the end of each Way is just the being whom all entering upon the first stage of the argument agree at the beginning to call God, and whom they agree must exist as cause if we can show that the universe is an effect.[57] Having, then, established in the Five Ways that the universe is an effect, we end by concluding that a being we all agreed to call God exists. I admit that it is not clear from the Five Ways alone that there is only one cause of the world. I included the Five Ways under Quaestio 2, not because I regarded the whole argument as ending where article 3 finished so that I could pass on to some other topic in Quaestio 3, but because in Quaestio 2 I was concerned to show that reason on its own can know God, not by actually proving that I can myself, but by producing evidence to show that non-Christian philosophers had come to some knowledge of Him.[58] I certainly did not intend anyone to think that, because I did not add a fourth article to Quaestio 2, reason unaided by faith could not in principle come to know more about God than is contained in the Five Ways. In brief, I never intended article 3 to decide or finish anything about God's existence once and for all: I intended it to present the challenge to reason with which it concludes and with which the theologian confronts reason, that, in the full sense of the term, the universe is contingent and depends on necessary being.

5. In philosophy we can and must add the second metaphysical, but purely philosophical stage to complete the total argument for the existence of God which is accessible to reason provided it is equipped

---

[57] *Summa Theologica,* I, qu. 2, art. 2, ad. 2.

[58] Many of the criticisms of the Five Ways made by Van Steenberghen seem to presuppose (a) that I intended the full proof of God's existence to end with article 3, and (b) that I intended to give a purely philosophical proof of God's existence.

with an adequate metaphysics of existent being. But once again Thomist philosophers need to think this stage of the argument out for themselves, and not just reproduce as pure philosophy the reasoning of Quaestiones 3–11 of the *Summa Theologica,* which, as I have said, contains the reasoning of a theologian based on divine revelation. I argued that in God Being and essence are one and the same on the basis of revelation, not on the basis of anything I had proved in the Five Ways. I lament the rationalist argument, sponsored by Leibniz and Wolff, and criticized by Kant, and still more the influence this line of argument has had on many of those who claim to be my disciples, for it has led them to think that I, too, presented as pure natural theology and as established by pure reason, all that I wrote in Quaestiones 3–11. The disagreement that exists amongst the modern Thomist philosophers on the interpretation of my argument for the existence of God has its roots in the way they first of all isolate the Five Ways from the rest of the text of the *Summa,* and then regard Quaestiones 3 onwards as pure philosophy, dealing not with the teaching of divine revelation about God, but with the pure philosophy of God's essence. I had better add that the *Contra Gentes* was also written as a theological work, and it would be quite false to think that because it was written as a kind of apologetic it is therefore equivalent to what nowadays can be regarded as a purely philosophical natural theology. Though I am in favour of philosophers constructing a natural theology to meet the urgent need of modern times, I must deprecate not only the habit some Thomist philosophers have of regarding me as having provided the world with the 'traditional' philosophical arguments fully formed once and for all, but also the unscientific habit they have of taking my theological arguments from the *Summa* just as they stand to construct the second stage of the argument they need. They ought to build the second stage of their argument on the first stage they have themselves constructed, and only take from the *Summa* what they can develop from, and what is consistent with the first stage of their argument. It is significant that Thomist philosophers do not try to establish in the first stage of the argument the real distinction between being and essence in all things within our universe while showing that the universe is an effect, and proceed from this to show in the second stage that the cause of the universe is the being in whom there is no distinction between being and essence. If they reconstructed the first stage of their argument on these lines, they could then show by reason alone what necessary being is, and complete the argument by showing that in necessary being being and essence are identical. In a purely philosophical argument for God's existence the real identity of being and essence in God ought to develop from the proof, established by reason alone, that they are really distinct in all particular things, and not be 'imported into' the argument when the first stage is finished in the way I introduced it in Quaestio 3. In other words, in a purely philosophical argument the third Way would have to be replanned to introduce the proof for the real distinction for all things in this world.[59] It is extraordinary to find Thomist philosophers sparing no pains to establish the real distinction in metaphysics, but failing, when they come to natural theology, to see how it ought to be employed within the first stage of the argument for God's existence.

Just as in the thirteenth century I insisted that theologians should take note of philosophy in discussing what we can know about God, so too, but by contrast, I would suggest that nowadays philosophers ought to consider the teaching of the Christian Revelation about the Being of God, and be scrupulously careful not to confuse what reason can know about God by its own reasoning powers, and what we can only know as certainly true on the authority of God's word. A regard for theology as the science of revealed truth is always of capital importance, and especially in discussing problems which many of the contemporary analysts enjoy discussing about the meaning of statements theologians make about God's love, mercy, justice and providence. Let us grant for the sake of argument the truth of the principle they invoke when discussing the theme of 'theology and falsification', namely, that a statement can only be informative if we know not only the facts or events which make us state it as true, but also what kind of events and facts would make us deny it as false, for if we were to advance some statement as informative and true no matter what happened to be the case, we would not in fact be saying anything informative at all. Some philosophers seem to forget that when the Christian affirms as he does that, for example, God loves all men, he does so because he knows this to be true from revelation and not because he has

[59]cf. F. Van Steenberghen: *Ontologie*, pp. 94–104.

convinced himself of the truth of the statement by mere reasoning; he is basing the truth of his statement on the deeds done by God, especially in the person of Jesus Christ, and on the truths revealed about God to man by the prophets of old, by Jesus Christ and His Church. It follows, therefore, that these statements of belief about God's love could only be falsified on the supposition that God should annul the whole of His divine revelation and the work of Christ's redemption, or on the supposition that God had refused to reveal Himself to us or to redeem us as He did from the plight of sin and its consequences. As none of these conditions can ever be realized, though we know they might have been, it follows that the Christian's belief in God's love cannot in fact be falsified as it has been proved true once and for all by God Himself, no matter what calamities befall us in the order of nature. The purely natural evils from which we suffer, and which are brought up in evidence against the truth of statements about God's love for, or His provident care of man cannot possibly falsify statements expressing truths revealed to us by God, though they certainly present the Christian believer with more or less serious difficulties which he discusses in connexion with the whole problem of evil. Purely human evils of physical and temporal sufferings bring home to the minds of a Christian the problem he regards as more ultimate than that of physical suffering, namely, that of sin, which is the most radical and mysterious of all forms of evil because it is man's defiance of and rebellion against God. Sin must be the worst of all diseases and disorders, an evil in comparison with which physical suffering almost pales into insignificance. Thus for the Christian the problem of evil, great as it is, merges into the vastly more serious problem of why God permits the deadliest of all evils which is sin. This, however, is a problem many analysts just overlook. In brief, then, it is quite impossible to discuss these problems, so far as they affect the truth of the Christian faith, by reason alone, and as they hold such a prominent place in contemporary discussions about God's existence and Being, the philosopher needs to know something about Christian theology. He needs to study the way in which a theologian claims to establish the truth of the statements he makes about God, and so form some idea of what the science of theology really is. Many philosophers who discuss the problems of theism know very little, if anything, about theology. The kind of discussion, mentioned in chapter 1 of this book, about the verification and falsification of theological statements shows that often enough philosophers understand neither the nature of the problems they raise about God, nor the ways in which the problems need to be considered. I would therefore make a plea not merely for Thomist philosophers to construct a sound natural theology based on reason alone, but also for the restoration amongst philosophers of the kind of investigation of theological problems about God which I envisaged in the *Summa Theologica,* taking the form of a dialogue between Faith and Reason. Such a dialogue might aim at showing clearly what we can discuss by reason alone, and equally what we cannot decide by reason alone. There is reason to think that Thomist philosophers have not succeeded in making either of these capital points sufficiently clear to the philosophical world at large.

6. The conclusion of the argument, 'therefore God exists', is to be accepted as final and irrevocable, as true for all time and under all conditions. In concluding that God exists and in claiming that in God we have an explanation of the existence of finite things, we are not just accepting God's Being as a convenient but provisional explanation of the being of the universe which we can accept for lack of anything better but which we might have to revise at some future time; nor are we, as Mr MacIntyre fears, advancing God as a kind of hypothesis like the scientific hypotheses advanced to explain observed phenomena. As Mr MacIntyre says: 'the essence of a scientific hypothesis is that it should suggest observations or experiments which will enable us to decide whether a particular phenomenon is to be explained in one way rather than another'.[60] A scientific hypothesis is of its nature only a provisional and partial explanation of phenomena, which in time may quite easily give way to other hypotheses. A metaphysical explanation, on the other hand, is of its nature a final and complete answer to the questions we ask about the being and existence of things. There is no reason at all to suggest that the kind of metaphysical analysis which the argument for the existence of God really is should not yield a conclusion that is metaphysically final and ultimate, unless, of course, one assumes that a philosopher must use the words 'proof' and 'explanation'

[60]Alasdair MacIntyre: 'The Logical Status of Religious Beliefs' in *Metaphysica Beliefs,* p. 196.

in the same sense in which a scientist or mathematician uses them. The argument for God's existence does not amount to a 'proof' in the modern sense in which a scientific hypothesis may be said to be proved, i.e. because it is found to work satisfactorily every time it is used as a basis for conducting experiments; nor is it a deductive kind of proof of the kind used in geometry to establish the truth of a rider from a theorem.[61] It is not a proof which would involve anyone who denied its conclusion once he had granted the premises in *evident* self-contradiction. The so-called 'proof' of the existence of God consists in a metaphysical analysis of the being of the universe, or in showing the necessity of viewing the universe itself in a certain kind of way which we may not find at all easy to do, and then arguing that when seen in this way as after all it really is (that is to say, as contingent), we cannot but conclude that the universe must depend existentially on the self-subsistent being which we show must be the God of the Christian revelation.[62] I agree with Father Copleston when he writes that in my view:

> One is involved in a contradiction if one affirms the proposi-
> tions 'there are things which come into being and pass away', and
> 'there are things which change', and at the same time denies the
> proposition 'there is an absolutely necessary being', and 'there is
> a supreme unmoved mover'. *But the contradiction can be made appar-*
> *ent only by means of metaphysical analysis. And the entailment in*
> *question is fundamentally an ontological or causal entailment.*[63]

Some writers say that we ought to think of the 'proof' of God's existence as a process, not of explaining or trying to find an explanation for the existence of the universe in the Being of God, but of metaphysical reflection on the universe which reveals the ontological necessity of God existing granted that contingent things exist.[64] It is quite true that the 'proof' does consist in such a metaphysical reflection, but I see no reason for saying that such reflection does not enable us to

---

[61] cf. B. A. O. Williams: 'Metaphysical Arguments', a paper in *The Nature of Metaphysics*, pp. 42ff.

[62] F. C. Copleston: *Aquinas*, pp. 41–46.

[63] F. C. Copleston: *Aquinas*, pp. 114–15 (italic is mine).

[64] cf. for example J. Lacroix's remarkable book, *Le sens de l'Athéisme Moderne*, p. 18ff.

understand both that God must exist, and that His existence explains the existence of contingent things, provided it is clearly understood that by 'explanation' we do not mean that God is some kind of super-hypothesis, but the Being which makes the universe intelligible to us in its very existence. God's existence is not accepted as a mere hypo-thesis because, for one thing, as I explained earlier in my talk, the point of the reflective analysis is to show that the mind has no possible alterna-tive but to conclude, 'therefore self-subsistent being exists'.

7. The Fifth Way which I gave in article 3, the famous argument from design, ought to be replanned and redesigned with the greatest care so as to be based first and foremost on man's place within the universe. I do not wish to raise the question of teleology here, as it demands another lecture. But I must say that the argument ought to be based on a sound metaphysics of man, the purpose of which ought to be to determine the end for which he lives within the material universe, that is to say, the destiny intrinsic to his nature and that for which he assumes responsibility in all his free activities. Secondly the argument must be based on the idea that, no matter how it has come to be as it is, and no matter what evolutionary theory may be advanced to explain the phenomena of development, ultimately the earth has been designed to be the place to be inhabited by men. In brief, the argument must establish that human life is life destined to be in the world, and that the world was ultimately formed that men might live in it as they do. The full argument for the existence of a personal God, Who knows and loves man, must be based not merely on the purely impersonal cosmological questions we ask about the universe, but also on the ultimate personal questions we must ask about our own human way of being, and about the causes, both efficient and final, of our very existence on the earth. In the modern world we cannot settle the question of the existence of God without showing that man can under-stand himself and his own being from what he learns God must be. The evidences of design in numerous particular things in which we used to be almost exclusively interested during the Middle Ages are barely sufficient nowadays as the sole basis for the argument to prove the existence of the God who made man and made man for Himself, and the universe for man. The teleology we need to stress in the con-text of the argument is that inherent in the structure of the universe on

the vastest scale known to us: the argument must be designed to show that man's life and nature cannot be understood unless conceived as set within the universe, and that the universe cannot be understood unless conceived as made to support human life. Whatever else may have come about by chance of one kind or another, we cannot reasonably hold that man's life on earth is itself merely the work of chance. To explain man's life within the universe by chance of any kind alone, is to make chance into the most incredible agent ever imagined, for it becomes more intelligent in its effects than any known intelligence. The argument must show that the modern scientific theories of evolution, no matter what form they may take, are not sufficient as complete and final explanations of man's existence on earth, nor of the earth being so plentifully supplied with materials of all kinds needful and useful for the ceaseless development of man's ways of living as he does on the earth. None of the evolutionary theories can prove that God did not gradually shape the universe and prepare the earth to be suited as it is for the maintenance of human life. The knowledge we have about the world and man would seem to warrant the idea that what development there has been in the formation of the earth and of living beings on the earth was designed so that man's position in the world is what it is. Human life is a life to be lived with other men, and men, by necessity of their nature, have to live with other men by means of the material resources with which the earth is abundantly filled. The idea of God comes to man not so much from his reflections of the material universe, but from his reflections on his situation within the universe, and the complete argument for God's existence ought to be based in part at least on showing that man's human situation is ultimately an effect produced by God, so that man cannot find the ultimate explanation of his own being anywhere but in God Himself.[65] But Thomist philosophers have so far failed to give serious thought to the need of proving in the first stage of the argument for God's existence that man's life in the world is an effect of mind, and in the second stage, of God's own mind. This is a theme to which very much thought needs to be devoted by many theists.

[65]cf. Michele F. Sciacca: *L'Existence de Dieu* (translated from Italian by Régis Jolivet) chs. I and IV, in which the theme of man and his position within the universe as a necessary basis for discussing the existence of God is admirably explained.

I find very unsatisfactory Dr Farrer's idea[66] that all we have to do as theists is to draw out the old reasons for accepting God's existence and restate them. There is plenty of scope for new ideas in natural theology, even after two thousand years of Christianity, and so long as man reflects on the universe and the ultimate mysteries of its being I am sure there always will be much to be said about knowing God that has never been said before.

[66]cf. p. 5.

# BIBLIOGRAPHICAL INFORMATION

(This is not intended to be a Bibliography in the currently accepted sense of the word, but merely to provide the reader with bibliographical details concerning works quoted or referred to in this book.)

## A. IN CONNEXION WITH CHAPTERS 1 AND 2

AYER, ALFRED J., *Language, Truth and Logic* (London, Victor Gollancz, second edition 1948).

BAILLIE, JOHN, *Our Knowledge of God* (London, Oxford University Press, 1939).

BARNES, WINSTON H. F., *The Philosophical Predicament* (London, Adam & Charles Black, 1950).

COLLINS, JAMES, *God in Modern Philosophy* (London, Routledge and Kegan Paul, 1960).

COPLESTON, FREDERICK (S.J.), *A History of Philosophy*, Volume 6, Wolff to Kant (London, Burns Oates, 1960).

EWING, A. C., *The Fundamental Questions of Philosophy* (London, Routledge & Kegan Paul, 1951).

FARRAR, AUSTIN, *Finite and Infinite* (London, Dacre Press, 1943).

HEPBURN, RONALD W., *Christianity and Paradox* (London, A. & C. Watts, 1958).

KANT, IMMANUEL, *Critique of Pure Reason* (translated by Norman Kemp Smith; London, Macmillan, 1950).

LAIRD, J., *Theism and Cosmology* (London, Allen and Unwin, 1940; and New York, Philosophical Library & Alliance Book Corporation, 1942).

LE ROY, EDOUARD, *Le Problème de Dieu* (Paris, Cahiers de la Quinzaine, 1929).

LINDSAY, A. D., *Kant* (London, Ernest Benn, 1934).

MACINTYRE, ALASDAIR C., *Difficulties in Christian Belief* (London, SCM Press, 1959).

PATON, H. J., *The Modern Predicament* (London, Allen and Unwin; New York, Macmillan, 1955).

RUSSELL, BERTRAND, *Why I am not a Christian* (Essays edited by Paul Edwards. London, Allen and Unwin, 1957).

*History of Western Philosophy* (London, Allen and Unwin, 1946).

*Wisdom of the West* (edited by Paul Foulkes. London, Macdonald, 1959).

SILLEM, EDWARD A., *George Berkeley and the Proofs for the Existence of God* (London, Longmans, Green, 1957).

SORLEY, W. R., *Moral Values and the Idea of God* (Cambridge University Press, 1935).

WEBB, CLEMENT C. J., *Studies in the History of Natural Theology* (Oxford University Press, 1915).

The following collections of Essays and Articles are important:

*Logic and Language* (edited by A. G. N. Flew. Oxford, Basil Blackwell).

First Series (1955):

RYLE, GILBERT, 'Systematically Misleading Expressions'.

WAISMANN, F., 'Verifiability'.

WISDOM, JOHN, 'Gods'.

Second Series (1955):

MOORE, G. E., 'Is Existence a Predicate?'

*Metaphysical Beliefs* (edited by A. C. MacIntyre. London, SCM Press, 1957):
MACINTYRE, ALASDAIR, 'The Logical Status of Religious Belief'.
*The Nature of Metaphysics* (edited by D. F. Pears. London, Macmillan, 1957):
RYLE, GILBERT, 'Final Discussion'.
WILLIAMS, B. A. O., 'Metaphysical Arguments'.
*New Essays in Philosophical Theology* (edited by Antony Flew and Alasdair MacIntyre, London, SCM Press, 1955):
PRIOR, A. N., 'Can Religion be Discussed?'
SMART, J. J. C. 'The Existence of God'.
FINDLAY, J. N.
HUGHES, G. E.     } 'Can God's Existence be Disproved?'
RAINER, A. C. A.
FLEW, ANTONY
HARE, R. M.     } 'Theology and Falsification'.
MITCHELL, BASIL
*Faith and Logic* (edited by Basil Mitchell. London, Allen and Unwin, 1957).
CROMBIE, I. M., 'The Possibility of Theological Statements'.
STEAD, G. C., 'How Theologians Reason'.


B.   IN CONNEXION WITH CHAPTER 3

DESCOQS, PEDRO (S.J.), *Praelectiones Theologiae Naturalis* (Paris, Beauchesne, 1935).
GARRIGOU-LAGRANGE, REGINALD (O.P.), *Dieu, Son Existence et Sa Nature* (Paris, Beauchesne, 1933).
GILSON, ETIENNE, *Le Thomisme* (Paris, J. Vrin, fifth edition, 1945). English translation under the title *The Christian Philosophy of St Thomas Aquinas* (London, Victor Gollancz, 1957).
*Being and Some Philosophers* (Toronto, Pontifical Institute of Medieval Studies, 1949).
*God and Philosophy* (Yale University Press, 1941).
*Introduction à la Philosophie Chrétienne* (Paris, J. Vrin, 1960).
GISQUIÈRE, EMMANUEL, *Deus Dominus, Praelectiones Theodiceae* (Paris, Beauschesne, 1950).
GRÉGOIRE, A. (S.J.), *Immanence et Transcendence* (Brussels-Paris, Desclée de Brouwer, 1939).
JAY, ERIC G., *The Existence of God, A Commentary on St Thomas's Five Ways* (London, SPCK, 1946).
MANSER, GALLUS M. (O.P.), *Das Wesen des Thomismus* (Fribourg, Switzerland, Paulusverlag, 1949).
MASCALL, E. L., *He Who Is* (London, Longmans, Green, 1943).
*Existence and Analogy* (London, Longmans, Green, 1949).
DE MORÉ-PONTGIBAUD, CHARLES (S.J.), *Du Fini à l'Infini* (Paris, Aubier, 1956).
PATTERSON, ROBERT LEET, *The Conception of God in the Philosophy of Aquinas* (London, Allen and Unwin, 1933).
SERTILLANGES, A. D. (O.P.), *La Philosophie de St Thomas d'Aquin* (Paris, Aubier, revised edition, 1940).
VAN STEENBERGHEN, FERNAND, *Ontologie* (Louvain, Publications Universitaires, second edition, 1952).

'Le Problème Philosophique de l'Existence de Dieu', articles in the *Revue Philosophique de Louvain*, 1947, pp. 5–20; 141–68; 301–13.

'Réflexions sur les "Quinque Viae"' from the *Acta III Congressus Thomistici Internationalis*, September 1950, pp 237–41 (Turin, Marietti, 1951).

'Sciences Positives et Existence de Dieu', article in the *Revue Philosophique de Louvain*, 1959, pp. 397–414.

VARIOUS AUTHORS, *Sulle, 'Cinque Vie' di S. Tommaso* (Rome, Officium Libri Catholici, 1954).


## C. In Connexion with Chapters 4–7

VAN ACKEREN, GERALD F. (S.J.), *Sacra Doctrina* (Rome, Officium Libri Catholici, 1952).

ARNOU, RENATUS (S.J.), *De Quinque Viis Sancti Thomae ad Demonstrandam Dei Exsistentiam apud Graecos et Arabes et Judaeos Praeformatis vel Adumbratis* (Rome, Gregorian University, 1932).

BOUYGES, MAURICE, 'Pour l'Interprétation des "Quinque Viae" de St Thomas d'Aquin', article in *Recherches de Science Religieuse* (1949, pp. 593–601).

CHENU, M. D. (O.P.), *La Théologie comme Science au XIIIe Siècle* (Paris, J. Vrin, 1957).
*Introduction à l'Etude de St Thomas d'Aquin* (Paris, J. Vrin, 1950).
*St Thomas d'Aquin et la Théologie* (Paris, Editions du Seuil, series 'Maîtres Spirituels', 1959).
'*Is Theology a Science?*' (Faith and Fact Book, London, Burns Oates, 1959).

CONGAR, M. J. (O.P.), 'Théologie' article in the *Dictionnaire de Théologie Catholique,* (Paris, Librairie Letouzey et Ané, 1943 and 1946).
*Bulletin Thomiste*, volume V. No. 8. Oct.–Dec. 1938, pp. 490–505 (Le Saulchoir, Belgium).

COPLESTON, FREDERICK (S.J.), *Aquinas* (Pelican Book, 1955).

DUBARLÉ, D. (O.P.), 'L'Existence de Dieu', from a volume entitled *De la Connaissance de Dieu* from the series 'Recherches de Philosophie' (Paris, Desclée de Brouwer, 1958).

FINILI, ANTONINUS (O.P.), 'Recent Work on the "Tertia Via",' article from *Dominican Studies,* volume VII, 1954.

HAWKINS, D. J. B., *The Essentials of Theism* (London, Sheed & Ward, 1949).
*Being and Becoming* (London, Sheed & Ward, 1954).

HAYEN, ANDRÉ (S.J.), *St Thomas d'Aquin et la Vie de l'Eglise* (Louvain, Presses Universitaires, 1952).

JAUNCY, G., *Modern Physics* (New York, Van Nostrand, 1948).

KNOWLES, DAVID, *The Historical Context of the Philosophical Works of St Thomas Aquinas* (Blackfriars Publications: Aquinas Society Paper, No. 30).

LACROIX, JEAN, *Le Sens de l'Athéisme Moderne* (Tournai, Casterman, 1959).

MARKUS, R. A., 'A Note on the Meaning of "Via"', article from *Dominican Studies,* volume VII, 1954).

MOTTE, A. R. (O.P.), 'A Propos des "Cinq Voies"', article from the *Revue des Sciences Philosophiques et Théologiques* (October 1938, pp. 577–82).
'Théodicée et Théologie chez St Thomas d'Aquin', article from the *Revue des Sciences Philosophiques et Théologiques,* January 1937, pp. 5–6).

O'DONOGHUE, DERMOT, 'An Analysis of the "Tertia Via" of St Thomas', an article in *The Irish Theological Quarterly* (April 1953, pp. 129–51).

PERSSON, PER ERIK, 'Le Plan de la Somme Théologique et le Rapport "Ratio-Revelatio" ', an article in the *Revue Philosophique de Louvain,* (November 1958, pp. 545–72).

DEL PRADO, N. (O.P.), *De Veritate Fundamentali Philosophiae Christianae* (Fribourg, Switzerland, St Paulus Druckerei, 1911).

DE RAEYMAEKER, LOUIS, *Le Philosophie de l'Etre* (Louvain, Editions de L'Institut Supérieur de Philosophie, 1946).

'Le Caractère Spécial de la Preuve de Dieu', an article in *Studi Filosofici interno all 'Esistenza', al mondo al Transcendente,* pp. 243–56 (Rome, Gregorian University, 1954).

SCIACCA, MICHELE F., *L'Existence de Dieu* (translated from Italian by Régis Jolivet. Paris, Aubier, 1951).

TAYLOR, A. E., *Does God Exist?* (London, Macmillan, 1947).

'Theism', article from *Hastings' Encyclopaedia of Religion and Ethics.*

WHITE, VICTOR (O.P.), *God the Unknown* (London, Harvill Press, 1956).

*Holy Teaching* (Blackfriars Publications: Aquinas Society Paper, No. 33).

## ADDENDA

GILSON, ÉTIENNE, *Elements of Christian Philosophy* (New York, Doubleday, 1960).

ROSS, JAMES F., 'God and "Logical Necessity" ', an article in *The Philosophical Quarterly,* pp. 22–27.

PENELHUM, T., 'Divine Necessity', an article in *Mind,* April, 1960, pp. 175–86.

# INDEX OF NAMES

*References to footnotes are indicated by a small n after the page number*

## INDEX OF TOPICS